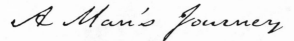

A Man's Journey
to SIMPLE
ABUNDANCE

SARAH BAN BREATHNACH
and friends

EDITED BY MICHAEL SEGELL

A SIMPLE ABUNDANCE PRESS BOOK

SCRIBNER
New York   London   Toronto   Sydney   Singapore

SCRIBNER

SIMPLE ABUNDANCE PRESS

1230 Avenue of the Americas
New York, NY 10020

I would like to gratefully acknowledge all the writers I have quoted from for their wisdom, comfort, and inspiration. An exhaustive search was undertaken to determine whether previously published material included in this book required permission to reprint. If there has been an error, I apologize and a correction will be made in subsequent editions.

—Sarah Ban Breathnach

DESIGNED BY ERICH HOBBING

Set in Adobe Garamond

Manufactured in the United States of America

1   3   5   7   9   10   8   6   4   2

Library of Congress Cataloging-in-Publication Data is available.
Ban Brethnach, Sarah.
A man's journey to simple abundance / Sarah Ban Breathnach and friends ; edited by
Michael Segell.
p. cm.
"A Simple Abundance Press book."
Includes bibliographical references and index.
1. Men—Conduct of life. I. Segell, Michael, 1951– . II. Title.
BJ1601 .B36 2000
158.1'28'081—dc21   00-045012

ISBN 0-7432-0061-6

See page 438 for a continuation of the copyright page.

There are no perfect men, of course, but some are more perfect than others, and we can use all of those we can get.

MERLE SHAIN

For the men who have loved me,
But especially for those nearly perfect few
who have let me love them.

SBB

CONTENTS

CONTENTS

PART THREE: RULES OF THE ROAD

PART FOUR: ISLANDS OF FAME AND FORTUNE

CONTENTS

CONTENTS

A Man's Journey
to SIMPLE
ABUNDANCE

UPON READING THIS BOOK

Man and woman He created them.

Book of Genesis

From ancient times we have been told that human beings were created in Spirit's image. However, as the acclaimed television journalist Bill Moyers reminds us, "being made in the likeness of God does not mean we were made to think alike."

Especially women and men.

One of my favorite parts of the Bible is the story of Adam and Eve. I find it fascinating that there are two startling accounts of creation in the Book of Genesis, and they completely contradict each other. One could be called Eve's recollection, which has God creating both masculine and feminine energy in a single breath. In Adam's version, of course, he comes first. This original "He Says/She Says" also amused Mark Twain, who wrote *The Diary of Adam and Eve,* tracing the battle of the sexes back to the observation, "The new creature with the long hair is a good deal in the way. It is always hanging around and following me about. I don't like this; I am not used to company."

To tell the truth, since I'm an incurable romantic, I actually prefer Adam's version because it's the original love story. After Adam is created, he wanders through Eden and then asks the inevitable question of his Maker: "Why are there two of every living creature but me?" God realizes that it's not good for man to be alone. I have always wondered if Spirit created a companion for Adam as an afterthought, or was He just waiting patiently for Adam to have an epiphany? Something or someone was missing.

So Adam is told to take a nap and when he does he has a wild dream. In it, God uses one of his ribs to craft the first soul mate. I think this imagery is exquisite. God removes a bone from the barrier that protects a man's heart to create the woman meant to fill it. The poet e.e. cummings describes this miracle best: "One's not half of two, it's two that are halves of one."

I think *A Man's Journey to Simple Abundance* deepens and broadens the eternal romance between Adam and Eve. Certainly, it was written in the spirit of bringing men and women closer together by revealing our similarities, not just our differences. Part owner's manual, part guidebook, *A Man's Journey to Simple Abundance* examines the private pilgrimages that occur in every man's life and the compass that steers him toward life's true north.

One of the most unexpected and meaningful compliments I've received about *Simple Abundance* is that it has enabled men to understand what's really important to the women they love—whether it's their wives, daughters, sisters, mothers, or friends. As one man put it, "You've given men the Rosetta stone." We've tried to accomplish the same thing here. I say "we" because this book has been a collaborative effort of the first magnitude.

There's a reason it's taken so long for there to be a men's *Simple Abundance.* The heart of my philosophy celebrates living authentically. Being a woman, I know how a woman thinks, feels, frets, and loves. But as much as I adore men, I understand as much about them as Eve did on her first day in Eden. Realizing and honoring the differences between the sexes, I knew that if there was to be a men's version of *Simple Abundance,* I'd need the right collaborator to help me explore the last great spiritual adventure, the quest for understanding male emotions. I found him in Michael Segell, the former "Male Mind" columnist for *Esquire* and the author of *Standup Guy: Masculinity That Works,* a personal and provocative dispatch from behind the front lines of the gender wars. Think of us as agents provocateurs dedicated to getting men and women together again on the page. All of the introductions before each essay were written by Michael Segell except for one, which I wrote. Frequently, though, the essays triggered such a personal reaction in me that I felt compelled to flash a feminine response afterward.

For my women readers, I believe this book will surprise you as much as it did me. To begin with, the format is completely different from the original *Simple Abundance,* which was written as one side of an intimate conversation between two women over the course of a year. In *A Man's Journey* there are more than fifty male voices illuminating what it means to be a man today with a courage and candor that is at times unsettling but always life-affirming. The topics the men explore celebrate how and where the sacred manifests in their daily lives, and often it's not where a woman might think. Some of the essays are philosophical, some heart-wrenching, some humorous, some ruminative, some just plain quirky, but all are compelling. Authenticity pushes us past our comfort zone, so please be open. The territory may seem unfamiliar at times. At the very least, after reading these essays, you and your partner can look forward to a year's worth of stimulating conversations (besides discussing the kids, money, chores, and how exhausted you both are).

For me, working on this book felt like living on a fault line of the soul; I never knew when my own tectonic plates were going to start shifting, and the aftershocks were equally profound. I believe you'll be as moved as I was by the deep emotional honesty of the writing, whether it makes you laugh or cry. Like the best books, *A Man's Journey to Simple Abundance* does both.

Toward the end of Adam and Eve's diary (as channeled by Mark Twain), the woman confides: "The Garden is lost, but I have found *him,* and am content." As for the man, he admits, "Wheresoever *she* was, there was Eden."

Man or woman, may this book bless you with equally surprising truths and extraordinary perceptions. Perhaps we will have another shot at experiencing Heaven on earth together. At least it's worth a read.

—Sarah Ban Breathnach, July 2000

INTRODUCTION

Not long ago, I was handed a copy of *Simple Abundance*. Within days of reading it, in one of those no-coincidence encounters that she writes about so convincingly, I met Sarah Ban Breathnach. I told her that much of the wisdom in her book about finding a realistic path to authentic success—success *as a person,* that is—was just as relevant and of as much interest to men as it was to the millions of women who had already grasped it. Sarah, of course, had heard this countless times before, and asked me whether I'd be interested in helping her put together a *Simple Abundance* for men—and, she hoped, for women who wanted to understand them better. It was an interesting challenge, for the profound differences in men's interests, talents, and concerns meant that the book would be dramatically different in style, tone, and content from her first. Some weeks later, after I signed on to the project, I was describing the difficulties I was having in deciding on a format to a woman seated next to me at a dinner party. "Well," she said, her smile doing very little to conceal her derision, "I don't see any difficulty at all. Isn't everything about men simple?"

It's the kind of comment men hear a lot these days. Turn on the television, and the characters in sitcoms and movies-of-the-week are either worthless wise guys or bumbling boobs. To judge by today's magazine covers, you'd think the only issues in men's lives are whether their pecs are big enough, their testosterone levels high enough, their erections hard enough. Can they meet the Ironman challenge? Can they locate the forty-six erogenous zones of the totally insatiable Modern Woman? Other media, too, give the impression that men, when they're not whining about lost entitlements, are demonstrating a historic lack of commitment to their wives and family.

What's wrong with this picture? Everything. The arbiters of what passes for zeitgeist—and I've spent many years in that role myself—rarely do more than skim the surface of the culture before making their pronouncements. There's an old rule in journalism that it takes three of anything to make a trend. So if a trio of disturbed boys in separate corners of the world commit hideous acts of violence, all boys will soon be a part of this alarming movement. If three men complain to a writer for a women's magazine that they've been reduced to girl toys, men everywhere must be flummoxed by and angry about their shrinking power and dominion in the postfeminist universe. As fun as it is to write about, the zeitgeist simply bears little relevance to the lives of the vast majority of us.

So here's a radical proposal: How about a book that explores the rich complexity of men's lives, and the goodness that underlies them? How about a book that, by the example of its many distinguished contributors, offers guideposts to achieving the kind of authentic success that Sarah Ban Breathnach articulated so brilliantly in *Simple Abundance*?

For despite my dinner companion's view, men's lives are anything but simple. We fall in love just as hard as women, and are just as desolated when our hearts are broken. Though we have different ways of showing it, we feel a fierce loyalty to and love for our wives and families. Less demonstrative than women, and less regular in our attendance at church, synagogue, or zendo, we nonetheless lead spiritual lives of quiet intensity. We have a reverential interest in and appreciation of the natural world and an instinctual understanding of the mechanical. We're playful and purposeful, competitive and curious, bound by an innate male code to produce, protect, and provide. We derive great pride and self-esteem from our professional lives—that is to say, from our skill and competence, from the respect we deserve and the rewards we earn. And we like to have fun.

INTRODUCTION

The fifty essays on the following pages, contributed by people as
diverse as a backwoods hermit, test pilot, professional big-game
hunter, champion surfer, mystical rabbi, and some of the finest writers of our time, explore, often movingly, the richness and color of
men's lives. The stepping-stones that Sarah identified on her own
journey to Simple Abundance—gratitude, simplicity, order, harmony,
beauty, and joy—also serve as trail markers in this book, only here
they are navigated by a variety of writers who offer a personal and
uniquely male perspective on these passages. To wit: *Gratitude* is
expressed by a devoted husband whose wife has been stricken with
a deadly illness. *Simplicity* is the lifelong pursuit of a Zen master who
wishes to experience the world purely, "as it is." A brilliant computer
programmer looks at the role that *order* plays in his work and life. The
natural world serves as the medium through which an eminent religious scholar achieves *harmony* with the past, present, and future. A
novelist articulates his definition of womanly *beauty.* And cultivating life as an act of love is the only way a wise and learned psychologist knows how to experience *joy.*

I hope (and know, really) that on the following pages many
men will recognize, perhaps for the first time, their authentic selves,
stripped of the posturing, conceits, emotional armor, and macho
impedimenta that normally obscure the view. Despite our individual uniqueness, most of us depart on our journey through manhood
with similar baggage, stumble up to the same crossroads, and have
the same destinations in mind. Along the way, we find that our interests, preoccupations, and goals gather into discrete clusters. They
make up the six sections of this book. In the first, "Latitude and Lon-
gitude," a sextet of writers identifies the important foundations that
fathers, brothers, kids, and wives provide for them. "Private Pilgrimages" delves into men's complex interior lives, exploring fear, vul-
nerability, grief, the sexual self, and the mystifying, often
overwhelming moods men are subject to—and to which they subject the women in their lives. "Rules of the Road" examines some of

the most important, and often morally complex, obligations of mature manhood—to mentor, nurture, protect, and to be a man of conscience and duty—while "Islands of Fame and Fortune" explores the vicissitudes of ambition and fame, disappointment and failure.

Most men take their recreational life as seriously as they do their professional—thus "Diversions and Detours" and the importance that hobbies, sports, hunting, cars, women, and other obsessions play in the manly pilgrimage. Finally, the authors in "True North" identify what constitutes, for them, the real rewards of authentic success and the human condition.

Wherever you are on this miraculous passage, you'll find yourself with some fine traveling companions in the following essays. If you're well launched, you'll be treated to a fond look back upon your early voyages as well as a preview of the joyous sojourns that remain. If you're on your way "home," you'll see yourself, happily, on nearly every page. And if you've yet to begin the trip . . . well, the important thing is that you get on board.

You'll be surprised whom you'll meet along the way.

—MICHAEL SEGELL

PART ONE

LATITUDE AND LONGITUDE

*Going from—toward; it is the history of
every one of us.*

HENRY DAVID THOREAU

MOTHERS

My earliest memory: my infant brother is nursing at my mother's breast on his first day home from the hospital. I crawl into bed with the two of them, jealously observing the sweet spectacle until I can take it no longer and try to displace the interloper from her bosom. My mother banishes me from the bedroom and I slink off, the mortal wound leaving a permanent scar on my psyche. More than four decades later, I've yet to forgive my brother.

A mother has a relationship with her son and he with her that has no parallel. She gives birth to the other, the masculine mystery, and in her eyes he often becomes a manly version of herself. For many men, Mark Winegardner included, this is only a good thing.

Like Mother, Like Son

Mark Winegardner

All women become like their mothers. That is their tragedy. No man does. That is his.

OSCAR WILDE

In the spring of 1968, when she was twenty-eight years old and had not yet been to college or become her family's breadwinner, and our family still lived in a double-wide house trailer on the grim, sun-baked outskirts of a town in northwestern Ohio, my mother took her big black Remington manual typewriter out of the hall closet, lugged it into the kitchen and onto the laminated table. It landed with a thud and its bell dinged. The tabletop was still damp. My mother did not eat breakfast, but it was she who'd wiped the table.

It was hot. She cranked open the jalousie windows. She positioned the fans. She lined up new pens in a neat row. She wondered if my father and I would ever leave.

I was six years old and oblivious. Nowhere in the textbooks and workbooks my mother had just received from the Famous Writers School did it cite pathological self-involvement as a key trait of the working writer. Had it done so, my mother would have recognized me as the family's best literary hope (instead, she alternated between imagining that I'd grow up to be president of the United States or else land in prison for some kind of crime of the evil-genius variety—this being the era when such destinies still seemed mutually exclusive). She watched as I gathered up my schoolbooks and ran down the long gravel driveway and caught the bus. I was just old enough not to turn around and wave. I was in first grade, but already too cool to love my mother. Besides, kids who turned around and gave Mommy a wave got on the bus and got pummeled.

My father was the next to leave. She kissed him good-bye and watched as he drove down the driveway and headed off to work. He was a straight-commission salesman at Winegardner's Mobile Homes, which sold house trailers, travel trailers, and outboard motors, and which his father owned.

My sister, who'd just turned two, was a sleeper. She could sleep until noon. A kid like this made it possible for my mother to do what she was about to do: embark on a career as a writer.

On a whim, and impressed by the legitimacy and gravitas of the "Guiding Faculty of the Famous Writers School" (which included Bennett Cerf, Rod Serling, Bruce Catton, and Red Smith), my mother had mailed in a coupon from *McCall's* magazine, asking for information. She didn't really think she could become a writer, but she'd always loved to read. Like most literate Americans, she hoped one day to write a novel. She dreamed of doing it once her kids were grown. My father told her there was no need to wait—a sentiment echoed by Faith Baldwin of the Famous Writers School's Guiding Faculty, who, in the ad my mother had seen, said she thought it a pity that more women didn't get into the exciting and lucrative field of freelance writing.

My mother had read her assignment in her handsome two-toned, buckram-bound textbook and every word of her first complimentary copy of *Famous Writers Magazine* and was ready to start. She stared across the blank page, out the back window, past the one-car garage and attached carport, across a cornfield, where there was a trailer park that her father-in-law owned and into which any house trailers her husband sold were likely to be parked, hooked up, and skirted, and their owners installed as tenants. My parents, in contrast, owned the lot where we lived. We were not tenants. My mother, child of an alcoholic father and a prima donna, half-crazy mother, had grown up in rented dwellings her whole life. Until this double-wide, on this lot. Someday, her husband would buy his father's business. Someday—maybe someday soon!—she'd begin to make money from her writing, and they could buy a decent house in town. The world out there was crazy, crazy, crazy: a terrible war in Vietnam, loud rock and roll, facial hair, flaming brassieres, riots, protests, assassinations—none of which she endorsed or could understand. But close to home, things made sense. She looked at the swing set and the plastic toys strewn across her own backyard. The car in the garage was a late-model Buick. She had children she imagined to be smart and good-looking, a husband who was spitting distance from becoming a good provider, a beauty-shop appointment at 2 P.M., and a talent worth developing.

She took out a stenographer's notebook. Maybe it would be easier if she wrote the first draft longhand. She took a tip the Famous Writers School had given her: just start with the word *The* and keep going. She wrote out the word *The*. Her penmanship was stellar. Had she gone to college, she would have wanted to become a teacher. She had blackboard-caliber handwriting.

A month before, on an aptitude test, my mother had written an essay about my belief—fueled by the comic books I'd been reading—that I could fly. She insisted I could not fly. This drove me to put on my Superman underwear and climb up onto the roof of the carport, and run off it as fast as I could, arms extended, shouting out my personal superhero motto, which has been lost to history. I injured nothing but my fantasy life. The essay had been evaluated by a balding man who was pictured next to his sleek electric typewriter wearing thick, serious eyeglasses and smoking a cigarette. He'd published a newspaper column that was syndicated throughout eastern Virginia and a book that recounted his experiences in the Pacific theater. His letter was signed personally. In it, he said that "you, Mrs. Gary Winegardner, have talent worth developing."

He'd given her a B, which unnerved her, since she'd gotten straight A's K through 12. But the Famous Writers School "field representative," who'd come to the double-wide himself to sign her up, explained that this was an elite school. That B was the highest grade he'd seen a prospective student get, even counting the three students he'd personally enrolled who'd gone on to publish novels. He told her that the Guiding Faculty would be among the people grading her work (a lie). He said the student/teacher ratio was 10 to 1 (it was almost 1,200 to 1; the school had only 55 teaching faculty, as opposed to 800 "field representatives"). He said that 75 percent of students began to publish within the first year (the real number was more like 1 percent—less if tiny religious magazines and shopping circulars didn't count). The tuition, which she could pay in small monthly installments, would be $900. (At the time, a creative writing course at an American university would have cost about $40. The Famous Writers School had 65,000 students, probably more than were enrolled in all the creative-writing classes in all the universities in America. My mother may have been scammed, but she had a lot of company.)

My mother crossed out the word *The,* then tore out the page, neatly folded it, threw it away, poured herself a cup of coffee, sat back down, took a deep breath, and began:

"If someone had told me two years ago that I would be studying writing today," she wrote, "I would have laughed in his face. Yet the seed for a writing career was planted before I was ten years old, even though I was unaware of it at the time."

As far as I'm able to tell, no one who ever signed up for the Famous Writers School ever became a famous writer, or even a really good one. But the number, I'd bet, is higher among those bilked students' children.

Especially the children whose mothers took the course.

Here's a paradox to chew on: it's much more common for the children of famous male writers to become writers than it is for the children of famous women writers, yet for writers who were raised in households in which neither parent was a writer, it's far more common for the literary influence to have come from the mother.

What that means I did not, at first, have a clue.

Obviously it's a notion skewed by all the generations of mothers who did not typically work and of fathers who did not typically spend much time reading to their children. In recent years, it's skewed by the fact that the audience for books of serious intent has become overwhelmingly female.

That was about as much as I could figure out on my own, and so, for the past few years, I've been doing sloppy, anecdotal research on the subject, running my paradox past my writer friends and acquaintances and quite a few of my nonwriter friends, too, looking for answers. Failing that, and being an English major and not a statistician, I settled for a half-baked theory.

Which is this:

Whatever profession a father pursues, if he's successful, at least one of his children will rebel against it and then, over time, drift semisheepishly toward it, as if it were home. If a father is a failure at anything other than sports (and often even then), all of his children tend to treat his chosen field as if it were a curse.

If a mother is a success . . . well, here, until lately, we're forced to generalize from a smallish sample. The grown children of successful working mothers seem neither unduly attracted nor repelled by her profession (my own mother would, later, become a wildly successful corporate comptroller, which is great, but from where I sit comptroller is a job for which it's impossible to feel much passion). But if a mother's ambitions are thwarted?

Consider each and every stage mother.

Look at all the mothers of American presidents who were smart, strong, feisty, justice-wielding, ahead-of-their-times women.

Ask your doctor sometime if his or her mother ever dreamed of becoming a doctor. Ask if Mom was ever a nurse.

Half the college professors I know had mothers who were schoolteachers.

As for me, the seed for my writing career was planted when my mother enrolled in a fraudulent writer's school.

For her first assignment, my mother wrote about her childhood love of telling or making up stories about pranks, crimes, wacky relatives, and haunted houses. She wrote about the family vacations she took and how they, too, built a foundation for her new career: "We have visited thirty-four states in the last nine years, and I like to write long, detailed letters describing our adventures on these trips and write them to our friends and relatives." She wrote that Faith Baldwin, in the Famous Writers School ad in *McCall's,* "seemed to be speaking directly to me."

She sent that essay in, along with another assignment, in which a cute little freckle-faced boy runs away from home but is returned safely. Neither of them was literature, but both were better than all but a very few college freshmen could muster. She got a B- on the former, a C+ on the latter. (In a college freshman comp class today, they'd be borderline A/B.) The comments were surprisingly unfraudulent.

Over the next few months, my mother completed five more packets of assignments, which were graded by five different instructors (the comments always came with a photo of the person and a bio of his/her impressive-sounding but finally pretty low-level publications). Her grades stayed about the same, but her writing got better. This was a woman who'd never had a college writing or literature class, yet—by the time she got beaten down by the mediocre grades, the loneliness of correspondence school, the realization that it takes more time to write than even the weariest two-year-old can be counted upon to sleep, and the very useful knowledge that writing fiction is about six billion times harder than she'd thought it was—the work she was doing would have put her in the middle of the pack of a good undergraduate fiction workshop. The comments from the Famous Writers School faculty were as good as you'd get from a mediocre professor in a so-so creative writing program. I give my mother all the credit for improving.

That summer, she and my father managed to buy a brick house in town. The house needed a lot of work, and my mother wrote the Famous Writers School and asked to be let out of her contract. They refused (a bluff, since the last thing this racket needed was a day in court). My parents had the trailer sales's lawyer write an angry letter, and my mother stopped paying, stopped writing, and that was that.

She did not stop reading—I cannot remember a moment in my childhood when she did not have a book going. She did not stop taking me to the library upon demand. She did not stop lavishly funding my wish list from the Weekly Reader Book Club.

A little over a year later, an exposé of the Famous Writers School appeared in *The Atlantic*. My mother was too busy to read it. She was in the middle of putting together a deal so that she and my father could buy the trailer sales. He became the president of the company. She taught herself how to be an accountant so she could run the finances. He was a crummy manager; soon she was forced to run the entire business. She did as well as possible, given that the Arab oil embargo sealed the doom of small-town RV dealers. Throughout all this, she didn't even pay herself a salary.

The Famous Writers School went bankrupt in 1971. The trailer sales hung on until 1979.

The next year, my father began a career as a failed insurance salesman, and my mother became a cost accountant at a factory. It was the first year she'd been the family breadwinner, the first year she voted Democrat, the first year she started calling herself a feminist. All these things would continue unremittingly for the rest of her life, which also continues.

She got the first in a dizzying series of promotions, and she and my father moved. By then, my sister and I were grown. My mother started taking college classes.

In 1988, my sister graduated from college, and started doing what my mother had grown up wanting to do: teach school.

The same year, I published my first book. It was an American cross-country travel book, inspired by and to some extent chronicling our adventures on long-ago family vacations.

The year after that, my mother finished her college degree. She graduated first in her class.

✦

I'm always shocked by the ferocity with which memories previously "buried alive" unexpectedly revisit; they're like a second cousin (thirty years removed) who drops by, refusing to budge until you've fed her and agreed that those summers spent sharing the hammock at Granny's were the best of your life, even if they were really the worst.

I hadn't thought about the Famous Writers School in decades until I read Mark Winegardener's winsome recollection of his mother. Now the epiphany it provoked is astonishing. I've realized that there was a period during the sixties when our family rhythm, not to mention our menus, revolved around the "assignments" that came in mysterious large envelopes addressed to my mother, who also was enrolled under Bennet Cerf's and Jessamyn West's tutelage. During those weeks, dinner was always a one-skillet splendor—Spanish rice, beef Stroganoff, and noodleburger—the memory of which puts Hamburger Helper to shame. Mom had the preparation of these fast, furious, and fabulous one-dish dinners down to ten minutes of sleight of hand, all while devouring her current literary challenge. With a clarity that is heartbreaking, I can see her now: standing at the stove, stirring with her right hand, reading her literary "hope" held aloft in the left.

During the next couple of weeks while she'd be percolating, pondering, and procrastinating, we'd eat casseroles (tuna, soup can surprise, sweet and sour, south of the border) prepared early in the day, slowly baked in the afternoon, and served piping hot at 6 P.M. If Mom was really blocked, she prepared her favorite comfort meal, which is sure to be my last culinary request: soup beans, mashed potatoes, coleslaw, cornbread. A successful completion of that month's assignment meant we were all rewarded with Sunday food, even on a Wednesday: fried chicken or pot roast, followed by chocolate cream pie. Failure to live up to her own impossible expectations meant soup and sandwiches for a week, or at least until the next envelope arrived. How horrible it must have been actually to pay to be told your work was mediocre at best! It explains so much about my mother and our family dynamic.

If it is true that reparation for the sins of the father

becomes the karma of the sons, how many unfulfilled mother's dreams become their children's destinies?

My mother never published a single word, nor lived to read the book I was born to write.

But now, at least, the next time I'm asked why I became a writer, I'll have the answer: "My mother encouraged me."

—SBB

FATHERS

When my father died, a new relationship was born. I could drop all my defenses, peel away the scrim of resentment and anger that prevented me from knowing and seeing him clearly, and form an honest perspective of our relationship. I was able to honor him at last, terrible faults and all. How sad it is that so many of us seem to know and appreciate our fathers better in death than in life.

In the years since his father died, Christopher Dickey has been getting to know him better, too. By every account, rumor, and self-admission, the cantankerous Southern poet James Dickey was a difficult man. Such men have no idea how terrifying they are to their sons, little men-in-training. When he was old enough, Chris mustered the courage to reject his father and spent the next couple of decades merely resenting him. As James neared the end of his life, Chris returned to care for him, learning more than he ever thought possible about the indestructibility of the father-son bond, no matter how tortured, which he movingly chronicled in Summer of Deliverance: A Memoir of Father and Son. *And since his father's passing, he has learned some important things about himself as well.*

The Family Album

Christopher Dickey

*How many of the people I know—sons and daughters—have
intricate, abstract, expressionist paintings of their mother, created out of their own emotions, attitudes, hands. And how many
have only Polaroid pictures of their fathers.*

ELLEN GOODMAN

The closet between the kitchen and the laundry room was still
locked the week after my father died, and it took a while to find
the key. In that low-eaved house by the lake in South Carolina,
there were so many keys. They were buried in cluttered drawers,
strewn on dusty bookshelves, crammed into cheap cuff-link boxes
among discarded military insignia. There were keys to briefcases
and suitcases, typewriter cases and guitar cases, and there were Phi
Beta Kappa keys. My father, so proud of this academic distinction
he'd earned, liked to carry extras. There were keys to other homes
we'd lived in when I was a child and offices at universities where my
father had taught poetry; keys to cars that were sold, or given away
in fits of largesse, or crashed when he was drunk; keys to doors and
filing cabinets in places unknown and unremembered by any of us
who were here, now, alive. And, finally, hidden away by the maid
who took care of my father the years when he was dying, here was
the key to the closet by the kitchen.

There was no obvious treasure left inside. Once there had been
silverware, but all of that was pawned and lost when my father's
second marriage was ending. What remained, pushed back on a
high shelf, was the baby book my grandmother started in 1923, the
year my father was born.

Its pages were made of heavy black construction paper and no matter how carefully I turned them their edges crumbled and came loose in the string binding. The photographs were simple, sunlit pictures shaded in brown and white. I had seen them before, but then my father was alive to laugh with me at his scrunched-up infant face or his sailor suit or the yearbook picture of Mrs. Osterhout, his elementary school principal, defaced with beard and glasses by his rambunctious pen. Here is a clipping from the school newspaper that says second-grader Jim Dickey was a member of the "Make Yourself Do Right Club." What could that mean? I look around to see if there is anyone I can ask. But of course there is no one in the house now—no one anywhere—who would ever have known. There is nothing to do but continue turning the crumbling pages. Class picture follows class picture, and it is not until my father is almost a teenager in seventh grade that I begin to recognize him with any certainty. He is standing there at the back of the crowd on the top step of the E. Rivers School entrance, tall, square-shouldered, and smiling. It is the smile that I recognize.

Now as I look at them the photographs are filling up with adolescent life. Young Jim Dickey, captain of the high school track team, is stripped to the waist and radiant with the sun, or he is in front of the house and all dressed up for a date with one of the pretty high school girls glued to these black pages. The energy of his youth draws me in. The thin white edges of the Kodak paper become window frames and I feel as if, through the strong sepia light, I might find a holographic revelation—change the angle just a little, just a little—to get a better look at this lithe boy soaring Apollo-like over a backyard high-jump bar, or this sneering running back clutching a football, or this young cadet on his way to war with the insolent grin that wasn't quite hiding his fear.

"What a handsome kid," I say out loud. The phrase lingers in the empty house. It is something he used to say about others. About my son, for instance. "What a handsome kid."

I did not know my father the handsome kid.

I knew some of the places where the pictures were taken, because I spent a lot of time in my grandparents' house when I was little. I knew that driveway where the boy in the tweed suit stood with his sister and brother for an Easter Sunday photograph. Those steps in front of the place, the yard in back, they were part of my life. I even knew where the sawdust pit was dug to receive the angelic high jumper when he returned to earth. But the jumper himself, that child-boy-man in the pictures, I had never seen him alive.

Most of us have a moment after reaching middle age when we think we know our fathers not just as fathers but as fellow men. Our own teenage resentments that linger so long suddenly give way to a sense that we've seen and done a lot of the same things as our fathers. They are old, but not so old. We are younger, but not so young. If we don't understand everything about each other, at least we understand each other's circumstances. And there's also this: we actually knew our fathers when they were the age we are now. Maybe we were just kids, but we can remember glimpses of how they looked, how they acted, who they knew. No measure of memory, however, will take us back to the time when our fathers were teenagers full of dreams and fears, juiced up on testosterone, trembling at the prospect of a first kiss, feeling their way through to a future that was all expectation and no accomplishment. To reach them there requires an act of the imagination or, perhaps, of the spirit.

In the months after my father died, destroyed by drink and gasping for breath at the end of his seventy-fourth year, I set out on a long search for the man I'd lost. I was writing a book about our life together and our life apart. When I was young he'd written a novel, *Deliverance,* that was made into a movie and made him, for a while, famous. The experience corroded everything in our lives. For most of two decades I blamed him for all that ever went wrong in our family. I left home and left him behind while I became a foreign correspondent covering other people's wars. I came back to him—we came back together—only in the last couple of years of his life. In that time, and after he died, as I worked on my memoir I realized that what went wrong between us had only a little to do with his fame, or with *Deliverance,* and a lot to do with that kid in the crumbling old album. That boy I didn't know was the person who haunted my father, the ghost that drove him. The same ghost had haunted me, and driven me from him.

Other fathers introduce their phantom youth into their children's lives. Maybe they do it by instinct, even by accident. But my father was methodical about it, whether we were watching football (that game he played so passionately and so briefly in high school and college) or reading together the work of other poets (A. E. Housman's violently sentimental "To an Athlete Dying Young") or reading some of the most memorable poems that my father wrote himself— about a boy riding his motorcycle to meet and make love to a girl in the back of a junked car; or older men talking high school football; or fathers looking for their own youth as they play with their young sons. He just could not bear to let those years, that life, that energy of the handsome track star slip away from him. He wanted to recover it all in his writing, his drinking, and in me. God, I was jealous of that young, unknowable father/ghost in the photographs.

For years after my father's funeral was over and my memoir was finished, I couldn't bring myself to look at those friable pictures. They lay in a box under my desk at home. No key was needed, but I didn't have the heart.

Then, just the other day, I opened the picture-book again. In the interval, the poet James Dickey had come alive once more in the public consciousness, which was something he certainly would have wanted. But his image had been oddly, sometimes hideously twisted. He belonged, it seemed, to the Make Yourself Do Wrong Club. A mistress who'd been scorned long ago wrote a spiteful little book in which she talked about his drinking, his faithlessness, his baldness— his baldness!—and any other little curse her long-held fury could conjure against him. My own memoir, *Summer of Deliverance,* had been widely reviewed, and in almost everything written about it a fraction of a sentence from the first page was quoted: "My father was a great poet, a famous novelist, a powerful intellect, and a son of a bitch I hated." So even though the book was about love and reconciliation, anger was the headline. As a journalist, I should have known that would happen, and I was sorry for it. But there was more, and worse, to come. A mean-spirited selection of James Dickey's letters had been published. A dreary biography had appeared that claimed my father's entire world was a lie, and assumed that all the bawdy tales told about him at faculty cocktail parties were the truth. After a while, I and my brother, Kevin, and our young sister, Bronwen, quit reading this stuff. To others it seemed sensational, or ludicrous, or bathetic. To us it had the stench of exhumation, the ugliness of desecration. To clear the air I would go back to my father's poems and novels, which are as fresh and powerful as ever, and then I went back at last to the sepia, sun-streaked world of his youth.

As I opened the album in my own home, far from the house in Carolina, which is now torn down, that boy who haunted James Dickey, and who haunted me, was no longer a threat and no longer a stranger. I knew more than the smile. I could see into the eyes and recognize them, too. I knew the best of what he would become, and I could put aside the worst. I hadn't forgotten anything, but I'd forgiven everything, because what time had taught me was just how much I missed him. How much I loved him. Other pictures of my father, some taken with cameras, some remembered, some imagined, clicked through my mind like a slide show, but I kept turning back to the track team captain, the backyard Apollo. Now, when I say his name out loud, that is the image I see, and it is not defaced by age, or drink, or anyone else's pen. That was the man my father had wanted to be, to remain, to re-become. Why not? If there is a happy afterlife, then this is the man he is.

I look into those young eyes and say, "You are a great poet, Dad, and in your own way you were a great father." I am alone in my own home, but it does not feel empty. "Your sons and your daughter love you as much as you could ever hope they would," I tell him. "And, Dad, it's true, you are a handsome kid."

✦

"It doesn't matter who my father was," the poet Anne Sexton observed, "it matters who I remember he was." Reading Chris Dickey's moving meditation prompted me to wonder why we inflict pain upon ourselves when we remember our past only in isolated snapshots. What if the photo that pries itself loose from the dark pages of memory isn't flattering? If that's the case, perhaps we need to keep turning the pages of our personal family album until we can find images captured through the lens of compassion. No parent could ask for more than the gift of considered love, a remembrance that "forgets nothing and forgives everything." And will we "shutter" to think of what our children's photogenic recall might be in the years to come?

—SBB

GRATITUDE

How does a man feel when his wife becomes seriously ill? Angry, afraid, sad, surely, but just as often confused. Faced with a crisis, our instinct is to reach for the blunderbuss and obliterate it, but disease presents a shifty target. The take-no-prisoners male response to a loved one's distress can itself be distressingly ineffective, even counterproductive.

Roger Evans, a commercial real estate developer in Sun Valley, Idaho, understands this better than most of us. In 1989, his wife, Laura Evans, learned she had advanced breast cancer. She underwent a radical experimental therapy that nearly killed her but beat the disease, then she was diagnosed with a brain tumor, a glioblastoma unrelated to the earlier cancer, just a few weeks shy of the new millennium. Laura had surgery, chemotherapy, and radiation treatments in San Francisco, then the couple returned to Sun Valley to get on with whatever the rest of life had in store for them. A glioblastoma is an aggressive cancer, and the prognosis grim. The average period of survival after diagnosis is fifty-one weeks.

Cancer doesn't discriminate, nor, unlike lightning, does it refuse to strike the same person twice. Still, it's hard not to feel that the disease has been particularly, gruesomely cruel to Laura. A well-known sportswear designer and outdoor enthusiast, Laura got interested in mountain climbing in the eighties and was a member of the American support team that summitted the Himalayan peak Kanchenjunga in 1989. After receiving the grueling bone marrow transplant that saved her life, she founded a breast cancer support group in central Idaho in 1990 and, three years later, the Expedition Inspiration Fund for Breast Cancer Research. Throughout the nineties, Laura led teams of breast cancer survivors on climbing expeditions, including one to the summit of Argentina's 22,841-foot Aconcagua, which was documented by the PBS New Explorers series. Her story, which she mov-

40

ingly detailed in The Climb of My Life, *has served as an inspiration to cancer survivors everywhere.*

Laura is a bright, beautiful, life-loving woman who seems to glow with an almost supernatural life force and lights up everyone around her. Not surprisingly, Roger has considered himself a lucky man ever since he met her thirty years ago, when she was a senior at Stephens College in Missouri and he was an admissions officer—"a fox in the henhouse," as he referred to himself. In long discussions at their home, often with Laura at his side, and on the ski lifts of Sun Valley, Roger described the welter of emotions and responses he's experienced during Laura's latest health crisis, resulting in the most complex and fortifying one of all: gratitude.

Love in All the Right Places

Roger Evans

If the only prayer you ever say in your life is thank you, it will be enough.

MEISTER ECKART

Two weeks before her fortieth birthday, at a time when she'd never been healthier or more vigorous in her life, my wife, Laura, was diagnosed with Stage 3 breast cancer, which had metastasized to her lymph system. I felt helpless. The week before, my mother, who had just visited us for Thanksgiving, had died unexpectedly of a heart attack. When Laura got her diagnosis, I felt that, as much as I could, I'd have to back-burner this grief I felt for my mom. Now, someone else close to me was in a life-threatening situation, but I felt I had a chance for this crisis to have a much better ending. In fact, when I look back on it, I can honestly say I never doubted we'd get through that one. I don't know if it was a naive belief that because my mom had been taken I was owed one or what. Even though I knew clinically what Laura was up against, I just had this confidence and resolute feeling that cancer had picked on the wrong person.

Fortunately, that initial sense of helplessness quickly gave way to a desire to play an active role that could lead to a solution. I knew that, as much as I was needed to provide emotional support, I could contribute more. So I told her to try to get her mind in the right place, concentrate solely on staying mentally and spiritually strong, and I would take on the medical research into the disease. I networked with friends, doctors, other people who'd had cancer to find the best medical team and the most promising treatment protocol. I researched the alternatives and left the decision to her. She decided on a bone marrow transplant, which meant she would need a lot of blood, so I wrote a cover letter to friends asking for blood donations and worked with the hospital to make sure she got every unit she needed.

Throughout the decade since that battle we've felt this blissful kind of protection: We'd taken on this monster, emerged victorious, and so we shouldn't have to fight it again. Life couldn't be so unfair as to do this twice—particularly to someone who has spent the last ten years of her life trying to help other people get through their own battles with cancer.

So in November 1999, when Laura began experiencing headaches, which she'd never before had in her life, and was quickly found to have a six-centimeter tumor in her brain, it was a total shock. Doctors told us that if the tumor were a recurrence of her earlier cancer, her prognosis would be much better than if it were a separate, primary tumor. It was kind of odd to be quietly cheering for and supporting as the best of the alternatives a recurrence of the deadly disease she'd already faced down once.

The tumor was a glioblastoma, a cancer that has a history of relentlessly coming back. We traveled to San Francisco so she could receive treatment from top specialists and she immediately underwent surgery. We stayed in the guest cottage of a friend of ours, traveling to the cancer center every day so Laura could receive radiation. And we struggled to process what had happened. We were overwhelmed by a host of reactions and emotions. But paradoxically, the feeling we spent the most time with was an unexpected one: gratitude.

Under the circumstances, in the face of a disease that typically results in death within a year, how could we possibly feel grateful? I wasn't grateful for the diagnosis, of course. In fact, I was stunned. At heart I'm a pragmatist and I knew I needed to spend a little time with the unfairness of it all, with the disbelief that I felt. I knew I had to work my way through that before I could focus all of my energy on what our plan of action would be. Everyone faces a crisis in his or her life. When it becomes clear that you can't undo it, the important thing is how you respond to it.

What I mean is that once the crisis occurred, everything else in our life quickly took a very distant second position to our relationship and to the urgency of treating the illness. I shut down my office and told my partner we were going to California to do everything we could about this thing. I was free of all work responsibilities—free of every responsibility in my life except one, which was to be with my wife from morning till evening. And that gave us an opportunity to experience a closeness that, even in the normal intimacy of our life together, is just so rare. We were thrust back into the warm center of this mutual support network that every loving couple strives to create and it brought us closer than ever. In these extreme circumstances, when we could have been worried and depressed, we were enjoying being in each other's company more than we ever had, and we felt this powerful sense of gratitude, almost like a benediction. The quiet, one-on-one time gave us a chance to gain some perspective on what had happened, regain our emotional equilibrium, but it also reminded us of how much we liked just being with each other. Amid the bad news there was this special blessing: the powerful realization that what we had together was very precious, very hard to come by.

I've never felt that Laura needed me more than she needs me right now. And I think of how awful it would be for somebody to face this on his or her own. Then it really hits you—just how precious life is, and how uncertain, with no guarantees. I'm grateful we're able to share what we already know, that we love each other a lot, that there's nobody else we'd rather be with, and that no matter what happens we'll be able to draw strength together from our love.

I've always admired the role model Laura has been for others, never more so than now. Throughout both illnesses, she's exhibited this fundamental fearlessness. In the face of a difficult clinical prognosis, she has an admirable inner peace. She's not sad, she's not afraid of dying, she's maintained absolutely unflagging high spirits throughout this whole episode. She wakes up every day with a smile, looks at the bright side, doesn't get caught up in depression or self-pity. You realize that everyone, sick or well, can at least try to make the choice she makes. A day is going to occur whether you fight it or not. You can choose to get caught up in the dreadful, sad, negative side of it or you can treat it as a good day, a special day, the only one exactly like this you'll ever have. It's the simplest choice in the world, regardless of how you feel. When people ask me how I'm doing, I can say I'm doing well because I'm inspired and empowered by how well she is doing.

Not that I'm not afraid. I dread having the the best part of my life taken away from me. I dread being alone, without my anchor, my partner. I fear how different life would be, which is a tacit acknowledgment of how good it's been. I fear the way in which my life will be forever changed, fear not being able to recover after losing the companionship, support, love, and comfort I've relied on for so long. Yet oddly, this fear, too, gives way to a feeling of gratitude, for I realize that my marriage has been the single best thing I've experienced in my life.

I'm also afraid of how well I'll hold up if at some point I have to watch the person I love so much suffering the painful physical effects of the disease. I want to do everything I can to help and support her, but I'm concerned about how well I'll be able to do that. Many times when I'm by myself, I hope I don't have to find out the answer.

I've never been much involved with institutional religion, but I pray every day now. I pray to God that He will get Laura through this, get her well, because she has so much good left in her to give to the rest of the world and she can enrich so many other lives. I don't know whether I have a pipeline to the Almighty, but I know I can't not take advantage of the opportunity to help. Both Laura and I believe in the collective power of prayer. She often feels its surges of energy and warmth.

For myself, I pray for peace of mind. I've refused to accept the inevitability of this. We're still of the mind that through the power of her will, her strength, her friends' prayers, and her doctors' help, she'll find a way through this thing. Even in the face of unfavorable odds, that attitude is important to our mental health. Accepting death, letting go, no hope for recovery? I'm not there yet. Have I accepted the gravest outlook? No.

Thirty years ago, we made a commitment to each other to treat life together as an adventure, a story with many different chapters. This is just the latest one. Regardless of what happens, there will be more.

✦

One of the gifts for which I am continually grateful is that while we can ask for our joys, we cannot choose our sorrows. Roger and Linda Evans's love story is a powerful reminder that gratitude's deepest mysteries are often revealed when we are struggling in the midst of personal turmoil—when we stumble in the darkness, rage in anger, hurl our faith across the room and cry ourselves to sleep. "Sometimes only gratitude can bind us to what eludes our grasp—our past, our beloved, our world, our fate," the English writer Simon May reminds us. "Gratitude can be our ultimate openness to the world; or it can be our last defense against misfortune—and perhaps the strongest."

—SBB

DAUGHTERS

We love our children equally, don't we? Well, yes, the particles of love in our heart devoted to our kids are divided into neat, equivalent bundles. But we don't love each of our kids in the same way. There's the firstborn, destined to occupy a special position in the family hierarchy and whose arrival forever alters his father's perspective on his past and future. There's the first son, whose appearance, despite his father's professed neutrality about the gender of his newborn, jolts him with unimaginable pride. And there's his little girl, whose sweet femininity, innocence, and generosity seem, for reasons he can't quite articulate, too, too heartbreaking.

To a large degree, our boys are known quantities—of exuberance, mischief, and uniquely male talent. Our girls, though, like their mothers, represent the other, the unknown. They require an unusual effort, albeit one joyfully undertaken, to understand. A father can never know his daughter the way her mother can. But he can teach her other things, deflate his own mystery, and share with her his particles of love, as adventure writer Geoffrey Norman discovered, in a very special way.

Like Father, Like Daughter

Geoffrey Norman

Fame is rot. Daughters are the thing.
JAMES M. BARRIE

The anchor line ran off below me at an angle, deeper and deeper, until it disappeared. As I swam along on the surface, waiting for the other divers to enter the water, I could make out some mottled shapes below the point where I lost the rope. They were patches of coral and sand at about ninety feet—pretty deep for sport diving. But we planned to go much deeper; over an edge on the coral reef and then down a sheer face of limestone. Down and down, through the vivid blue water that reached a depth of two miles here. We would level off at 165 feet and stay for five minutes.

"We" in this case meant my wife, Marsha, my two daughters, and I. We were in Andros, the largest and least populous of the Bahama Islands, staying at a little barefoot resort where my wife and I had come alone, a few years earlier. We had liked it so much—the first-class diving and the casual, unhurried mood—that we had promised ourselves we'd return, with the kids, when they were older.

So, now that Brooke was thirteen and Hadley ten, here we were, making a wall dive, which is something divers do for the sheer sensation of falling into the abyss, the wonderful sense of weightlessness and soaring that must be what it feels like to be in space.

It is safe enough if you are trained and do it properly, but there are risks. My chief worry this morning was nitrogen narcosis, or "rapture of the deep." Breathing compressed air at depth results in an accumulation of nitrogen, which affects people differently. Some divers experience symptoms of intoxication—a feeling of euphoria and a loss of judgment. Divers who are "narked" have blithely gone on, deeper and deeper, riding the sensation until they have gone too deep to make it back to the surface. A few divers have even taken the regulator out of their mouths and drowned.

I'd been narked a few times, but merely ascended a few feet, the way I'd been trained, until the euphoria passed. Now, as I looked down the anchor line, I wondered if my daughters would remember their training if they got in trouble. I'd convinced my wife that they would be fine and I had believed it myself. But now I was nervous. They had both done some diving but neither had been this deep before. They had said they wanted to make this dive and persisted when I said I thought maybe they were not old enough. The younger girl, Hadley, knew exactly how to punch my buttons. "I'll bet you wouldn't be worried," she said, "if we were boys."

We had arrived at this place—my daughters and I—by both design and accident. Like most parents, my wife and I wanted to spend time with our kids and it was easy enough at first. Later, it got easier for my wife, harder for me. I was okay with events like *The Nutcracker*, which we went to see in New York or Boston from our home in Vermont. But I was a flop at the mall, which is where, increasingly, it seems most families spend time together. I don't like shopping, and I hate malls.

Still, I liked spending time with my little girls, and since they had been barely old enough to stand we had gone on family hikes up in the Green Mountains around home. I had always preferred the woods to town, and soon it was plain that they liked the woods, too. They liked to go exploring, weren't afraid of getting lost, and considered a porcupine sighting a big thrill. They learned to pick berries; both got attacked by yellow jackets and learned you got over it. We went on family camping trips and they carried packs that were, for their size, big and heavy, but never complained. They skipped down the trail ahead of their mother and me, singing. They liked to gather and chop wood, which made them ideal camping companions—certainly better than a lot of grown men I'd been with in the woods.

Since we lived in Vermont, they had both learned to ski before they were in the first grade. The four of us spent many hours at a local mountain where the amenities were austere but the terrain challenging. We liked to play Follow-the-Leader and by the time the girls were nine and six, Marsha and I couldn't keep up with them. They were bold skiers and when Brooke, my older daughter, made the transition to a snowboard, she promptly broke her arm. Hadley, when it was her turn, took a hard fall—an "eggbeater," she called it—that put her in the hospital for a possible skull fracture and a CAT scan. Turned out it was just a minor concussion and she was back on the mountain the next day.

I warned, cautioned, admonished—no father likes seeing his child hurt. Still, I admired the way they shook off the injuries and came back, just as bold. I liked even more the way they let me ski with them and the way the family would get back to the house, after a day on the mountain, divide the chores, then sit down in front of a fire to eat dinner.

I taught Brooke and Hadley to fish and to shoot because they asked me to. They never became hunters but they liked fishing and Brooke, for some reason, enjoyed cleaning fish whenever we kept some to eat. When I was a boy, girls like mine would have been called tomboys, and it wouldn't necessarily have been a term of endearment.

At first, I was merely glad for their interest in "my" sports. Later on, when they were a little older and Marsha and I had their peers, the Internet, and the MTV culture for rivals, I gave thanks to God for it.

You worry about an adventuresome kid pushing the edge and breaking some bones, even winding up crippled or, possibly, dead. A neighbor of mine had a daughter who was killed in a mountain-climbing accident and he was, understandably, never the same. But those fears are manageable up against the dread you feel when you consider all the possible forms of slow death that are out there waiting to seduce a kid today. When Brooke was in the early years of high school, one of her classmates dropped by the house one day. The girl seemed remote, almost aphasic, and I asked Brooke about her.

"She's been like that," Brooke said, "ever since she got out of rehab."

A junkie, and not even old enough to drive a car.

So when my girls wanted to learn how to scuba dive, we happily took them to the Bahamas resort we liked so much. They were too young to be certified in the United States, but the people who ran this resort were Canadians and excellent, safe divers. They would let the girls dive if they could show they were good enough. Before we left home, I tutored the girls on what air does under pressure, how the body responds to depth, why you need to ascend and descend slowly, clearing on the way down and breathing steadily on the way up—the basics. They were better pupils than boys their age—more attentive, more diligent.

At the resort, we were soon making thirty- and forty-foot dives over coral together. Brooke and Marsha came face-to-face with a small shark. Hadley made a point of learning the species of fish and coral we saw and carried plastic cards looped around her wrist to help with the identification. I was content to let them stay at that depth, but they pushed to go on some of the more ambitious dives.

"We're careful," Hadley said, "ask Tom."

"They're very good," Tom, the resort's head divemaster, said when I asked him. "I think they could do more."

So they did. We all did a couple of night dives. They were not especially deep but they required an extra measure of concentration. We sat on the deck of the boat afterward, looking at the stars and the glow from the bright lights of Nassau forty miles across the water. Neither of my daughters said anything about preferring to be over there, away from their parents in more youthful company.

"Isn't this neat?" Brooke said.

"Can we go on the deep dive tomorrow?" Hadley added. They didn't back off and I liked that.

"We'll see," I said, the totally noncommittal answer every parent learns to rely on.

After a couple more days, when we were at the end of our stay and I was at the end of my resistance, we went out across the reef for the 165-foot wall dive.

"Keep track of your air, your depth, and your buddy," I said nervously, "and if you feel like you are getting narked, then ascend a few feet until you feel all right. Understand?"

They both nodded solemnly. No eye rolling or shoulder shrugging. Which was a payoff all by itself.

Once we were all in the water, I looked to each of them, made a circle of my thumb and forefinger for the OK signal. They gave me the signal back. You can't make out expressions through a dive mask and regulator but I imagined I could see excitement and confidence in their eyes. But, then, I often saw things in their faces that were not there. Dads are bad about missing, or misreading, signals, especially from daughters. I pointed to the anchor rope and we started down. I followed them, noting how confidently they swam.

We reached the bottom and followed Tom out toward the ledge; seemed to sail out over it and then drop down into a vast blue void. My eyes went from Hadley to Brooke to my gauges. Then back to Hadley. The girls drifted along ahead of, and slightly below, me. We went beyond 110 feet, which is the recommended limit for sport diving. And we kept going.

When we reached 165 feet, we hung there for a while, neutrally buoyant, looking back up at the surface, penetrated by shafts of sunlight. We were under tons of water and five atmospheres of pressure, enough to squeeze our lungs to 20 percent their normal size.

I got an OK from Brooke, an OK from Hadley.

After a few minutes, we started the ascent. A foot a second, breathing normally so as not to embolize, all the way up to ten feet, where we hung off for a couple of minutes in a precautionary decompression stop.

"That was so neat," Hadley said when we were back on the boat.

"For sure," Brooke said.

"We'll do it again," I promised. I was as giddy as they were. And very proud.

*   *   *

We still talk about that dive, years later. Just like Brooke and I still talk about the days we spent inside a tent, enduring seventy-mile-an-hour winds on our way up a 23,000-foot mountain. Hadley and I reminisce about the time in Alaska when we were on a salmon river together and a grizzly rose on its hindquarters out of the grass, twenty or thirty steps from her. The bear looked her in the eye and they stood there, eyes locked, for a seemingly endless period of time before the bear lowered itself back into the grass and ambled away.

A woman I once met at a party gave me a hard time about taking my daughters on that dive. It was an imprudent and risky thing to do, she said, and suggested that I was compromising my daughters' safety for my own foolish, macho reasons. She could have made the same accusation, I suppose, about the climb I made with Brooke and the Alaska trip with Hadley and a dozen other adventures we've undertaken together and enjoyed (and survived) over the years. What I couldn't think fast enough to tell that woman is that, yes, those things were a little risky at the time.

But nothing compared with the risk of not doing them.

✦

I had a visceral, polar reaction to Geoff Norman's account of adventures with his two very lucky daughters—equal parts envy and horror. Having been raised by my Southern mother to bloom as a hothouse, pot-bound plant instead of a wildflower, I was as surprised as anyone when, at age forty-five, I gave myself permission to spend the rest of my life as an adventure seeker. But this radical departure in personal decorum is always accompanied by as much trepidation as enthusiasm. So the thought of what life might have been like if I'd had a father who was a pal instead of a loving, distant presence is bittersweet.

"Fathers help their daughters become comfortable as to who they are as a girl and later as a woman," Jonetta Rose

Barras writes in her profound exploration of the father-daughter dynamic, Whatever Happened to Daddy's Little Girl? *Their relationship "helps to develop his daughter's confidence in herself and in her femininity . . . helps her to shape her style and understanding of male-female bonding . . . and introduces her to the external world, plotting navigational courses for her success. . . ."*

And Geoff just thought he was taking Brooke and Hadley out for a water adventure.

On the other hand, if I'd been their mother, I would have throttled him at the first mention of our ten- and thirteen-year-old girls plunging 165 feet below the surface of sanity. But I would have said that about our sons as well.

And, of course, no one would have listened anyway.

—SBB

SONS

We are all sons, we all have fathers who live on through us. Even more so, sometimes, through our sons.

Separate and Shared Agenda

Michael Segell

A good idea—sons.
ERIC SYKES

The boy, awkward and gangly, faces into the wind at the ship's bow, his bony shoulders drawn tight, shielding himself more from human contact—from me, anyway—than from the salty gusts of spray kicking up from the ocean surface. We've driven an hour to the eastern tip of Long Island, boarded a noisy trawler whose operators guarantee a whale sighting, if we're lucky, even a mucousy shower from a cetaceous blowhole, and hauled another hour across the water until time has slowed to a crawl. Neither of us wants to be here. We're on a forced bonding mission, but it's going badly. When I look at him, I'm too keenly reminded of my adolescent self, and feel a wave of shame and disgust. When he looks at me, he sees, in addition to an alien adult, a man who's trying to replace his father.

Of course, it's not true that I'm trying to replace his father, a good man, but I have fallen in love with the boy's mother. It happened more than a year ago—a hallucinatory, giddy, and deeply familiar event that very quickly severed the tethers of two lengthy marriages and promised a whole other way of living, feeling, and seeing. At first, the children—two of hers, one of mine—had found the new arrangements kind of exciting. There was Mom's house and Dad's house and Mom's boyfriend's new apartment and Dad's girlfriend's new place. Though we weren't all living together yet, the kids sensed we would soon blend, which meant to her five-year-old daughter that she would no longer be the youngest and to my two-year-old girl that she would no longer be an only child—exciting developments for both of them. But the boy, his adolescent antennae precisely calibrated, immediately sensed—correctly—that his mother's new friendship had preceded his parents' split. And he still doesn't much care for that.

Yet he's a good boy, very decent, very kind and responsible, ter-rifically bright, very loyal—one big reason for his distress. His mother tells me he will come around, just give him time, and to reach out a little. As I stare at his back, hunched against the ocean chill, I know that there's nothing I've ever wanted more than to make this all work, and that my success in penetrating the boy's protective shell is essential. I just have no idea how to do it. I don't know how to reach out a little.

What does a son learn from his father? How to be a father, among other things. But what if the father was distant and melan-cholic, and what if the son, matching his father's withdrawal step for step, was just a little too rebellious and resentful, not to mention stubborn and willful? And what if a tragedy, the loss of the father's beloved firstborn son, widened the gulf between this second-born son and his dad? How can he know, later, as a father himself, how to reach an angry teenager who reminds him so much of himself at the same age? Where is the internalized paternal mentor he can con-sult to guide him into the boy's roiling adolescent world and make a connection? What does he know about reaching out a little?

I know nothing.

* * *

What can we do, the boy's mother asks after we become the inevitably blended family, other than show the children how we feel for each other? We can feel guilty about leaving their other parents, about the discomfort and confusion we have brought upon them, or we can happily model a marriage that has heat and romance yet is steady and for all time—the one thing we truly know. It's what we wish for them, too, is it not? Let them take this picture inside them, not the other. Our gift to them.

So I give the boy time and space. He loves his mother, and I love his mother. We have that in common, it's a beginning. And the feeling, an oblique memory of a similar dyad, percolates. I can place it, finally, by reversing roles with the boy. I am the toddler on the kitchen floor, watching my father walk in the back door, sweep my mother into his arms for a backbreaking kiss. I am the ten-year-old at the top of the stairs, listening to them talk quietly well into the night. And I am the hormonal fourteen-year-old, inexplicably estranged from my father, yet still deeply admiring of his respect and love for my mother. Even at three, ten, fourteen I know that, above all else, I want this, too.

I have reached out a little to the boy. And my father has reached back—his gift to me.

Repair continues, for the boy and for me, for our separate and shared agendas. It happens slowly, incrementally, in ways that can't be predicted. Lacing up my running shoes one day, I turn and find the boy waiting by the door. He's going out for the high school track team and wonders if he might be able to accompany me around the park. I slow my pace for a few months, but soon enough I can't keep up with him.

He wants to know one day, if he's really careful, whether I'll let him play my drum kit, an old mother-of-pearl trap set I bought when I was his age. Weeks later, he's jamming with a quartet in the living room—though only when I'm not around to hear.

Will I help him buy a suit? He doesn't know how it's supposed to fit. He also wants to learn to play squash. Maybe we could run to the gym and I could give him a few pointers.

He is imitating me, my wife tells me. I should be flattered. It's a good arrangement. I am not his father, he is not my son. The remove neutralizes our father-son-like interactions, renders them easy and harmless. He can listen and follow when he chooses, with no serious consequences if he doesn't. He has his father for discipline. And I get to practice having a son, with few repercussions from my mistakes. If I have a boy of my own one day, maybe I'll have learned to reach out a little.

He will arrive soon enough, accompanied by a twin sister. The girl's gender is identified first, the boy's, after much silent pleading with the cosmos by their newly pregnant mother, a few days later. She desperately wants this for me, she whispers in my ear while delivering the news. I can repair my past by shaping his future. Meanwhile, I should get a second job.

They are love children, worshiped by the older blendees, who now all have a brother and sister in common. The boy, tall, strapping, handsome, is old enough to be the babies' father. He watches his mother and me play with the babies on our bed, then takes them to his own room to tickle and cuddle them on his. Like his stepfather, practicing to be a dad. He rehearses adulthood in other ways, too. One night, I awaken just before dawn to muffled giggles, stagger to the bathroom. The boy is showering with the Swedish au pair. As I tiptoe back to my bedroom my heart brims with unexpected pride. And envy.

The boy is home from college, the babies—they will never shed the title—in preschool. At dinner one night, the five children together for the first time in months, the boy asks the twins how many kids they'd like to have. The little boy, who giggles when his twin sister is tickled and cries when she's hurt, says he'd like three but his sister wants four. It's something they're going to have to work out. Their mother informs them that brothers and sisters can't get married and have babies, that they're going to have to marry someone outside the family. The little boy is shocked. His parents play and hang out together, sleep in the same room, argue and make up—just like him and his sister. Aren't you and Mommy twins? he asks.

The boy has graduated now and has a serious girlfriend. They come around often, holding hands and kissing and patting while the twins smirk and roll their eyes. The little boy, a prankster in school, has nonetheless charmed his female teachers, who seem incapable of staying mad at him for long. Big and little girls love him, and he knows it. His mother, alluding to the benefits of growing up in the constant presence of a female, says he's going to be a great husband. He has definite ideas about what men do for women, and what women do for men.

It's shortly before Christmas and the five children plus girlfriend gather for dinner. The little boy, in a hyperexcited state, proclaims about Santa Claus's unbelievable stamina and power. All year he directs an operation at the North Pole that guarantees delivery, in a single night, of millions of toys to millions of kids. What a man. His twin sister, prefeminist but assertive, pipes up. She wants to know what Mrs. Santa Claus's job is. Her little brother, younger by six minutes, has a quick response: Her job is to relax Santa when he gets home. A new euphemism for Mommy and Daddy's locked bedroom door on a late Sunday afternoon is born. *Mommy's relaxing Santa.*

Somewhere, my father is smiling and congratulating himself. One part of his job, at least, he did very well indeed.

SIBLINGS

Men have always had the hard jobs—hunting fearsome beasts, fending off marauding rival hordes, protecting and rescuing loved ones from danger. The nature of these grim challenges has required them to be able to quickly forge deep and loyal bonds with one another—stifle competitive instincts, set aside differences, and instead become a fraternity of men. Siblings *very accurately describes the connection among members of police forces, fire departments, fighter squadrons, search-and-rescue units, even sports teams. But does the strength of this bond equal that of genetic brotherhood? Some time ago, on the cusp of manhood, the novelist Richard Bausch, an identical twin, learned the difference between the two.*

Mirror Image

Richard Bausch

One man in a thousand, Solomon says,
will stick more close than a brother.

RUDYARD KIPLING

One cold late afternoon in the early dark of the winter of 1966, I marched with a lot of other young men in a freezing rain to a big, hangarlike building the United States Air Force was pleased to call the "dining facility" for an institutional meal of fish sticks and french fries. It was Friday. The weekend was here; we would have two days of relative freedom. My twin brother, Bobby, and I were in one of the tech schools, Survival and Survival Equipment.

This was the old defunct Chanute Air Force Base, in Rantoul, Illinois. There was an unofficial war in progress on the other side of the world. We had joined the air force, like almost everyone else, to avoid being drafted into the army, because everybody in the army was getting sent over there—the drill instructors called all of us draft dodgers, among other things—and we believed, most of us, that even if we did end up going to Asia, we wouldn't be slogging through the jungle carrying a rifle and getting shot at. But no one was happy to be here at this base, either, and everybody did a lot of grousing and complaining. Especially Simpson.

Simpson's mother had won some sort of lottery in the state of Vermont, just after he'd been sworn into the air force. They had enough money to have sent him off to the best schools—or, if it came to that, to Canada or Europe. Anywhere but where he was. Simpson talked a lot about getting out.

The first time I saw him he was perched on his knees, on the top bunk of my brother Bobby's room. "I can get out," he was saying. "Anybody can get out if he's willing to do anything. You know what I'm gonna do? I'm gonna let myself off this bunk and fall knees first. Break both knees." We waited. We were at least as curious as we were horrified, though I don't believe we really believed he would do it. He didn't. He just went on talking about it. He talked about finding a way to make the air force see that he wasn't right for them. And when, one afternoon, the top sergeant said that, after waiting forty-two weeks to begin what would be a fifty-two-week training program in missile technology, Simpson had only twelve more weeks to wait, Simpson responded by saying very quietly, "Oh, well, pardon me while I go out of my fucking mind."

That evening in the chow hall, Simpson sat with us. We understood that in all the important ways he was already quite mad. On his forehead was a bandage from that morning, when he'd injured himself on the chow hall door. He'd said to Bobby, "Listen, tell everybody I've been acting crazy. Will you do that?"

"Okay," Bobby had said.

And Simpson got up on his toes and walked headlong into the hydraulic door hinge, bloodying himself. He lay on the floor groaning, dazed, but conscious enough to say, "Oh, I've been acting crazy. Tell them, Bausch. Tell them how crazy I've been acting."

Bobby said, "He's been acting crazy."

Now, we were eating fish sticks that tasted fishier than fish ever should taste, and talking about where the air force might see fit to send us when we were through with training. Bobby and I wanted to be sent someplace near home, which was Virginia. Our main hope was Andrews Air Force Base, in Maryland. Or Bolling Air Force Base, in Washington, D.C. We had read recently that Bolling was scheduled to be closed down, and we were not holding out much hope for Andrews. We were both a little depressed, along with being tired and scared. Simpson was chewing his fish, staring off, and then he looked directly at me. "Don't you understand?" he said. It was as if he had been going over all of it in his mind. "They're gonna get us killed. They have the power to get us killed, man. And there's not a thing we can do about it. And it's for nothing. It's save the world for time-release deodorants! This isn't even a war."

"Calm down," I said. But I felt a little stir of panic. I tried not to show it to Simpson, who seemed at times to be taking his cues from us, from our responses to him. The disbelief in our eyes made him all the more determined to show how nuts he was. I ate my dinner, such as it was, among the hundred other young men, and as I ate, I felt the enormity of the government, its sheer size, as if it were a massive living thing out in the winter dark, skulking toward us. Then it seemed to me that there was no life in it at all; it was a thing with gears and wires and parts. I had a moment of feeling my little life in the cogs of the giant machine.

I looked over at Bobby, who had stopped eating, and was listening to another boy tell a joke I knew he had already heard. He was going to be polite, I could tell, and laugh anyway. He did. He glanced at me, and then looked down.

Simpson kept looking around himself in terror, not hearing the joke, oblivious to the laughter around him, worrying his one thought: he had no control over his life and he could be killed and it would mean nothing.

"If I'm crazy," he said, "don't they have to discharge me?"

"They might put you in jail," I said. I'd had the thought myself.

Another of us at the table, a squat, acne-scarred boy named Weinberg, who was unlikely-looking as a soldier or airman, with his round framed glasses and double chin and pudgy features, leaned toward us and said, "Somebody killed himself in Fifty-ninth Squadron today. This morning. They found him. He took a whole bottle of aspirin."

This news went up and down the table. Simpson turned white. "Well," he said in a defiant tone. "I'm not gonna do that to get out."

It was as if he were rejecting somebody's suggestion. We finished with the fish, and made our separate ways out into the cold. I was with Simpson and Weinberg; Bobby had gone off with a couple of others, who were telling jokes. I had wanted to go with them, but felt proprietary toward Simpson, and Weinberg, too, who was so clumsy and out of it. Also, I was a very religious boy, and at the time I was trying not to put myself in the way of the dirty jokes I knew Bobby and the others would be telling.

So I was with Simpson and Weinberg, and they kept talking about the suicide. From the beginning of our time in the air force, only two months now, but all through basic training and on into tech school, there had been rumors of suicide, of boys cutting their own throats or taking a lethal dose of something or jumping from the roofs of barracks because of the mental strain. Only that morning a drill instructor had said: "If you pansy-assed dodge drafters get to feeling like it's too much and you decide to kill yourself, don't make a mess in my barracks. Go out in the field and get your blood on the grass."

Probably this was said in reaction to the news from Squadron 59, which would have reached him long before it reached us.

"Do you think it really happened?" Weinberg asked now.

"I'm not even close to thinking about it," said Simpson. Which made me believe that he was. We went along the flight line in the wind and cold, and there were several dozen of us, trailing along. Darkness in the Midwest, I was finding, is an entirely different matter than in Virginia, mostly because of the flatness of the land; so much of the sky is visible, you can see a storm coming from ten miles away. You can see many more stars on a cold winter's night, and when there is snow coming, as it was on this night, the moon shines on it all and makes it look like a prodigious advancing wall of blackness on a field of bright gray.

"Look at that," Weinberg said. "Goddamn, I wish I'd never done this." His voice was tight with dread, and I thought he might begin to cry. He was shivering; we were all shivering.

We went on toward the central square, like a town square or plaza: stores, including the commissary and the pharmacy, a barber shop, a bank, the base library, the Airmen's Club, and two theaters. There was a crowd of other airmen there, some waiting for the theaters to open, some waiting for a place in the Airmen's Club, some waiting to use one of the phones that were all in a row just across from the commissary. You could feel the loneliness and the wanting to be elsewhere in the very air, all those boys away from home. The line was very long at the telephones. I stopped there, not sure how I wanted to spend the rest of the evening. I might go to one of the movies; I wanted to see what Bobby had in mind. But I couldn't find him in the crowd. There wasn't much to do, of course. We were all crowded together into this self-contained city on the plains of Illinois, homesick and cold. Our kind were dying in larger and larger numbers in a place whose names we could not pronounce. But nobody said anything about the war. Poor Weinberg coughed, and I thought of the tears in his voice. Simpson slapped his hands together to work some heat into them and talked aloud about how suicide was not an option, though he was certainly out of his mind. "I'm telling you," he said. "I'm out of my fucking mind. It's a true fact."

I didn't want to think about it anymore. This was the weekend, and two days of freedom stretched out before me. I looked at these two, and at the others, who seemed to be aimlessly wandering around in the square. I felt as if there were some infrangible connection between us all. Brothers. They were all in that moment essential to me. The first flakes of snow began to waft down out of the now starless dark.

To Weinberg and Simpson I said, "What do you guys want to do?"

"I want to go home," Weinberg said, almost crying. "I wish I could go home."

He wandered off in the direction of the commissary, where he would buy bread and canned meat for his time alone in the barracks. That way, he wouldn't have to go out again into the cold. He would die three months later in a bomb explosion on the streets of Saigon.

Simpson followed him, muttering about madness. I don't know whatever happened to Simpson.

I let them both go, and turned in that crowd, and Bobby came toward me out of the dark, saying my name. Someone had killed himself in another squadron. We were all brothers. I felt it keenly, with a physical pang; but here was my brother. In one instant, I had a sense of the wide, terrible, dangerous world of manhood, full of killing and violence and requirements, the need for toughness I didn't have. And I thought of how it would be to lose him, who knew me, and knew where I was tender and where I hurt, and what I was afraid of, and understood all of it because he was so much the same. He came toward me, and muttered something about hating the cold, and the same tremor was in his voice that I had heard in Weinberg's. For a hard minute it was as if he *was* Weinberg, and I was nowhere near, no one to help him, or speak to him with the understanding of brothers.

I knew that I would never forget that moment, or me in it, as long as I might live.

I don't even remember what we did later that night, whether we went to one of the movies, or hung out at the commissary, or walked over to the Airmen's Club to drink the twenty-five-cent beer and watch television, or simply went back to the barracks, to read, or play guitar, or sleep. I don't remember anything else about that weekend, and so it is lost forever. I remember my brother walking toward me out of the cold dark, his face obscured by the hood he wore, and his flight cap pulled down over his eyes. I remember that as he came out of the crowd of others and spoke, I experienced an ache like grief, and an inexpressible joy at his presence, and fear at what the world might do to us, fright at what the future would do.

Just then, I wanted time to stop forever. It was thirty-four years ago.

THOUGHTS FOR THE ROAD

Ten Things I Wish I'd Said to My Father*

Greg Bestick

1. Please don't eat bacon and eggs for breakfast every day.

2. Tell me what it was like for you as a kid. Seriously, I want to know.

3. I thought I'd have more patience with my kids than you did; I was wrong.

4. Even though the words of fatherly advice bounced right off me, I remember them now.

5. You had a bigger impact than you thought you did and than I thought you would.

6. I wish we'd had a few more laughs and a few less arguments.

7. I didn't do any better balancing the job and the family than you did.

8. However it turned out, it wasn't your fault.

9. It turned out all right.

10. Thanks, Dad. I love you.

*and if there's still a chance, I will.

PART TWO

PRIVATE PILGRIMAGES

True pilgrimage changes lives whether we go halfway around the world, or out to our own backyard.

MARTIN PALMER

VULNERABILITY

A heart is an extraordinary thing, muscle charged as though by divine spark, billions of cells firing in a perfect, single rhythm—the very embodiment of life force. It's entirely appropriate that we should use the word metaphorically to describe some of man's finest attributes—courage, inner strength, the desire to press on and do right. But is there more than just a syntactical link between a man's heart and his "heart"? Writer Charles Siebert thinks so, knows there is, in fact—even when the heart in question is dying.

A Broken Heart

Charles Siebert

*Every day I grieve for your great heart broken
And you gone.*

ELAINE FEINSTEIN

I was twelve years old that summer morning back in 1967 when the ambulance first came and rushed my father to the hospital with severe, squeezing chest pains, radiating up into his neck and down into both arms. He had just come downstairs to the kitchen of the newly built Colonial that our family had moved into five years earlier from our overcrowded brick row house in Flatlands, Brooklyn. Already the whine of chain saws and lawn mowers could be heard across the still freshly cut suburbs of Westchester County. My father was anxious about getting out to manicure our own little corner of it. He'd always seemed a stout, healthy man, his only prior illnesses being the rheumatic fever he suffered as a child in the early 1920s, and the bout of malaria he barely survived in 1945 while fighting the Japanese in the jungles of New Guinea. Just two years later, he'd marry my mother, settle into a career as a traveling salesman for a small electronics firm, and go on to beget a perfectly symmetrical (from my middle child's vantage point, at least) set of seven children: two girls and a boy before me, two girls and a boy aft.

He was sitting in his usual place that morning, at the head of the kitchen table for one of our family's typically huge weekend breakfasts, a heedless array of eggs, bacon, sausage, rolls, butter, cream cheese, pots of coffee, and mounds of doughnuts, my father's Chesterfields set right beside his cup and saucer: a veritable still life from a world before warning labels, a world when ever-burgeoning families like ours piled into Vista Cruisers and hurtled headlong and seat belt–less down highways, without a thought about things like cholesterol, or caffeine, or tar and nicotine, none of which—as we would learn from the legions of doctors who would try to help my father in the years between that first bout of heart failure and his final, fatal one in 1980—had any direct, causal effect on his particular heart condition anyway. My father didn't suffer from coronary artery disease, the kind that results in arterial blockages and heart attacks. In fact, he had, as one of his doctors put it, "the cleanest arteries he'd ever seen for a man his age." My father's problem, it would eventually be determined after years of testing, lay in the heart muscle itself, an inexorable thickening of the chamber walls, which, over time, would impede the heart's pumping action, making it work that much harder to compensate and thus, like a weight lifter's bicep, thicken even more.

That morning back in 1967 was to be the first of his heart's many revolts against its own increasing dysfunction. I remember so clearly now, I think, because I was the only one in my family who wasn't there. My father and I became, in a sense, inextricably bound to each other that day by the fates of our disparate hearts. We became, as I suppose all fathers and sons ultimately do, unwitting partners in an ongoing drama of diminishment: life's inevitable apportionment of physical and psychological setbacks, the lesson from which my father, I now understand, always expected me just to take to heart and quietly live by.

Even as he lay on his back in the ambulance, watching the tree branches blur past the windows, I was off hiking with a group of fellow Eagle Scout candidates through the cool, piney umbrage of the Adirondack Mountains, about to have my own heart truly tested for the first time—tested in an entirely different and yet, between my father and me, no less significant way. Our troop leaders had said nothing to us about where we were going that day or what lay in store. That, of course, was the point: a group of loud-mouthed, endlessly posturing adolescent boys about to be chastened by a well-orchestrated bit of terror, about to discover what we were made of by the way we responded to one of life's sudden bad turns.

I remember coming to a small clearing. A hand went up at the front of our single-file brigade, and then, one by one, the file was disappearing into the earth near the base of a huge white pine. The opening was no more than three feet across. It looked like an outsized foxhole dug under one of the pine's roots, but once inside there was a brief earthen landing that quickly gave way to a steep ten-to-fifteen-foot drop along a narrow ledge.

No one hesitated, each of us edging eagerly down out of daylight into the earth's dank chill. Soon it was just our frenzied voices and flashlight beams coursing over the crags of a massive underground cavern, the walls sweating water everywhere into the icy stream beneath our boots. On we marched, in single file again, that first room giving way to another slightly smaller one, and then the next, the water rising up slowly around us as the cave walls began to draw in closer, and now there wasn't nearly as much chatter, our initial curiosity and sense of daring getting slowly choked by fear.

I remember us all repeatedly looking over our shoulders, weighing the immediate rewards of a hasty retreat against the certain, lasting humiliation such a course of action would bring—one which a troop leader had positioned himself at the rear of the line to guard against anyway. "No," you could almost hear us collectively thinking to ourselves as we shivered on through the rising water, "there is only the going forward. They, our troop leaders, the older ones, they must know what they're doing. They must know ways out of this."

In the end, of course, there would be only one, those progressively diminishing cave rooms directing us toward a dead-end wall of rock. I saw the line of heads before me making a sharp turn left through a long, shoulder-width corridor of opposing rock ledges that eventually melded in an inverted Y above our heads and then, to everyone's horror, plunged below the water line, the only possible exit route left to us at that point eerily illuminated by the outside daylight wavering in and around our legs and waists.

There was much crying and screaming. I grew insular, felt deeply alone, a way I've often felt as the middle child of a large family, as though I'm forever caught both on the outside and at the very vortex of all the commotion. I could see, as I stood there, quaking, the point of keeping calm, even nodded, trancelike, at those in our ranks who were suddenly stepping forward, assuming leadership roles, assuaging fears. But I saw a real good case for panic, too, and might well have indulged in it if not for the boy right behind me. Ralph DaSilva—my bunk mate—and the meanest, most intimidating, foulmouthed kid in camp. He went to pieces, had to be pulled to the back of the line and finally cradled by the rear-guard troop leader through the underwater passageway back out to daylight. Ralph DaSilva scared me, I think, into at least some semblance of bravery.

And where, I've often wondered since, was my father at that precise moment, being carted, perhaps, into the emergency room, asking himself if this was the last of daylight he'd see, his own heart pressing him, just as those cave walls were me, toward the one, inescapable outcome? I'd get the news as soon as we arrived back at camp that day—a real-life crisis following so close upon the heels of that morning's crafted one—and was promptly put on a bus home to join my family.

He was sitting up in bed when we were allowed to see him the following day. You can't make much sense of illness as a child and certainly can't abide it in your parents. I remember feeling quite impatient with the whole thing, wanting him to get up and come home, an attitude not unlike his own. I can still see him, the look of anger and shame in his face over being in that hospital bed, and back there again four years later when he'd somehow manage to come through another massive bout of heart failure, the one after which the first physician to tend to him actually told my mother, "Even if he lives, your husband will probably be a vegetable all his life."

I was a junior in high school by then, a starting lineman on the first undefeated football team in our school's history. I remember being so caught up in all my pursuits that I was fairly oblivious to the gravity of my father's condition, the typical teenage spell of self-involvement which my father—gracious man that he was—actually got mad at himself and his illness for threatening to break. It was my coach who insisted after the season's fourth victory that we take one of the school's clunky eight-millimeter projectors to the hospital and replay the entire game for my father in his room. His cardiologist was there, too, I think to monitor my father's heart in case of any undue overexcitement. He sat up in bed, watched, proudly, even the decidedly unglamorous conquests of his offensive-guard son. When the lights came up again, he turned to his cardiologist and, in that guileless, foursquare American staccato spoken by those of my father's generation, said: "Hey, Doc, when can I get the hell outta here?"

No one, not even the cardiologist who eventually came up with the precise daily cocktail of drugs that would right my father's heart rhythms and bolster its pumping action enough to prolong his life, expected that he would live for another ten years. That he did so is, I think, testimony to the kind of heart that there is no way of monitoring or measuring except through a person's behavior, the way one responds when the walls start closing in.

I wasn't around him much over the course of those last ten years. His job would take him and the younger half of the family from Westchester out to western Pennsylvania and then suburban Chicago. I stayed back east, living with a friend's family to finish out my senior year of high school and then going off to college, where, to my father's utter incomprehension and dismay, I'd chosen to turn down the myriad athletic recruiters who'd contacted me to play ball, and began to devote myself to writing poetry.

"Why not journalism, at least," he'd often say to me. "Sports writing. You'd be so good at that."

Over the course of those last years, he'd never discuss his illness with me. Whenever we talked on the phone, or saw each other at Christmas and I asked him how he was feeling, he'd say he was fine. Every so often his heart would fall out of rhythm again and he'd be rushed to the hospital to have it shocked back into line and his medications readjusted, like tuning a dying engine. A heart transplant, the only thing that could have saved him, was not a viable option then. He knew he was running out of time and yet refused to let that ruin what time was left. That, I've come to understand, was part of the subliminal lesson learned that morning in the Adirondack cave, how not to be defeated by the fact that life forces you and all your accrued experience and knowledge, into ever-diminishing quadrants.

I'd learn this all over again from my father one winter near the end of his life. I'd gone out to Chicago to have surgery on the knee I'd injured rather ignominiously in a drunken backyard touch-football game near the end of my college years. My high-flown literary aspirations notwithstanding, I still fell at that time under the aegis of my father's medical coverage. Laid up for months of recuperation and physical therapy, I got a too-close view of the dire struggles my

A Broken Heart

father had been so determined to hide from us: the severe shortness of breath whenever he stepped out into Chicago's bitter winter chill, the pains and tightness in his chest and neck when he walked too fast through a shopping mall or an airport terminal.

Then, late one night, as I sat up in bed reading, I felt just beneath my breastbone this slight, taut raveling of the heart muscle, and then its sudden furious unraveling at over two hundred beats a minute. Unable to catch up with it or my breath, I felt certain that I, like my father, was dying, that my heart, at a preternaturally young age, was literally going out to his, was assuming via some mysterious act of osmotic empathy, his heart's sickness. I must have looked a sorry sight to him and my mother, sitting in the downstairs den, watching, as they did most every night, Johnny Carson, their stout son suddenly appearing in the doorway, a breathless ghost on crutches.

With all he'd been through my father was the first one to me. He made the call to the emergency room and rushed me there in his car. There was, it turns out, true urgency behind this visit, the very real threat faced by those wearing a cast after major surgery of a blood clot forming and traveling to the heart. Once the doctors discounted that, however, it was determined that I'd suffered a good old-fashioned panic attack. The diagnosis wouldn't change for four subsequent late-night visits, by which time I'd severely tried the patience of a number of doctors and, far more regretfully, begun to shame myself a bit in my father's eyes.

One afternoon at work he would have another severe bout of arrhythmia and be rushed to the hospital yet again for electric shocks and tests. That particular stay lasted a week. In the course of it, I was sitting outside his room one day with my mother when his doctor came out the door. She asked him to listen to my chest by way of finally putting my fears to rest. That, I think, was the turning point, the moment when I suddenly saw myself panicking in the cave; when I realized that for the sake of the brave, quietly dignified man in the room behind me, I should start to get a grip. I remember actually asking him at one point in the throes of my heart hysteria how he did it, how he lived from day to day knowing how frail his heart was.

"Well," he said, looking a bit startled by his clever son's fatuousness, "what choice do I have?"

I was, again, far away—a teaching fellow in a master's of fine arts program in Houston, Texas—the February morning when I got the phone call everyone in my family had long been dreading. So many presentiments of it we'd gotten over the years, and yet it had become our habit, the very one that my father had fostered in us, not to see the encroachment of the walls, to keep going on the assumption that more time and light awaits just up ahead. Only months before that final phone call came he'd have to have his heart's wayward, faltering rhythm righted one last time. I remember much about that day as well. I was at the Houston campus, being told by my professor that my first poems had been accepted by a major magazine. I ran back to my apartment to call my father with the good news, the only time in my life I phoned him at his office. His secretary answered. She was crying. She said he'd just been rushed to the hospital.

There is a way, I remember thinking to myself at that very moment, in which you and he will never leave behind the lessons of that first morning years ago when he was rushed away in the ambulance and you emerged on the far side of the cave only to hear the news of him: the simple lesson, for example, about how a in life triumph is often closely attended by a tragedy and the need to push past it. When I tracked down his hospital-room phone number to find out how he was feeling, he was, as ever, putting the best possible face on things, sitting up in bed, eagerly receiving my news, telling me how proud he was.

We drown when our hearts fail, drown in ourselves. People tend to think of their bodies in solid, two-dimensional terms, as static arrangements of parts to which the heart, a simple, monorhythmic pump, supplies the blood. We are, really, each of us, barely contained, shifting seas of fluid that the heart, like a deft helmsman, keeps us at once adrift; keeps us buoyed up in a kind of continuous, dynamic suspension.

They were to go on a trip that day, he and my mother, February 1, 1980. They were taking a train to St. Louis to visit old friends. He'd been—she has told me this a number of times since—particularly clingy all that night in bed, never wanting to let go. When my mother finally did that morning in order to get ready, she heard from the bathroom her name being called and then a soft moan as he fell back upon the bed, his heart fully spent and my father no longer able to tread his own body of water.

You swim hard, as I remember it, and yet calmly toward the light, all the cries, all the echoing fuss, fading; just yourself now and your life's deepest caresaswim there before you, bidding you on. And you go, the way he'd taught me all his life, always go forward, for more light, even as the darkness finally descends.

My father didn't live long enough to see any of my poems in print, but at his wake I decided to place a copy of one in the left inside pocket of his suit, directly over his heart. Entitled "Fathers and Sons," it's, about the December night, a year before his death, when I was driving from New York to Chicago for Christmas even as my older brother was flying there, and the younger, still living at home, awaited our arrival with the rest of my family. The words came to me all at once, so rapidly and uniformly it seemed I was taking dictation from someone else, a force, a presence, call it what you will, but so strong that I was too frightened to remain in my apartment when I was done, was heading out the door as soon as the last refrain was complete:

> And I come to him
> as breath,
> the way breath travels,

almost aware of itself,
driving through Ohio in late December.
It has rained and now ice coats the dead woods.
A full moon gives glow to the road
and on both sides, miles of frozen branches:
crystal network of expanding lungs,
this night, my father, breathing.

And I come to him
as thought,
the way thought travels,
drone of a distant pulse,
flying over the Midwest in late December.
Moon lights the ghostly curve of earth's skull.
Below, a wide lake of dark gives place
to a startling city, miles of patterned lights:
tense hum at the base of the brain,
this night, my father, wondering.

And I come to him
as blood,
the way blood travels,
vigorously dreaming,
living in this house with him in late December.
Coldest winter for years, the pines, full, warm,
around the house's brittle frame, have bend
in their branches for what the winter moon brings:
blood's dream for open arms,
this night, my father, waiting.

✦

When I feel shattered or scattered, it's often because I'm
missing a part of myself and I don't know what it is. So I

search for misplaced or misbegotten memories where I'm sure to find them—between the lines of someone else's writing. So many times, when I'm going down for the third time, books have become my life preservers. My sense of gratitude is palpable when another writer rescues and restores me through the sharing of joys and sorrows, promise and pain, triumphs and travails. I might cry tears of recognition, but I can also breathe again, which is why I have come to regard the best kind of writing as word-to-word resuscitation.

However, as I finished reading Charles Siebert's exquisite heart-to-heart essay about "the enlightening duet of diminishment" between him and his father, I found myself unexpectedly tense. Right around the end of the first paragraph I started holding my breath. I also have a tendency to tense up and hold my breath in a dentist's chair, especially if there's a thin metal probe searching for rogue pockets of decay that need to be routed out into the open. What's hidden cannot be healed.

You might not have responded as I did to this particular essay, but any time you have a visceral reaction to something you've read, pay attention (especially if you want to slam the book shut). Think of it as your future extending an invitation for a heart-to-heart between your present and your past. Your body is the go-between. Of course, it's glorious when we agree with another writer's observation; it's evidence that we're not the only genius on the planet or the only one feeling this way. But don't discount anger, annoyance, or even vague unease— the easiest to ignore. Be willing to reread the trigger passages slowly and meditatively. Then put away the book and mull over the message.

When I allowed myself to become as vulnerable to Charles's regrets and guilt as he was, I realized that in the past decade I've pushed down a lot of inarticulated rage and *unexpressed grief. There were always deadlines to meet. Books to write. Speaking engagements to keep. No choice, I thought, but to move on.*

It's no coincidence, then, that my breathing constricted and my chest hurt while reading and editing a meditation on love and loss. In Chinese medicine the chest cavity—the lungs—is considered the sacred repository for the unresolved. It was a psychological and spiritual challenge for me to respond with the same amount of respect and courage as a reader, as writing the essay must have required for Charles Siebert. But I'm grateful I did. I can breathe clearly now.

Zora Neale Hurston believed "there is no agony like bearing an untold story inside you." Sometimes, thank God, it's not necessary to write all our stories. We also live on the pages created by strangers. So whether you write your own stories or read them, honor them all. The past asks only to be remembered.

—SBB

SIMPLICITY

Near the top of the mountain, the road dips, bends, then snakes through a small grove of redwoods. The dense tree canopy blocks all ambient light, so that when you emerge on the other side of the grove, you feel as though you've passed through a portal into another world. It's a fitting way to approach the Sonoma Mountain Zen Center, because people there view reality just a little bit differently from the way most of us do.

This is certainly true of Roshi Jakusho Kwong, the center's abbott. A short wisp of a man of indiscernible years, Roshi has a perpetual quizzical smile on his face and a presence, in the most fundamental sense of the word. He leads me from the car to the dining hall, where we are joined by his wife, Laura, and four students, all middle-aged men, who have been getting a "tune-up" at the center for the past couple of weeks. As I sip miso soup, the group asks me where I've been, how I got here, what the journey was like. Each response, however polite and mundane, elicits uproarious laughter. You made a wrong turn? Utterly hilarious. You forgot your umbrella? Fall-down funny.

This is the way it is with Zen people. They're always laughing. They try to simplify their vision, bring nothing from the past to the present, eliminate projection, expectation, and, most important, ego from their participation in the world. They experience it simply as it is and consequently it is absurdly funny.

Their way of seeing defines simplicity. While the rest of us lead lives of ever-increasing complexity, theirs is an example, however raucous, we would often do well to emulate.

As It Is

Roshi Jakusho Kwong

Like all Holmes's reasoning, the thing seemed simplicity itself when once it was explained.

SIR ARTHUR CONAN DOYLE

When I was in my twenties I was studying to be an art teacher at San Jose State University. One night, driving home alone, I was in a terrible car accident in which I was almost killed. I remember well the highway patrol paramedics transferring me onto a gurney when I felt myself falling, falling, falling. Fortunately, I recovered and took a job as a mailman to strengthen my legs, which had been shattered in the accident. By the time I returned to teaching I had grown a goatee, along with new thoughts and ways of how to live a meaningful life. It was the fifties, the period of the beats, which my wife, Laura, and I identified with—but it was also the era of McCarthyism and conformity. My supervising art teacher insisted that I shave off my goatee and cut my hair. We also had profound differences about teaching—he wanted to preserve the conventional status quo while I wanted to try an open, creative style of instruction in the hope of easing the division between student and teacher. I had no choice but to leave the school. This was very important, because it was the first time I stood up for myself and for what I believed. I then vowed to embark upon a path that would infuse my life with deeper meaning.

I took a job in the commercial art world as a sign painter and window-display artist to help support my family. Laura and I had been talking about trying to find an alternative way to live—developing a simpler, clearer, purer way of seeing and experiencing the world. One day I read in a Japanese newspaper a story about Suzuki Roshi, who was the first Zen master I ever met. Suzuki Roshi was the founder of the San Francisco Zen Center, the first Zen monastery in the West, and author of *Zen Mind, Beginner's Mind,* one of the most cherished and popular books about meditation in the West. He was asked why, if he believed in liberation from the ego, from the self, he kept a bird in a cage, whereupon he immediately opened the door and the bird flew out, circled the room, and disappeared through a window.

I was very taken with that and became one of his beginning students. I saw something in him that was pure, childlike, spontaneous, fresh, joyous, and nonjudgmental. He had piercing eyes and an unbelievable presence and was full of strength. I had never met anyone like him before; it was scary and wonderful at the same time. I feel that if you can see a quality in someone else, that means you must have it, too. It's like a flower—if you recognize a flower's beauty, it's because you are beautiful at that moment. Or it's like a mirror: to see clearly, you have to be clear. In order to love you have to be loved, starting with yourself. How could it be otherwise? After all, where else could these abilities to see and love come from? From this simple truth it's possible to glean great things.

Given the historical enmity between China and Japan, my father was deeply worried about, and offended by, my decision to be ordained. How could I be studying with a Japanese man? Later he partially accepted who I had become and agreed to come to my ordination, but he refused to share lunch with us.

Suzuki Roshi also asked me to discuss my decision with Laura, knowing my new commitment would change our lives and family. By then we had four boys. And in fact the first thought I had when my head was shaved during the ordination ceremony was how my oldest son would feel about it. Ryokan, who was named after a famous Zen monk and poet, was just turning thirteen and was very sensitive about the image his father projected. When I was at home shaving my head he would pass by and say, "You're doing that *again*, Dad?" It really hurt my feelings. I told him, "This is the life I have chosen." Ryokan never said that again. Still, I made him feel self-conscious. Once, I went to his baseball game and he was pitching. He hit six batters. The rest of the parents accepted me for what I was, but the kids were understandably affected. When we drove to town my sons would all hide in the backseat. They didn't seem to understand so well then but they're very proud of us now. After ordination, Suzuki Roshi asked me to be one of his successors. The year before he died, Roshi began training me in confidence.

"As it is" is a phrase that's used a lot among Zen practitioners. It refers to active or discriminating awareness, embracing the way things are, whether it's a single brown leaf dancing in the wind blown from an oak tree, a personal defeat—or your son's conflicting feelings about you and your shaved head. It's seeing things without projecting your judgment and expectation upon them. If you just *see* a person then you don't judge him or her and the relationship remains open. When you experience reality as it is, you don't try to make a straight thing out of something crooked. When something is sad, it's really sad. And when you're hurt, you feel really hurt. It's about cultivating simple, clear vision so that you can see the vast complexity of things, states, and emotions as they are. That's all!

So Zen, the active acceptance of "as it is," is not always so easy to practice. There's a practice here at Sonoma Mountain of sitting through the night once a year. Suzuki Roshi introduced the tradition to us. It's modeled after Buddha's enlightenment on December 8, when he finally resolved to sit in one place for seven days. The first night we did it, in 1973, I sat full lotus on the cold concrete floor. The bell rang to begin and five minutes later the bell rang to end. Four hours seemed like five minutes. So every year since then I've tried to reproduce that experience and have been completely defeated. Sometimes I'd sit down and feel happy, sad, agitated, restless, or exhausted, even though I had no reason to be. It's not how I wished to be during meditation but that's exactly how it was. And it took me maybe twenty years before I could accept that whatever is during that all-night sitting is just as it is. Then I was freed from my preconceptions of what I believed should happen.

For an ordinary person an example of this problem could be the need to repeatedly return to the same place where he took his first happy vacation and expecting the experience to be exactly the same. I imagine for a heroin junkie it's like chasing that first high. For someone who has been spurned, it's like trying to re-create the same relationship with each subsequent lover. But you can't chase impermanency; everything is changing. The reality that surrounded that perfect sitting, that perfect high, can never be duplicated. It occurred at one specific point in time, and that moment is gone. It's the same with everything.

Now when I'm sitting on the cushion, what I find is that I'm . . . sitting on the cushion. There's no discriminating awareness. I'm not expecting a big buzz or a little buzz. Any buzz will do, or none at all. It's not that important. And because my conditioned thinking mind is not being cultivated, I can have access to my inherent, basic goodness. There are no major hindrances, such as greed, anger, or ignorance.

Every time you use a calculator, you have to clear it. If you don't, you will have many numbers superimposed upon your present reading. Similarly, when the complexities of the past are superimposed on the present, you can imagine all the distortion, confusion, and suffering that arise. When you see life with awareness—"as it is"—your energy is free-flowing and you don't seem to be overwhelmed by many things. When you realize clear, simple vision, you rediscover your inherent compassion and wisdom. Thus your relationship to all things (material and immaterial) changes. When you forget the self, when you step out of the box, you can laugh at yourself. Because there's a generous sense of spaciousness, you will experience a great joy, peacefulness, and a deep feeling of gratitude.

And when the conditioned self is forgotten, this big self becomes merged in the process of being and experiencing. Remember when you learned how to tread water? The more you concentrated on trying to achieve buoyancy, the deeper you sank. It's only when you start feeling the water and forgetting the self that buoyancy happens. The ego has to get out of the way before you can learn and realize things. You have to empty your cup so you can fill it. It's true of myriad things—learning to waltz, skiing, riding a bike. The process leads not only to learning how to ride the bike but also *having the realization* of riding the bike!

This point is very rare. This is the actualization or practice of Zen. The simpler you are, the less obstruction you experience and the greater access you have to the truth.

Some people have asked me, if such simple and clear vision is so desirable, why are we not evolving in such a way that simple vision becomes a favored human trait? Why is evolution not helping us achieve clear, simple vision? Because that's not the goal of the regular world. The spiritual world's direction is toward the realization of truth, which is the absence of greed, anger, and ignorance. And I'm not sure that evolution shares those goals.

❖

Like Roshi Kwong, I am also frequently asked, "If simplicity is so desirable, why does it so easily escape our grasp?" More often than not, this desperate entreaty has been posed by a rabid pack of normally amiable, clever, and competent women who have been on the Simple Abundance path for two or three years, yet suddenly find themselves mysteriously on the verge of nervous breakdowns (which led them to drive two hours seeking advice from me). These are the same women who have been evangelical about the curative powers of a certain pink book and couldn't wait for their husbands, lovers, brothers, and sons to experience the serenity they have found in its author's suggestions.

Why has simplicity escaped the grasp of those of us who should know better?

In a word: entropy. Or hubris. Take your pick. Last week for me it was hubris; forty-eight hallucinatory hours of arrogant pride in which I was guilty of perpetuating the superwoman myth—being all things to everyone else. On the third day, I awoke and couldn't drag my sorry carcass out of bed. I told everyone I was sick. I was. Of the pretense. So I stayed out of sight, then slowly roused from my stupor. Inch by inch I came to my senses by making sure that every other word uttered was no until I recovered my equilibrium. But it was a close call.

However, entropy is the word that explains best the complex chaos that engulfs me today. How about you? According to writer and scholar Stephen Mitchell, entropy is what scientists call the phenomenon of the "irreversible downward slide of events: life becomes death, order becomes disorder, princes become frogs." It's also another name for the mother martyr syndrome, whereby women transform themselves into harridans. Children cower. Men shake their heads and go hunting. Or fantasize about it.

Buoyancy may very well occur when the self is forgotten while trying to float in water or master a spiritual practice. But if you find yourself on dry land—frazzled and remembering the good old "simpler" days when you had only three or four things that needed to be finished yesterday, rather than fifteen or sixteen—then you have forgotten the self for too long. That's self as in self-preservation or self-nurturance. Self-sacrifice is not how the soul soars, even if, through the best of intentions, we become overwhelmed and overwrought.

So the next time you're asked where you've been, how you got there, and what the journey's been like so far, if you can't remember the last time you had an hour of idle solitude, met a friend for lunch, or made love, give your questioner a contemplative moment to sip their carry-out miso soup. Take a deep breath and exhale fully. Smile. Then remind everyone within listening range that it's not necessary to go halfway around the world to count the cats in Zanzibar, when the kitty litter in your own basement needs to be changed.

—SBB

THERAPY

A doctor I was once seeing—okay, he was a psychiatrist—occasionally mentioned that I was "allergic" to my office visits. This was a brilliant move on his part, for now I didn't have to feel guilty and defensive about the resistance I was putting up to sharing my troubles and worries—exposing my "weakness"—with anyone. A man who manages to make it onto the couch, he knew, is a very delicate creature and needs coddling, or he will be lost to the shrink forever.

Like me, Daniel Menaker, author of a very funny novel about psychoanalysis called The Treatment, *never quite managed to overcome the allergy he developed in the shrink's office. Nonetheless, he managed (also like me) to take away from the experience some very valuable information about himself and his place in the world. The "allergy" may even have been worth it.*

Vision Quest

Daniel Menaker

Fortunately, analysis is not the only way to resolve inner conflicts. Life itself still remains a very effective therapist.

KAREN HORNEY

In the winter of 1970, I was twenty-eight years old, a fact checker at *The New Yorker*, sharing an apartment with a friend from college. Not long before I got my job at the magazine—I was then a high school English teacher—my brother had died of a blood infection, which he contracted after routine knee surgery. A few months after his death, my girlfriend of many years' standing went home to the South, shocked by my family's tragedy and tired of trying to be an actress and tired of our static relationship. My parents made the best they could of their shattered lives, and I saw them a lot, but basically I stumbled through my days, entirely dismayed. My brother Mike had, far more than our sweet but feckless father, set an example for me. He meant the world to me.

One night that winter, I woke up suddenly and sat up in bed. I felt a cold dread come down and settle around and within me. My heart beat violently, I felt faint and clammy, and I was terrified—of what I could not have told you then nor can I now, even after a few thousand hours of lying on a couch and talking about it. And since I had no idea that what I was experiencing had a name and was, sadly, not uncommon, I thought I was surely going to die. I woke up my roommate. His father was a psychoanalyst. He knew what was going on with me. He gave me some scotch. I calmed down, and after an hour or so went back to sleep.

This experience was so fearful—I believe that no one who has not had this kind of out-of-nowhere panic attack can understand how real and frightening such an episode is—that I immediately began to live in terror of its recurrence. I somehow managed to go on with my work and even do it well. In fact I probably threw myself into it to try to get my mind off this new horrible condition. But the anxiety became generalized and began to affect everything I did. It would threaten to overcome me again when I went out to lunch with someone, the few times I had dates I'd never be sure I'd be able to get through them, and I could not sleep.

I had before then lived a life so cocky and so ignorant of this kind of affliction that I regarded those who exhibited its symptoms with casual disdain. So now I had disdain for myself, to go along with the awful symptoms. I could not believe I was so "weak." I tried to discard this mental knave of spades by force of will. It didn't work.

I went to a regular doctor. He told me I had an anxiety disorder and gave me Valium. I took a little in the morning and a little in the evening, and I began to be able to manage—but not much more than manage—the derangement. Valium would help me in a crisis, I knew, and, after a while, using it regularly had me staring blankly at, say, the pencil holder on my desk for minutes on end, so I stopped. But my psychological molecules had been scrambled, and I was still pretty miserable and, well, nervous all the time, so I finally gave in—as I put it to myself—and started seeing a psychiatrist. He was a kind, smart man, a fellow Knicks fan, and he put me on the couch. So it began.

Luckily for me, manly disdainer that I had been, the culture of the early seventies not only sanctioned but encouraged "feelings" and "getting help" and even "alienation." Half the people I knew— men and women—were in therapy or analysis. The *New Yorker* had a medical plan that paid 80 percent of the cost of therapy or analysis not only for its employees but their families. The nature of one's treatment, and its substance—the seductive mother, the withdrawn father, the lack of attention paid to all us complainants (my disdain lingers) at crucial moments in life, a manipulative boss, problems with commitment (a lot of that)—became common conversational fare. This sociological sea change helped reduce the shame I felt about my affliction, but not by much.

At that time, far less was known about the medical nature of anxiety and panic disorders than is known now, and talking was considered the only valid course of treatment available, with tranquilizers as a stopgap measure. Cognitive behavioral therapy and "flooding" (in which the patient is exposed to onslaughts of whatever it is he is phobic about) were little known. There was no Prozac. So, if you could afford it, you went to the doctor and you talked, sitting up or lying down, in an effort to understand what was ailing you, and in the hope that the understanding would lead to improvement.

Because I was a man I had a hard time "getting in touch with my real feelings." The kind, round-faced analyst with glasses did the classical analytical thing—"Mm-hmm" and "How do you feel about that?"—and he offered some interpretations of the meager material I presented—interpretations that I was not really ready to hear. But I did the best I could to dig around below the surface of my agitated mind. And what I came up with, generally speaking, was anger—anger from the present, the recent past, and the sometimes distant, sometimes sharply immediate era of my childhood. And I was afraid of that anger, especially since it had played a part in the athletic accident that had led to my brother's knee surgery. I also mined an angry fear of separation and abandonment that may have begun with an illness in infancy that put me in the hospital for a month with almost no contact with my parents. (Boo-hoo, I am tempted to say to myself—the old disdain—but there you are.) At the bottom of it all was a conviction that I was simply no good.

Reciting these problems bores and depresses me, and I try not to discuss their particulars with anyone with whom I am not intimate. Even she can't keep her eyes from rolling just a little when the neurosis curtain begins to rise, and who can blame her? So I'll sum up my five years with the kind man by saying that I began to discern certain repeated patterns in my behavior with my family, my brother, my colleagues, my alleged superiors ("alleged" represents one of those patterns all by itself), my girlfriends, and my therapist, and I began to see that these patterns often had as much to do with my own psychodynamics as with external circumstances. And I started to write, in part as a way of conjuring with what had happened to me. But I still yearned to recover my prepanic, more confident self; despite the permission given to men by the times not to have to be constantly "manly," down deep I still wanted to be a "man."

Two scraps of material come immediately to mind from those five years (a lot more would come rushing in if I gave it a chance): One is the kind psychiatrist suggesting, after hearing about an anxious moment, that I "try to relax." This struck me as hilarious: This is what your expertise consists of, I said to myself disdainfully. Then it struck me as wonderfully oxymoronic: try to relax. Now it seems to me poignantly and even profoundly apt: it distilled into three words the more futile aspects of what we were up to.

The other scrap is that the New York Knicks won their only two NBA championships during those five years, and that the kind man and I talked about them a little—about Bradley and Debusschere and Reed and Frazier and Monroe and Barnett—when all else failed.

"Why do you suppose you started with the two white men on that team?" the next, far from kind man—whom I saw, for another five years, in my early forties—would ask, were he to read that sentence. I was still damaged goods, but I had learned how to handle myself better in my dented condition, learned to rebutton-up my confessional vest, learned that part of my problem was just the general state of trying to be a grown-up man with all the discontents that accompany responsibilities and civilization. The kind man and I had gone as far as I could go at the time, so, without his blessing, I stopped seeing him.

But a couple of years later I had clawed my way through my antagonism toward all authority and was a senior editor at *The New Yorker,* and I was ready to get married at last, have kids, get on with it in general, and I thought it would be useful to have some more "help." I wanted some fine-tuning, I wanted to see if there was any possibility of living without chronic anxiety instead of living with it.

It's hard now for me to believe that I kept seeing this guy for five years. He was so hostile toward me, it seemed, and this hostility so regularly galvanized my own inclination toward anger that our sessions more closely resembled collisions than collaborations. He ridiculed my docility about certain financial inequities at *The New Yorker,* he shortened the time of our session—from an already minimal forty-five minutes to forty—without any discussion of the change, and he was critical of most of what I said in his office and most of what I did outside it: my efforts at interpretation, my getting married, my wife's and my decision to have children.

Here is one specific—and crucial—example of how vexed our relationship was. One night, about four years into this second analysis, I dreamed that this doctor and I were on a bus together, talking like friends, about ourselves and the other people on the bus. The burden of our conversation was that he and I and the other passengers were all not only in the same bus but in the same boat—the human condition, filled for all of us not only with rewards but serious problems. Finally, my stop came along, and we parted on warm terms. After I told the doctor about the dream, he was very quiet. I filled the silence with a self-effacing comment about the dream, expressing a wish to deny that I was "only" a patient. Silence again. Then he said, "I don't understand this dream. It is a perfect termination dream"—I didn't know there was any such thing—"but it couldn't really be." My heart had leaped up, despite his skepticism, at hearing the word *termination*. Why couldn't it be? I asked. "Because you are by no means ready to terminate," he said coldly. Ah, but now I knew that I was—and I did, a few weeks later.

Oddly enough, out of all this psychological mess, I made some kinds of progress; whether it was a result of carving out some autonomy and maturity for myself or of simply growing up a little (and more than a little late) I shall never know. My anxiety remained, but I developed more strategies for coping with it. But repeated exposures, with Dr. Kind and Dr. Unkind, to the idea of patterns and the unconscious connections between one thought and another, one action and another, one person and another heightened my awareness of *coherence*—first within myself and, gradually, in the words and actions of others. It was like reliving, as

an adult, the emergence of a student's appreciation of literary interpretation. And, in fact, analysis has been enormously helpful to my
writing and editing. Overall, the couch taught me to look for the
truth lurking beneath appearances, the reality looming behind
denial, the gravity darkening the casual.

And it led me to some real conclusions. For instance, when it is
rooted in ignorance, my tendency to be scornful of others' ideas or
activities almost always stemmed not from real superiority, of
course, but from fear and anxiety. (Thus my initial scorn for therapy.) And it almost always included a repressed desire to be part of
what I held in contempt. Now instead of scorn I feel joy when I can
conquer my anxiety and learn or do something new, deep sadness
about my limitations when I can't.

Psychoanalysis has also helped me understand other people's
conflicts. I've learned to use this understanding in both a calculat-
ing, seductive way and in the service of genuine affection and
respect. An example of the latter: A good friend of mine stopped by
my office when I was at *The New Yorker* to say hello. I asked what
he was up to and he said he'd just written a Talk of the Town story;
it was going to be published but he "modestly" dismissed it as
rather inconsequential. Because I recognized and sympathized
with the insecurity behind this dismissal, and because I knew how
seriously all writers take even their most neglible productions, I
told him that he was a wonderful writer (which he was) and that I
was sure the Talk story was, like all his work, worthwhile. A smile
of appreciation and relief broke out on his face.

An example of calculation: Well, never mind; suffice it to say
when I detect in someone an evidently unconscious anxiety about
something, I can steer our conversation toward an opportunity to
offer (often false) reassurance about whatever is troubling her. A
commercial writer wants to be considered a literary writer, I can
tell—maybe she criticizes real literary writers—but she can't bring
herself to acknowledge this fear that she's not. I lie and tell her she's

a good literary writer. I find this manipulation shameful—and not exactly rocket science (except, perhaps, when the insecurity presents itself subtly and indirectly). Or I can bring to the surface something that has been swimming around underneath a conversation—that is, break the ice from below. Or I talk about ordinary life with extraordinary people. The higher they fly, the more they appreciate the chance to come down to earth, if the offer to do so is made deferentially.

These psychological wiles, when they are no more than wiles, leave me feeling empty and phony, like a human oil can. But when sincere, they are not wiles but a manifestation of love, and they represent the knowledge, gained at least in part through years of often uncomfortable and tedious self-examination, that we are all indeed on the same bus, in the same boat.

This sense of connection and recognition and respect makes me feel less like a man—at least the prepanic "man" I once was—and more like a human. Efforts to achieve compassion for oneself often lead to compassion for others, understanding of oneself to understanding of others. When they work (far from always), therapy and analysis—for men in particular—paradoxically assist people in seeing themselves from the point of view of others. "Paradoxically," because so much of what goes on in this business, especially at the outset, has to do with the self, not others. The driver who cuts you off, the woman on the train who is talking too loudly, the colleague who steals your idea, you yourself when you spoil a conversation with a joke—good therapy will turn you into a better observer, a novelist, of such people and events. You may not forgive them (or yourself) but you will see them in greater depth and with better perspective than you did before.

It's doubtful that I'd ever have become a writer without having undergone psychoanalysis. Without analysis, it's doubtful I'd have come as far as I have in my profession, purged the poison of racism that remained in me, gotten married, had kids, seen my parents for what they were and weren't, been able to love anyone as fully as I can now. My illness, which is a real and sometimes debilitating illness, has cured me of other illnesses. (When you say to someone, "Don't be so neurotic," it's closer than you may realize to telling someone else who is about to faint from a blood-sugar disorder, "Don't be so diabetic.") And it has also taught me to at least try to be honest—when I'm not busy manipulating, that is. And in this regard, if someone were to give me a choice between all this insight, this broadened definition of what it is to be a man, this compassion, the skill and significance (if there are any) in these very words—a choice between my analyzed self and my former, oblivious, limited self—I'm sorry to say it would be a very tough call.

✦

"Men, as a general rule, shy away from therapy because there is no obvious way to keep score," the writer Merrill Markoe observed. Most of the men I know who have gone into therapy caved in only when their life did. When they couldn't stumble out of the debris and depression, they sought a second opinion on what their options might be. If he could choose again, what would be Daniel Menaker's call? As a woman, I'd hope it would be for his "analyzed . . . less disordered, more limited self," but something makes me sense his choice would be to retain and wallow in his manly misery.

Will you please tell the next man you see (especially if you love him) that for a grown-up woman, the sexiest thing about a man is emotional courage?

As far as I'm concerned, the sanest people I know—women and men—have spent years in therapy. I've certainly found a lot of psychological insights on the couch, as well. Lately, though, I've discovered many more in alternative therapies. These days my three favorite forms to instigate introspection are cinematherapy, audiotherapy, and bibliotherapy—lessons learned by going to the movies, listening to different kinds of music, and reading books that touch and speak to me. An added bonus? The pleasure of sharing them with others and gaining their insights as well.

—SBB

BALLS

The boy—he is a young man, really, but to me ever a boy—lies on the hospital gurney, deranged from the lingering mortifications of anesthesia, while his mother weeps quietly in a corner, spilling great tears of relief. The boy has been gutted like a fish from sternum to pubic bone, his stomach muscles pried apart, his thoracic lymph nodes meticulously probed, dissected, and sampled. He's clean, the surgeon has announced, the cancer never escaped the diseased testicle, which was removed two weeks before in a simple procedure, and he can expect a complete cure. His mother, now composed and smiling, moves to the boy's side. Everything's fine, she tells him. The boy's eyes cannot focus, but he longs for touch. "Kiss my forehead," he mumbles, raising his hand to point to the spot. His finger reaches his nose and slips down his cheek. His mother and I laugh. It's been a while.

Now comes the hard part. In nascent manhood, will he feel like half a man? Will he be embarrassed in the locker room? Though sexually functional, will he be reticent in romance? Shy in bed? How will the psychological fallout present? How much does a guy define himself by his reproductive equipment?

The boy moans. Encroaching consciousness means encroaching pain. His wandering eyes find mine. "Kiss my forehead," he says. "Tell me you love me."

I do. I do.

You Only Need One

Gallagher Polyn

Macho does not prove macho.
ZSA ZSA GABOR

I don't know whether you have breasts, but if you're a man—a young man—and they've developed unexpectedly, you will find yourself concerned. Add a daily enlarging testicle and, in proportion, a growing share of your day will be devoted to some very unusual speculations.

At college, when these physical developments occurred in me, I tried to view my case through a veil of energized conceit. Leaving conveniently aside the problem of my budding bosom, I thought that my growing right testicle, which was as hard as the core of an avocado, was responsible for a horniness and joie de vivre never before known to me. But, as Chevy trucks implies in its hit ad song, I felt my "like a rock" nut was a new spring of manliness, not a potentially fatal carcinoma. I even wondered when there would be complementary enlargement in my left nut, adding more vigor to my daily life of study, drinks, exercise, and sexual reverie.

I was indulging a crude *cojones* theory, whereby bigger balls equate with being a greater man. It turned out to be medically naive—and absurdly dangerous. I'm thankful, for in my case any empirical support for such a theory will be necessarily half strong. An inevitable confrontation with medical authorities revealed that I had testicular cancer, or TC, as we survivors can say. My right testicle, once the supposed fount of my vigor, has since been removed.

*   *   *

My diagnosis returned me to the womb. At least a few months and some elaborate invasive procedures were required to correct me, though, thankfully, at little risk. I took a leave from school. My family doted on me. Work disappeared. Reality was suspended. I was starting over. My only job, like an infant, was to survive. That time was a rip in my life, a perfect interregnum. Today, I am twenty-six going on three.

I hadn't often thought about my balls before then. They were neither too small nor too large. They generally followed me in whichever direction I traveled. I didn't seek their special inclusion in sex play. Apart from an occasional, poorly aimed fist from my kid brother, they tended to stay quiet. In healthier days I would sometimes hold the connection of a testicle with its duct between two fingers, noting the pain at only light exertions of pressure. They are fabulously fragile things, considering their metaphorical significance. I seldom feel my remaining testicle now. I'm not frightened, but it could be bad luck.

A long, bilious pink scar extending from my sternum to below my navel is my record for the public. When just freshly inscribed, I thought about getting a snake tattooed to garland this angry, tumescent branch. I imagined myself on the beach luring the eyes of women to this strange thing. Perhaps I felt I had to compensate. I could no longer ejaculate. After the operation, erotic dreams in which I emitted gallons of semen became frequent. A snake-free normalcy has returned to me now. Apart from occasional qualms about retaining the plural noun *balls* in self-reference, I've coped.

Cosmopolitan males, if they notice my wounds in locker rooms, betray no interest. Rural folks are different. The summer after my final operation I worked as a volunteer in a remote village of the Dominican Republic. In the evening, I'd bathe with men I'd befriended working in the fields, soapy rinse from our basins splashing into the town's drinking supply as wild boys swung in the trees. My scars and missing testicle were always great curiosities. Obligatory question-and-answer sessions took on the form of group meditation. While I annotated the marks on my body, the others would drop their heads in ruminative trances to pore over their own.

These Dominican meditations turned into confessionals when older men would describe genital afflictions I scarcely could have imagined. One regular would always point to himself, and with a clown's grimace intone, *"No me sirve"*—literally, "It doesn't work for me." Through all this, the young boys would jump up and down, grinning and holding their crotches as if for protection. The men took care to remind them to be polite and not to laugh at me. After all, how would they like it if it happened to them? I knew that if it ever did happen to any of these guys, they were dead.

There have been minor humiliations, all of them occurring at my fertility clinic, where I stored sperm in case nerves that control ejaculatory response were damaged during the operation (which appears to have happened). The day before surgeons split open my abdomen, the head of the clinic, Pam, met and escorted me to a low-lit room with a cup. I thought she must have played some part in selecting the furnishing of my room. Its signal décor element matched her accent perfectly: leather. The last time I remember having a big-time ejaculation (erections and orgasms are no problem) was in that onanist's pit, eyes fixed on a woman's ass undulating on a video screen before me. Before walking out, I hitched my belt extra high, Jimmy Stewart style, to repair my dignity. I believe she actually snickered as I passed! She maintains her control of me through custody of my potential heirs and heiresses, made plain when my semen-storage bill arrives.

At first I did not think much of fertility. Even immediately after excision of the diseased testicle, and then again after the gruesome exploratory surgery, there was somehow conserved an avidity for the female form, or at least its promise. I remember a beautiful, young black nurse attending to me within hours of my testicle's removal. I made her blush with my pathetic flirting. Did she know my status? After my second surgery, my groggy eyes keenly sought the bottoms of eligible post–op room nurses. I would have had a lot to offer, belly slit open, half-shaven pubis, and my scrotum still shrinking to fit my remaining testicle. These experiences convince me that men do not "think with their balls." We require only one. This raises the question: What untapped genius lies in the other half of the team?

I continue to brood on my new state. Though never much of a fighter, I'm very wary of physical confrontation now. Sometimes I think I might like to be in law enforcement. That would require my wearing a protective cup. I've worried that in some future arena, enemies would attempt to silence me totally by severing my remaining testicle. I have been victim to the frightful recurring mental image of my penis being severed or otherwise mutilated.

Sometimes I feel like a joke has been played on me that I will never fully be able to understand. Like an Alzheimer's sufferer, I fear I may never know what I'm missing. When I have a rare visit of anger, I also feel free. I wonder how I can turn on anger when I need it. Have I been rendered unable to rage?

For the rest of my life I shall require checkup examinations by urologists. The office of my present doctor—first rate—is a veritable Ellis Island for prosperous elderly men. Most are there for prostate cancer, I suspect. Old grays from all over the world sit in the waiting room in Pasadena linens, Midwestern flannel, or Mediterranean wool. The suspension of the reality on the floor of the city below our skyscraper suite is further enhanced by a Babel of inscrutable chatter. My comrades are masters of appearing fully engrossed in their immediate surroundings while carrying on counterdialogues through slightly contorted lips with their silver- and golden-anniversaried wives. I've spent many hours locked in their intent gazes. Thus engaged, I've realized that it's not the woe of this "poor boy"—me—that they're discussing but more likely marital discord in their children, rudeness among the medical technicians, or the unfortunate side effects of the medication they're taking. They are like the megaliths of Easter Island, their old faces exquisite and defiant of individual psychology. Like Olympic athletes, they are but assembled tokens of the world's greatest varieties of male. This Olympiad is occasioned, however, by the hazards of being a man.

Given the unctuous concern of the family members who accompany them, I suspect that my comrades, too, have been crawling back from the womb. In their company, I think about my own future family. Will I bring my sons or daughters to my checkups if their mother is too busy to watch them? When I am an old septuagenarian gray, still fighting to preserve the manhood left in my remaining testicle, who will be my companion in the urologist's office? And what of the other men waiting with me then? For how long will they have been reborn? Men of twenty, thirty-three, fifty-five, eighty years of age—going on four, two, ten, and twenty-five.

✦

Does having a breast removed mean a woman loses her sex appeal? What about a man's testicles? Only if they allow it to. Two of the sexiest and lustiest people I've ever met had breast cancer and testicular cancer. Before they faced these crises, they were very attractive people. After they came through it, both emerged stunning—irresistibly magnetic to men, women, children, and animals. Why? Because the love of life became their aphrodisiac.

Simone de Beauvoir wrote in The Second Sex *that "one is not born, but rather one becomes a woman." In the same way Norman Mailer observed that "masculinity is not something given to you, but something you gain."*

You Only Need One

For man or woman, there are really only two essential sexual organs necessary. Find a man with an open heart and a woman with an open mind. Put them in a room together for one hour and you won't be able to pry them apart.

—SBB

FEAR

Several years ago, longer than we'd both like to admit, a bleary-eyed Tim Cahill walked into my office at Rolling Stone, *where we both worked as staff writers, dropped his suitcase on the floor, and slumped into a chair. He had just returned from a reporting trip to Guyana to cover the mass suicide of hundreds of sad souls who had fallen under the evil spell of psychoguru Jim Jones. Tim, a great bear of a man with a fierce look but a gentle heart, always volunteered for the most difficult or dangerous assignments, but this was one he regretted. He was absolutely shattered.*

He got over it, though, and over the next twenty years almost single-handedly popularized a brand of adventure journalism that is widely imitated in almost every men's magazine today. He has anthologized his thrills-and-chills pieces in Jaguars Ripped My Flesh *and* Pecked to Death by Ducks, *the titles of which hint at just how seriously he takes the macho posturing of many of today's self-described thrill seekers. Tim has some pretty cosmic ideas about the role that risk plays in a man's life. He's also had to face down fear, as he admits here, in the unlikeliest of venues.*

The Bravest Thing I Ever Did

Tim Cahill

We must travel in the direction of our fear.

JOHN BERRYMAN

I can't remember the host's name, only that the show was a pilot for ABC television, and that it was to be called *Stories*. I was a guest on the program. During each and every commercial break I got up and vomited in a wastebasket set discreetly off camera for the purpose. Worst case of stage fright in television history, probably.

It was a talk show–type format, but rather formal, with four of us sitting around a coffee table, complete with little cups of coffee, all of us wearing coats and ties.

I have never worn a tie since. It's been over ten years now.

The show was filmed at seven in the morning, but we were to look as if we'd just finished dinner and were having a spontaneous discussion. My impression was that some network exec had attended a dinner party in which the conversation had been about something other than television and had thought: Hey, wow, good television.

The host said that one of the best episodes they'd filmed so far had to do with people who had seen or had contact with flying saucers. These folks told good stories.

There were two other guests at the coffee table. One was Hugh Downs, the distinguished ABC commentator, a gentleman adventurer who once dove in a cage while great white sharks cruised by outside. The other interviewee was Dick Bass, who, at the time, was the oldest man to climb Mount Everest. We were to tell hair-raising stories of manly courage, or so I gathered. My job was to blather on about various adventures I'd written about in the past, before a sudden and vividly loathsome awareness of personal extinction had confined me to my own house for two months with a condition subsequently diagnosed as panic disorder.

Now, the entire concept of a fearless adventurer suffering panic for no reason at all is high comedy on the face of it. I knew that. There was a part of me, just observing, that thought, This is actually the story of *Stories,* happening right here on camera: big adventure guy paralyzed by fear, for no apparent reason.

Sometime after the second commercial break, when it became achingly obvious that I was suffering through a bout of intense emotional torment, Hugh Downs, a nice guy who is as calm and reassuring in person as he has always been on the small screen, sought to hearten and comfort me. "You know," he said, "the great Ethel Merman once said, 'Stage fright's a waste of time. What can they do, kill me?'"

I thought: Thank you, Hugh, you blithering simpleton. Ethel Merman is *dead.* Does that tell you something, anything at all?

A stagehand counted down from ten and the filming started again. The host asked, "What would you say your closest call was? Tim? Dick?"

He meant: Tell me a tale about when you came face-to-face with death and spit in its vile face. I could taste the bile rising in the back of my throat. Steel bands tightened around my chest, and I was possessed by a sense of vertigo so intense I could barely catch my breath. I was going to die, perhaps right then and there, but if not then, sometime, sooner or later. The perception wasn't simply academic. It was visceral. Death was nigh, and, contrary to Dr. Johnson's smug prediction, it did not concentrate the mind wonderfully.

Panic disorder strikes at least 1.6 percent of the population. It is characterized by feelings of intense terror, impending death, a pounding heart, and a shadowy sense of unreality. My own version featured several daily attacks of ten to thirty minutes in which I felt smothered and unable to catch my breath. There were chest pains, flushes and chills, along with a looming sense of imminent insanity. The attacks struck randomly, like lightning out of a clear, blue sky. The idea that people might see me in this state of helpless terror was unacceptable. I stayed home, cowering in my own privacy, unable to read, or concentrate, or write, or even watch television. My overwhelming conviction was that I was going batshit.

So when the producer called from ABC and asked me if I wanted to tell hairy-chested stories of virile derring-do, I said, "You bet." I thought: This terror thing has gone on long enough. I'm going to stroll right over to the abyss and stare directly into it. And I'm going to do it on national TV. Face the fear, boyo.

The producer had seen a picture of me climbing El Capitan, in Yosemite, on a single rope. It looked pretty scary. Could I talk about that?

No problem.

El Cap, I explained, is shaped rather like the prow of a ship, and my companions had anchored a mile-long rope in half a dozen places up top and tossed it over a rubber roller positioned at the bow of the formation so that it fell free for 2,600 feet. A half-mile drop.

We were all cavers. The rope-walking and rappelling techniques we used are common to this dirty, underground sport. Caves generally follow the course of underground rivers, and sometimes these rivers form waterfalls. Over the millennium, the rivers sink deeper into the earth, and the waterfalls become mostly dry pits, sometimes hundreds of feet deep. Many cavers like to "yo-yo the pits," which is to say, drop a rope, rappel down, and climb back up solely for the sport of it, never mind the exploration aspect.

That's what we were doing at Yosemite: we were going to yo-yo El Cap.

I recall standing on the talus slope at the bottom of the vertical granite wall with my climbing companion, photographer Nick Nichols. We calculated that the climb would take us five to six hours. Aside from a cruel weight of cameras that Nick carried, our backpacks contained some bits of spare climbing gear, a few sandwiches, and only two quarts of water. We intended to hydrate big time before we started and each of us choked down a gallon of water as we contemplated the cliff face.

Nick wanted me to follow him on the rope, for photographic reasons. His professional sense of the situation told him that the better picture was shooting down, at my terrified face, with the world dropping out forever below. The alternative was six hours of my butt against the sky.

And so we strapped on our gear—seat harnesses, Gibbs ascenders on our feet, a chest roller that held us tight to the rope, a top jumar for safety—and proceeded to climb the rope. There was a goodly crowd of people watching us from the road. Some of them had binoculars.

About an hour into the climb, Nick called down that he had some bad news. The water we had drunk earlier had gone directly to his bladder. I contemplated the mechanics of the situation and shouted up, "Can't you hold it?"

"Four more hours?" he whined. "No way."

"Why didn't you think of this before we started?" I said. I sounded like my father discussing the same matter with me as a child on a long road trip.

In time, we devised a solution that might keep me dry. I climbed up to Nick, unclipped my top jumar, popped the rope out of my chest roller, and climbed above the ascenders he wore on his feet before clipping back into the rope. In that position—with me directly behind Nick, my arms wrapped tightly around his chest— he unzipped and did what he had to do. It took an inordinately long time to void a gallon of water. The rope was spinning ever so slowly, so that, in the fullness of time, we were facing the road, and the crowd, and the people with binoculars. I feared an eventual arrest for public lewdness.

The television producer listened to the story and suggested the spinning yellow fountain aspect of the El Cap climb wasn't precisely what a family audience might want to hear. She wondered if there was any time during the ascent in which the choice was life or death.

Well, yes, in fact, a certain lack of foresight on my part presented me with a number of unsatisfactory choices. I explained that, as Nick and I climbed, the wind came up and blew us back and forth in exciting seventy-foot pendulum swings. This went on for some hours.

Had we simply dropped the rope off the prow of El Cap, the sharp granite rock would have sawed it in half, *snap bang splat,* like that. Instead, the rope was draped over a long, solid rubber tube anchored to the edge of the cliff wall. The final obstacle on the climb was to muscle up over the roller. This was tricky. The rope itself weighed several hundred pounds, and was impossible to drag over the roller. Instead, there was another rope, a short one, anchored above and dangled over the rubber. It was necessary to unclip from the long rope and clip onto the short one in order to make the summit.

It was a maneuver I had neglected to consider when I clipped into the long rope on the talus slope five hours before. I had been contemplating the climb, not the summit, and was concerned with a danger peculiar to this type of climbing. If, for some reason, a climber lost his top jumar and his chest roller, he'd fall backward, and end up hanging from the ascenders on his feet. There is no way to recover from this calamity. You simply hang there, upside down, until you freeze to death. Popsicle on a rope.

With this mind, I'd run the long rope through the carabiner that held my seat harness together reasoning that, in the bad, upside-down emergency, I might still be able to pull myself erect. What this rig meant at the summit, however, was that I was going to have to unclip my seat harness to get off the long rope and onto the short one.

But . . . a seat harness, as every climber knows, is the essential contrivance that marries one to the rope. Unclipping wasn't certain death, but the probabilities weren't good. I assessed my chances for over an hour. It was getting cold and late. The half-mile drop yawning below was sinking into darkness as the sky above burst into flame. This sunset, I understood, might well be my last, and I followed its progress as I would that of a bad bruise on my thigh: at first the sky seemed vividly wounded—all bright, bloody reds that eventually began healing into pastel oranges and pinks, which eventually purpled down into blue-black night. The temperature dropped. My sweat-soaked shirt was beginning to freeze to my body. I would have to do something.

Stories never made it to air. Not the adventure segment or even the one about flying saucers, which proves that sometimes the most fervent of our prayers are actually answered. Hugh Downs has retired from ABC, and Dick Bass is no longer the oldest man to have climbed Mount Everest. That honor now belongs to Georgian mountaineer Lev Sarkisov, who in 1999 reached the summit at age 60 years and 161 days.

And me? I haven't had a panic attack in ten years, knock wood. My doctor recognized the symptoms straight away and prescribed antianxiety medications that had an almost immediate ameliorative effect. He suggested therapy as well, but a pamphlet he gave me about panic disorder was pretty much all I needed. There were others, I learned, who have had to deal with uncontrolled anxiety. They included scientists such as Charles Darwin and Isaac Newton; actors Sir Laurence Olivier, Sally Field, and James Garner; writers Isaac Asimov, Anne Tyler, and Alfred, Lord Tennyson. Barbra Streisand and Sigmund Freud (natch) were on the list, along with the Norwegian Expressionist Edvard Munch, whose rendition of a panic attack is immortalized in a painting called *The Scream*.

The idea that I wasn't suffering alone—that the malady had a name—was strangely reassuring. Panic disorder feels like standing on the gallows, the rough rope on your neck, waiting, waiting, waiting for the floor to fall away into the never-ending night. But there is no rope, and no immediate threat. None at all. For some of us, these feelings are just another obstacle on the path of excess that the poet William Blake assures us leads to the palace of wisdom.

This is surely something to contemplate, but it doesn't get the grocery shopping done. In my experience, fear of collapsing into a puddle of terror at the minimart—agoraphobia—feels precisely the same as real physical fear in the face of an actual threat. The difference is this: there is almost always something you can do when confronted with an authentic life-or-death situation.

At the summit of El Cap, for instance, my companions rigged up a pair of loops made of webbing, anchored them off, and dropped them over the rubber roller. I placed my feet in the loops, and laboriously muscled the heavy, long rope up over the roller: a triumph of brute strength over clear thinking.

There was no thinking at all, really, not in the ordinary sense of brooding contemplation. Risk sets its own rules, and one reacts to them instinctively, with an empty mind, in a state that some psychologists believe is akin to meditation. And, like the meditative state, risk takers sometimes feel they've caught a glimpse into eternity, into the wisdom of the Universe, and into the curve of blinding light itself. Just a glimpse.

We didn't talk about that on *Stories*. Sitting there sweating, waiting to vomit during the commercials, I was incapable of saying what I felt: that the stories we tell are the way we organize our experiences in order to understand our lives. I didn't say that risk is always a story about mortality, and that mortality is the naked and essential human condition. We put these stories together—in poems and essays and novels and in after-dinner conversations—in an effort to crowbar some meaning out of the pure terror of our existence.

The stories are prisms through which we perceive the world. They are like the lenses we look through in the optometrist's office: put them together incorrectly, and it's all a blur. But drop in the correct stories, turn them this way and that, and—all at once— there is a sudden clarity.

Call it enlightenment and admit that none of us ever gets all the way there. We only see glimpses of it in a flashbulb moment when certain selected stories fall together just right. That's all. In my own case, I know that fear always feels the same, that it is about perceived mortality, and that while courage continually escapes me, appearing on one silly unaired television show remains the purest and the bravest thing I've ever done.

✦

"The next time you encounter fear, consider yourself lucky," the Buddhist nun *Pema Chödrön writes in* **When Things Fall Apart: Heart Advice for Difficult Times.** *"This is where courage comes in. Usually we think that brave people have no fear. The truth is they are intimate with fear."* Tim Cahill *knows fear, but so do we all. What do you think a baby's first cry expresses? Jubilation? Think again. It's stark terror. Fear in its most undiluted form. From our cradle to our grave, we're not meant to live without fear—in fact, we can't. It's a natural, primitive instinct, a remnant of our ancestors' necessary fight-or-flight reflexes, a spiritual gift that ensures survival.*

Today, of course, most of us don't have to fight off woolly mammoths. But making a cold sales call, starting a difficult conversation, or beginning to date again after forty-five has been known to bring on a racing heart, pounding head, and several trips to the closest rest room.

I'm not sure I agree with those self-help proponents who claim that mastery over fear leads to self-determination. I think that true self-mastery, the kind that doesn't abandon you in life's foxholes, means learning to coexist with fear. Fear has been very good to me. I don't think I'd be as healthy or as successful as I am if I hadn't started to view fear as an ally—an agent provocateur sent to stir things up, to push me past my comfort zone. More often than not, if I'm afraid of the next step, it means I'm supposed to take it. Change is on the way whether I like it or not.

I love the idea that the bravest thing Tim believes he's ever done is vomit his way through one unaired television program and live to tell the tale. What's fascinating about the tales we tell after we've not just faced our fears but embraced them is that we appear larger than life to ourselves and others. That's because we are. We've grown. "There is no hope without fear," the philosopher Baruch Spinoza reminds us. "And no fear without hope."

—SBB

VANITY

As a man of a certain vintage, I came of age at a time when long hair was worn as a badge of rebelliousness and independence. Naturally, I had to grow some, too, if only to irk my father and hockey coach. Of course, the idea that a ponytail was some kind of unusual fashion statement, a mark of independence, was preposterous; everyone had one. But such is the myopia of male vanity. It's hard to see beyond your own mirror.

The males of every species are the vain ones, sporting the classiest stripes, the most variegated feathers, the roughest ruffs, the plumpest plumage—all in service to the universe's great mating design. Humans are no exception. For some reason, a disproportionate chunk of male vanity is devoted to the quality of the tonsure. For a lot of men of my vintage, this has presented a problem over the accumulating decades. Fortunately, there is strength, and fashion, in numbers. We've declared—defensively and by default—that bald is beautiful. And so now we must believe it.

Most of us, anyway. Richard Liebmann-Smith, the quirky writer of the cartoon show The Tick, was until recently a hoary holdout, a devotee of what's known in some quarters as the turban wrap. But then he learned something all men should remember: Women don't care that much about how many hairs you have on your head. They care more about what's inside it.

A Man and His Hair

Richard Liebmann-Smith

The tenderest spot in a man's makeup is sometimes the bald spot on the top of his head.

HELEN ROWLAND

Recently, after years of agonizing internal debate, I finally went Full Shoogie.

Let me explain: I once doodled a drawing of a middle-aged couple in which the husband had one of those lightbulb heads like Ed Koch or Frank Perdue—totally bald except for a fringe of hair on the sides and back. It's a style sometimes called a monk's tonsure but which is better known as just plain bald. For reasons that escaped me even at the time, I named the pair Shoogie and Marie. Ever since, I've always referred to that terminal male-pattern baldness look as a "Full Shoogie," and to choosing to wear one's hair that way as "going Full Shoogie."

Not that there's really all that much choice. For those of us with little or no hair on the tops of our heads, the alternatives to going Full Shoogie—short of drastic and embarrassing medical, surgical, or toupee-ical procedures—are really only two: You can opt for the Yul Brynner/Telly Savalas/Michael Jordan shaved-head solution, cutting off your hair to spite your head, as it were. Or you can choose the Modified Shoogie—the much maligned "comb-over." In popular culture, unfortunately, the comb-over is universally iconic of the loser. It's generally seen as a desperate, transparent attempt to pretend that one still has hair where one clearly no longer does. Short of a really ridiculous rug, nothing is quite so reliable a lightning rod for snickers as a bad comb-over. But let me say this in defense of the Modified Shoogie: I don't believe it's usually a calculated attempt to deceive anyone, except perhaps the combee himself. Rather, I think it's simply a habit that hangs around longer than makes any aesthetic sense, like the continued wearing of short skirts by some older women.

From this you will correctly infer that I was a comb-over case myself, keeping the part in my hair long after there was much left to part. Which doesn't mean that I was in baldness denial. In fact, by my early thirties, not long before I married, with my hair already noticeably thinning (despite the outrageous length dictated by the seventies zeitgeist), I had already fine-tuned my self-image: instead of thinking of myself as a guy with hair who was losing it, I started seeing myself as a bald guy who just happened to have some hair. It was simply a matter of turning the half-empty glass into the glass half full. (I employed a similar bit of sleight-of-mind upon turning fifty, when I decided that I was a dead guy who just happened to be alive.)

If all of this fancy mental and emotional footwork strikes you as somewhat excessive as a response to the loss of a few (even a few thousand) hairs, you have to understand that in our society, baldness walks softly but carries a big stigma. According to no less an authority on the subject than Larry David, bald cocreator of TV's *Seinfeld,* there have been surveys in which 75 percent of women say they would never date a bald guy. Apparently there's just something about the shiny pate that's a deeply serious turnoff. Which may seem perfectly obvious and appropriate to you (especially if you happen to be three-quarters female) but which is something I've put considerable time and effort into convincing myself (and anyone who would listen) simply doesn't make sense. Consider, for example, the evolutionary perspective—the last resort of the hirsutically challenged—from which it's clear that women ought to see baldness as exquisitely attractive. The history of the human race, after all, has been a glorious ascent up and away from the hairiness of our ape ancestors. Baldness, in that context, can only be read as a proud badge of advanced evolutionary status, the permanent wave of the future. Think about it: Aren't all of those space aliens from superior civilizations—E.T. and the creatures in *Communion*—invariably depicted with huge, hairless domes? Talk about Full Shoogie! Those superevolved little guys are *total* Shoogie!

Then, of course, there's the testosterone factor. Male-pattern baldness, medical science assures us, is associated with elevated levels of that famous masculinizing hormone. Indeed, without testosterone, there wouldn't even be any male-pattern baldness. That's why, according to *New York Times* health guru Jane Brody, the one sure cure for baldness is castration. (Ms. Brody fails to cite any surveys about the percentage of women who say they would never date a castrated guy, but I'm guessing it would be well in excess of 75—not that the castrated guys would give much of a damn, though, I suppose.) The point is that bald men are hormonally gifted and you would think that women would be genetically wired to respond to baldness the way they do to muscles or money. But for some reason, it just doesn't seem to work that way.

That reason is probably the age factor. Unfortunately, along with all that elevated testosterone and advanced evolutionary status, baldness in our species also tends to be associated with increased age (or what I prefer to think of as maturity). Face it, you just don't see all that many guys in their teens and twenties walking around looking like billiard balls—unless they happen to be politically somewhere to the right of Hitler, in which case they're hardly burnishing the skinhead image for the rest of us.

In light of all this, my decision to go Full Shoogie was hardly one I could make lightly. My father had gone FS in his early twenties, long before I was born, long even before he was married. The only picture I ever saw of the man with anything even close to a full head of hair was his high school graduation picture. So for me going Full Shoogie meant identifying with my father, a mixed bag at best. The baldness per se wasn't the sticking point, but according to the implacable calculus of the unconscious, going Full Shoogie also meant signing on for his depression, heart disease, stroke, and early death. Naturally I was inclined to put it off as long as I could.

Yet inevitably the day came when I could no longer continue on my comb-over course in good conscience. Caught in the crossfire of multiple mirrors while trying on a pair of chinos at Banana Republic, I realized that the writing, like the mirrors, was on the wall.

I took a deep breath and headed for my neighborhood barber shop, a basic Sal-and-Vinnie operation with a striped pole outside. It's the kind of place where a haircut still costs less than ten bucks and where the barbers probably learned their trade in the army, if at all. (Well, you don't go to Harry Winston to set a half-carat diamond, do you?) I was expecting to get my regular guy but instead there emerged a barber I had never seen before. Being of a literary—not to say hysterical—bent, I was put in mind of that new crew Captain Ahab summoned out of the hold of the *Pequod* when he spotted the White Whale. Special hands for special work. When this new guy asked how I wanted it cut, naturally I refrained from blurting out "Full Shoogie." (He was having enough trouble with the English language as it was; I saw little sense in tensing up a man who would be wielding a pair of sharp scissors a couple of inches from my eyes.) Fortunately, he himself had already gone Full Shoogie; all I had to say was "like yours," making his work nothing so much as an induction into the club. Snip, snip, snip. He held up the mirror—front, back, sides. The deed was done. I had gone Full Shoogie. There was no turning back. (Even if I'd wanted to revert to my Modified Shoogie, there was little at that point left to modify; the hairs I had previously combed over would now reach only halfway across the top of my head—a look totally unacceptable even in an insane asylum.)

It turned out, however, that there was more to going Full Shoogie than simply submitting to the cut. After more than half a century of being combed one way, my new Shoogie was not about to accept the dictates of the scissors lying down. To my distress, the side that had previously been combed over kept popping up and sticking out, leaving me half Dwight D. Eisenhower, half Bozo the Clown.

It took more than a week of slicking and combing and spraying to get the thing under some semblance of control. But finally I felt my new look had begun to really come together. "So," I asked my wife at dinner one night, "how does it feel to be married to a man who's gone Full Shoogie?"

She peered across the table, carefully inspecting my pate. "Oh," she said, "I hadn't noticed."

✦

Who was it that declared, "Vanity, thy name is woman!" It wasn't Shakespeare and it wasn't Solomon. Be on the lookout for a bald guy.

For a lot of men, starting with Samson, self-worth is measured by the number of hairs on their heads. What is it with men and hair? Anyway, Larry David has a very plausible theory that bald men make better lovers because "the bald man is so thrilled to actually be in bed with a woman that he'll do anything and everything, and all with tremendous gusto." This could change a woman's perspective, especially if she's sensitive about her cellulite.

Vanity, thy name is human.

—SBB

MOOD

Several years ago, I was reading Robert A. Johnson's He: Understanding Masculine Psychology *and found myself returning to the same passages again and again. Johnson is a Jungian analyst and author of* She: Understanding Feminine Psychology, We: Understanding the Psychology of Romantic Love, *and other books. On a few captivating pages of* He, *Johnson examined mood, which he described as a kind of poor-quality femininity that is uniquely male, just as a certain kind of needling behavior in a woman is a type of poor-quality masculinity. A mood, Johnson wrote, "prohibits true feeling, even though [it] may appear to be feeling. A man overwhelmed by a mood is a sundial in moonlight telling the wrong time." Later, he writes, "An alert woman knows the instant a man in her life succumbs to a mood for all relating stops that very instant. A glazed look comes over the eyes of the man and the woman knows he has abdicated from any relationship."*

An alert man should, too, except that as the one possessed by the mood, he can't feel anything. And so he sulks. He is silent, not out of spite, but because he is unable to express himself. Women are mystified by this behavior, for it is not a part of their repertoire. Most men are mystified, too.

When he was a young man, Johnson was virtually paralyzed by his moods. After considerable work, he has since learned how they enrich his life. Now he shares the wealth.

The Tyranny of Gloom

Robert A. Johnson

Time cools. Time clarifies. No mood can be maintained quite unaltered through the course of hours.

THOMAS MANN

I s there a woman alive who is not utterly mystified by the gloom, the glowering cloud—the dark state of mind we know only by the oblique term *mood*—that descends upon a man without warning? Exists there a man who has not been blindsided by a funk that jeopardizes his happiness, his sense of purpose and meaning, and his relationships with the women he loves?

Moods are a phenomenon particular to men. Every modern man has suffered them to some degree, and every modern woman has been victimized by them. A mood can be thought of as a man's unconscious response to an uprush of emotion, which he typically characterizes as feminine and therefore tries to disregard. Our culture demands that a man be strong and rational, so when he feels vulnerable and emotional—*feminine* is the only word he can think of to describe such a state—he reacts, albeit unconsciously. He doesn't respect this in others and hates it in himself. But that unlived feminine life in a man demands its place. If it can't be honored legitimately—through conscious acknowledgment—it will be known illegitimately. It will present itself symptomatically, as a compelling mood.

Soon after the onset of adolescence, I was largely incapacitated by dark moods that would suddenly sweep over me, distorting everything. I saw the world, literally, as through a glass darkly. It was only by virtue of a rigorous sense of discipline that I managed to carry on my schooling and activities. But the discipline required to disavow this inner self destroyed any possibility of happiness and I felt miserable.

Carl Jung's system of typology helps illuminate the dynamics of a man's mood. He believed that people have four basic faculties—thinking, feeling, sensation, and intuition. Everyone has all four, but in each person they are weighted differently. The Italians are thought of as feeling people—hence the Italian man's reputation as a happy, feeling person. The Germans, Scandinavians, and English are thinking- or sensation-oriented people and ignore or depreciate the feeling function. When they experience feeling they are troubled by it and usually don't recognize its value.

Jung referred to the interior feeling content of a man's psychology as the Anima—she who animates, the giver of life and meaning. The Anima is largely responsible for a man's happiness and, equally, his dark feelings. If he degrades this feminine side of himself, which is customary in our thinking-dominated culture, then he jeopardizes his own happiness or sense of meaning. If a man is strong in the nonfeeling faculties, he will suffer bouts of moodiness but can probably get by with never having to address them. On the other hand, if he is endowed with a sensitive, feeling nature and tries to repress it, he will suffer a crisis.

I was born an introverted, feeling type. I loved music, literature, art; the big, boisterous sensational side of life did not much appeal to me. But I was raised by two extroverted, sensation-seeking parents who trained me into the best thing they knew—a highly engaged, noisy, competitive, unfeeling man. I didn't know anything else and the society around me contributed to my misconception about myself. Although I managed my way through a miserable adolescence, by the time I was twenty I couldn't function any longer; the system that had been imposed upon me simply broke down. I went through a crisis, dropped out of school, lost any sense of meaning in my life, and had to retrain myself by learning just how vital my feeling faculty was to my happiness and well-being. Eventually, Jungian analysis gave me the language and tools I needed to restore my native feeling function and escape the tyranny of functions that were not native to my inborn character.

Overwhelmed is the only way to describe the force and obstinacy of a man's mood. Its power over his rational faculties approaches that of mild psychosis. He can try to hide his mood, as I did, or deny it, but he has no control over this dark demon. Deceptively, the mood may take the form of an utterly irrational, manic sense of joy, which can quickly turn into explosive anger or unexplainable sadness. Every man knows the experience of feeling hopeful and confident one day, but waking the following morning to find everything inexplicably dark and gloomy. Eager to look everywhere for an explanation but inside himself, he will usually project his gloom onto something or someone else—his boss, his job, but more often the woman in his life.

Why would a man throw this negative energy at a woman he loves? Almost every man chooses a woman to live out his feminine side for him. She is more at home with the feeling, irrational dimensions of life. So he looks to her to provide him with a sense of meaning, to act as a conduit to his emotions, and thus holds her responsible for his happiness. In direct proportion to how much he denies his interior feminine life, he will blame her for his malaise. And he will most often do this at the worst possible moment—when caught in the vicious grip of a mood.

The ancient symbols for mood are the dragon and the witch. Mythology is full of stories of the young man who goes forth in all his male power and glory to slay the dragon that is devastating the land and returns a hero. In the same fashion, a modern man in search of maturity is required to make his heroic journey—confront his moods, bring them into consciousness, and not only halt their devastation but add their power to his personality. It can be a humbling, and often humiliating, experience. But the man who has lifted the veil from his moods and created an honored role for feminine values within his overly rational and hard masculine faculties is immeasurably strengthened in his character.

How does he do this? First of all, he must see the need. He must recognize that his feeling side is in conflict with his more rigorous masculine nature and that the conflict is preventing him from becoming a fully realized man. During a period of reflection, he must engage his mood—his witch, his dragon lady—and ask her what she expects of him and why she has chosen to make him miserable. He might inform her about the havoc she plays in his practical life and ask if she will compromise on her demands. She is likely so ignorant of his practical needs that she has no concept of how destructive her well-meaning intrusions are. In conversations with my own mood, my own dragon lady, I have often discovered that we share the same goals but understand each other so poorly that we get in each other's way.

A dialogue will then ensue in which the masculine and feminine sides struggle to find a vocabulary they both understand. As they become comfortable with each other's language—with the feeling content of the feminine, the rational and literal locutions of the masculine—they will slowly come to understand that they share the same needs and wants. With work, a man can build cooperation between his two warring personae. He can tame that tyrant, that dragon lady who once undermined his stability and power, and turn her into the source of his greatest strength. But this taming can be accomplished only by respectful cooperation with her. She is the creative side of his nature, able to imbue his masculine insights with spiritual power.

Just as with the heroic tales of old, the man who has conquered his dragons—his moods—becomes the possessor of the Holy Grail and the fair maiden of happiness.

When I was growing up I would frequently see my father flip a quarter repeatedly while staring off into the distance. I once asked my mother what he was doing and she said, "Thinking." Women were always the moody ones no matter what time of the month it was. Men were the thinkers.

Which is why I was as fascinated with Robert Johnson's meditation on men's moods as I was with the novelist Faith Baldwin's observation that men's private worlds are characterized by a multitude of terrains: "Deserts and oases, mountains and abysses, and endless-seeming plateaus. . . ."

Hand him a compass the next time that glazed look comes across his face and ask him which way he's headed.

On the other hand, when women are moody, think weather report. Today, variably cloudy. Possible showers. Didn't sleep well last night; up twice with children. Much tossing, turning, churning. Could be time of month, bills due. Heavy water retention. Alternating clouds punctuated by streaks of light, some levity but not quite sunny. During the afternoon, expect thunder and lightning due to deadline approaching, boss's frustrations, revised sales figures. Tonight, turning colder. Didn't resolve argument with husband over upcoming holidays. Possible frost late tonight, which will make for another unsettling day tomorrow.

Becoming aware of our emotional patterns is essential if we want to remain sane, functioning, and well-loved members of the human race. Every man and woman has a pattern, and everyone's different. If you really want to make love to your partner tonight, start tracking your patterns while there's still daylight so you can find your way home.

—SBB

CONSCIENCE

The Good Samaritan impulse runs strong in men. It's one reason that, since the Carnegie Hero Fund Commission was established in 1904 to honor extraordinary acts of bravery, more than 90 percent of the citations have gone to men. But where does a man draw the line between getting involved and just walking away?

For much of the nineties, photojournalist Greg Marinovich faced this dilemma nearly every day. Covering conflicts in Angola, Bosnia, Croatia, Somalia, Rwanda, Chechnya, and his homeland of South Africa, he was witness to unspeakable atrocities committed in the name of ethnic or national pride. He often wondered: Should his "moral victory" be confined only to exposing such crimes for all the world to see?

Greg was a member of a quartet of South African photographers— Joao Silva, Ken Oosterbroek, and Kevin Carter were the others—who were known as the Bang-Bang Club. They all worked for different agencies and newspapers but generally ran together covering the violence that followed Nelson Mandela's release from jail and, later, other conflicts around the world. In 1990, Greg won a Pulitzer Prize for photos he took of an incident he describes on the following pages. In 1994, Carter won the Pulitzer for a picture—indelibly etched in my own memory—of a starving Sudanese girl being stalked by a vulture.

Such work takes its toll on more than a man's conscience. In April of 1994, Greg and Ken were shot in Thokoza township in South Africa while on assignment. Ken was killed, Greg severely injured. Carter, just back from picking up his award in New York, had skipped the assignment to keep a lunch date. Four months later, wracked with guilt, he killed himself.

He knew where he would have drawn the line. He just wasn't there to do it.

The Burden of Truth

Greg Marinovich

In the depths of every heart, there is a tomb and a dungeon, though the lights, the music and the revelry above may cause us to forget their existence, and the buried ones or prisoners that they hide. But sometimes, and oftenest at midnight, those dark receptacles are flung wide open.

EDGAR ALLEN POE

On a sunny spring afternoon in August of 1990, at the start of a journey that forever altered my understanding of what it means to be a man of conscience, I felt a shiver of tension stretch across my back and down my arms as I tightened my grip on the steering wheel. I was scared—scared of what I might witness in the civil conflict that had exploded in the black residential ghetto of Soweto, just a twenty-five-minute drive from my home. I sensed I was jumping into a moral quagmire for which I was utterly unprepared. And I was right. By the end of this grisly adventure, I would learn more than I ever hoped to about moral victories—and defeats.

Although I had no professional news affiliation, I felt I had a social and political duty to cover the war going on in the Soweto ghettos. Supporters of the recently released Nelson Mandela and his nonracial African National Congress (ANC) were pitted against Zulu nationalists who supported the Inkatha Freedom Party. Fanning the hatred was the apartheid government's security forces. My uneasy stirring of excitement and fear increased as each hour's radio broadcasts told of a widening conflict.

As I approached the entrance of Nancefield Hostel, deep inside Soweto, I was confronted by dozens of armed, belligerent Zulu.

Armed with a variety of crude weapons, they wore red headbands and shouted insults and threats across a field at ANC supporters. I knew that the massive, decrepit dormitory complexes housing tens of thousands of migrant workers from the rural, tribal homelands across the country were being brutally purged of all non-Zulus. But I was entirely innocent as to what these facts really meant and naively decided to try and get pictures from the Zulu/Inkatha side.

After some time, a piercing, excited whistling echoed from somewhere deep in the massive hostel complex. The Zulus began running toward the noise. "What's happening?" I asked. "Nothing, it's nothing," a man answered, as he ran toward the sound, carrying sharpened iron rods and a cardboard shield. I followed another man lugging a piece of steel pipe. He paused now and then to blow into it, emitting a thin, trumpetlike sound. Was this a call to battle? I wondered. We came to a halt outside a dormitory where a score of men armed with sticks, spears, sharpened rods, and machetes gathered before a white steel door. Some peered cautiously through the windows, shying back as the curtains twitched. *"Vula! Vula!"* They were demanding that whoever was inside open the door. But there was no response. It remained stubbornly shut.

The mood of the crowd was strangely jovial. The men did not seem too bent on aggression, except when they shouted *"Vula!"* with an explosion of breath on the first syllable. They smiled at one another and at me: "There is a Xhosa inside. He has been shooting at us," explained one.

I had not heard a single gunshot in the time I had been at the hostel, but felt it was not the time to point this out.

The men grew impatient. They crowded and pushed at the door, which bowed inward, only to be jammed shut again. The contest was slow and deliberate, the strength of the men outside countered by an unseen force within. Eventually the door was pried open long enough for one Zulu to squeeze in. The door slammed shut after him. The door continued to resist the men outside, but then another man managed to slip through, and then another. What grim, silent battle was taking place inside, I could hardly imagine.

Then the door opened from the inside and a tall man raced out, waving a broom. His wild eyes looked directly into mine, from just a few feet away, but there was no comprehension, no connection, just a desperate attempt to escape. The Zulus and I took off after him, a pack hunting its terrified prey. After just a few dozen steps he went down. The attackers were instantly around him in a tight, silent circle, stabbing, slashing, hitting. These were sounds I had never heard before—the whispery slither of steel entering flesh, the dense thud of heavy fighting sticks crushing skullbone—but they made sickening sense, exactly the noise a roughly sharpened, rusty iron rod should make when pushed deep into a human torso. The victim's body quivered each time he was hit and jerked spasmodically when a jagged spear blade was tugged from the resistant flesh.

I was among the circle of killers, shooting with a wide-angle lens just an arm's length away. I was horrified, screaming inside my head that this could not be happening. But I steadily checked light readings and switched between cameras loaded with black and white and color, rapidly advancing the film frame by frame. I was as aware of what I was doing as a photographer as I was of the rich scent of fresh blood and the stench of sweat from the men next to me.

A few minutes later, the victim passed from living to dead and the frenzy of blows slowed to a sadistic punishment he could no longer feel. The man with the homemade horn blew monotonously into his pipe, emitting a coarse, unearthly sound. It was not a call to battle, I now understood, but a celebration of death.

"*Mlungu shoota!*" one of the dozen killers exclaimed as they finally noticed that I was taking pictures. The men sprang away, but within seconds they would surely realize that I was a defenseless witness to the murder.

Fear engulfed me. I prepared myself to do anything to survive—kick the dead man and call him a Xhosa dog, spit on the corpse. I knew I would be capable of desecrating the body to survive. "He was a Xhosa, he was shooting at us, a spy!" said one of the men. I readily agreed, quick to seize this chance to justify the killing, to save myself, even though papers in the dead man's pocket later showed he was a member of the Pondo people.

I had absolutely failed my own unspoken code of conscience. I knew that I was not responsible for the actions of others, but I had done nothing to try to save a victim of hate who was innocent of any crime but his ethnicity. And later that day, I would profit from his death by selling the pictures I shot. It was the start of a waking nightmare for me—the violence continued, and I continued to cover it, plunging headlong into horror and excitement. I hoped for a chance to redeem myself, to have another opportunity to act the way I hoped I could, to fulfill the internal picture I had of myself as a decent human being.

A month later, a skirmish in Soweto forced me to revisit my moral failure. The ANC supporters I was with had begun to attack an alleged Inkatha member who had inadvertently disembarked from a train right into the conflict zone. They began to stone and stab him. I was terrified that I might again witness a murder like the brutal killing at Nancefield Hostel a month before. It had been the first time I'd seen a person killed and I could still not shake off the guilt. He had died so close to me I could have reached out and touched him, yet all I had done was take pictures. As much as I wished for another chance to redeem myself, that Saturday morning seemed too soon.

The youths dragged the silent and unprotesting man they had identified as a Zulu to his feet and down a path to the street below. More people gathered round, mostly teenage boys, along with one or two older men and a handful of younger boys. The assault against the bloodied Zulu intensified. A man in a long-sleeved white shirt hauled out a massive, shiny Bowie knife and stabbed hard into the victim's chest. My heart was racing and I had difficulty taking breaths. Stepping across the chasm from detached observer to accountable participant, I called out: "Who is he? What's he done?" A voice from the crowd replied, "He's an Inkatha spy." I tried to see who was speaking, to make eye contact with an individual amid the killing fervor.

"Are you sure he's a spy? How do you know?" I asked. Another voice answered: "We know." It was the man in the white shirt, absolute certainty in his flat voice. But he had stopped the attack for the moment and was looking at me.

"What if you're wrong?" I said. "I mean, last month I saw Zulus, Inkatha, kill a Pondo because they thought he was Xhosa. Just here, at Nancefield Hostel. Maybe he is Zulu—yes, of course he is— but maybe he is not Inkatha. He could be ANC. Just make sure." The man nodded while I talked, watching me shrewdly. Despite the garbled way it came out, he understood.

But what I had to say did not matter.

I never heard the man utter a single word throughout his ordeal. He did not appeal for mercy, nor even look to me for help. He seemed not to recognize what was happening. I wondered if he was mentally deficient, drugged, or just dumb with terror.

My questions had worried the assailants, who hissed ominously, "No pictures, no! Fokoff!" I managed a weak defiance: "I'll stop taking pictures when you stop killing him." But the attack continued, moving down the street as the Zulu stepped ponderously forward.

Now, one person after another took turns inflicting grievous injury upon the defenseless man. A young man with a wisp of a beard stepped forward and stood on his toes to thrust a knife into the Zulu's chest. His victim just stared dumbly ahead as the knife plunged in, while I released the shutter and wound on the next frame. A part of me did not want to be a photographer just then, but as with the killing in Nancefield Hostel, I smoothly exchanged camera bodies to shoot slides as well as color negatives.

The progress down the street halted when the Zulu collapsed

into a sitting position on the pavement. Most of the mob was edging away by then and others had slipped behind me, probably to avoid being photographed. As I shot and cranked the advance, the man in the white shirt moved in again. In response to some vague sense of unease, I took a few steps back.

Later, a BBC cameraman who had been filming from farther away, would say, "Jesus, did you see that guy try to stab you?" I had lost my grasp of what was going on. The pictures I kept taking by rote would later substitute for the events my memory could not recall. One image is of the man in the white shirt stabbing his knife down into the top of the Zulu's head as he sits on the road, almost absentmindedly reaching up toward the source of pain.

My awareness gradually returned. The victim was flat on his back a few yards in front of me. The street was now empty. The man in the white shirt was standing next to me, my left shoulder brushing his right. He lifted his right hand, the one he had used for stabbing, and showed me a little cut he had sustained. He drew his breath in sharply to underscore his pain. A thin line of red traced a shallow incision no deeper than a clumsy shaving cut. I felt we were both acutely aware of how grotesque this instant of bonding was. The bond dissolved when a boy, no older than thirteen, walked across the deserted tarmac to the lifeless man and unscrewed the cap of a Molotov cocktail he was carrying. The boy methodically doused the Zulu with the petrol. Then he walked over to the man next to me. The kid knew what must come next, but he would not, or could not, do it himself. I pretended not to see him slip a box of matches into the older man's left trouser pocket and whisper in his ear.

The hissing and cursing around me grew louder, more menacing. But I was determined not to leave the scene. I had failed to prevent the man's death, but I simply would not leave and let them burn him, too. I stood my ground next to the man in the white shirt, both of us staring at the body, pretending to be oblivious of the matches in his pocket. But then an excited shout went up from near the railway tracks. Onlookers drawn by the drama and participants in the killing ran up the embankment and I followed them. A handful of residents were trying to attack a man in a blue shirt, but their assault lacked the conviction of the earlier mob, and it petered out.

There was a low brick building between me and where the Zulu lay in the street. Suddenly I heard a *whoof* and women began to ululate in a celebration of victory. I ran toward the edge of the elevation. The man I had thought dead was running, stumbling across the field below us, his body enveloped in flames. Red, blue, and yellow tongues licked the clothing and skin off his body. I lifted the long-lens camera. The human torch slowed and dropped to a squat.

As I focused, I noted that the early sun was right behind the burning man. I depressed the shutter, then pulled the camera away from my face for a second to advance the crank and frame my next exposure. A bare-chested, barefoot man ran into view and swung a machete into the man's blazing skull as a young boy fled from this vision of hell, from an enemy who would not die.

Those shocking pictures would be published around the world. This time, I had not entirely failed my test of humanity, but I had been completely ineffectual. The tangible results of my inaction and action were identical: both men had died brutally at the hands of other human beings.

Did I feel better this time? No. Worse. I had followed my conscience, but it had made no difference. I felt weaker than I ever had in my life, sapped of spirit, because I had triumphed over my fears and made my moral stand, but the result had been an utter defeat.

And how I wanted there to be a corresponding material effect, a victory for humanity. But neither the victim nor his assailants had changed their paths, nor had their fates been altered by my actions. Years have passed, and I realize that moral victories do not necessarily lead to any material consequence. They just are.

✦

Greg Marinovich's soul-wrenching essay is the most difficult reading I have ever done. For days after I read it, I couldn't get the images he'd conjured up out of my mind. They haunted me more relentlessly than any photograph.

To be frank, my initial reaction was revulsion. I am a woman who puts her hands up in front of her eyes when the scary parts come on in a movie. I rarely watch the nightly news because sometimes all of life seems frightening. When women hear stories of war, famine, disease, and death, it makes us want to do something. "Doing" is how women grieve and cope with the unspeakable. And when a woman can't do anything to "make it all better," even if it's just pushing away the disturbing headlines and turning off the television, she feels impotent, isolated, and overwhelmed. There are few things that a cup of tea, a casserole, a sympathetic ear, and an embrace can't alleviate, and this story is one of them.

So I really wrestled with whether or not I should include this essay in our collection. Here's why. For women, the words simple *and* abundance, *when used together, have come to mean serenity and safety. Greg's essay had completely the opposite effect on me. It rattled me. It disturbed me. It made me feel vulnerable.*

And then I realized that Greg brought me, this book, and our readers an exquisite gift—the one thing all of our extraordinary contributors were invited to bring to the project: his emotional courage. This book was intended to be a spiritual and creative safe house, a masculine "den" or sanctuary to explore what it means to be real, honest, true, and authentic.

It is so rare that men open up to women. When they put down the shield and shed the armor. When they fling open their hidden, barricaded dungeons of pain, remorse, regret, and guilt. When they indicate with a glance, embrace, tears, half sentence, or full confession that they no longer want to live in solitary confinement. For me that's what Greg Marinovich did on the page. In his photographs, his words, and his heart, he bears witness to the Swiss psychologist C. G. Jung's belief that "One does not become enlightened by imaging figures of light, but by making the darkness conscious." And I'm very grateful to be reminded of that.

—SBB

MEDITATION

The novelist and poet Jim Harrison has always traveled far afield of what he "knows." His novels teem with intimate knowledge of native cultures; a couple of his books have been written, remarkably convincingly, from the point of view of a woman. His work is without ego, without self, as though he's attempting a literary application of Heisenberg's uncertainty principle: perception is inexact because the object is changed by the very act of perception. How does he manage to remove himself so completely from his work, thereby creating more exact perception? By meditating on a red cushion in his granary, accompanied, on occasion, by his beloved dog.

The Question of Zen

Jim Harrison

Meditation is simply about being yourself and knowing about who that is. It is about coming to realize that you are on a path whether you like it or not, namely the path that is your life.

JON KABAT-ZINN

I often think that because I am quite remote up here in northern Michigan from others who practice, and am intensely stubborn, I learn so slowly that I will be dead before I understand very much.

But "Who dies?" is a koan I posed for myself several years ago. To know the self, of course, is hopefully to forget the self. The especially banal wine of illusion is to hold on tightly to all the resonances of what we see in the mirror, inside and out. In our practice the self is not pushed away, it drifts away. When you are a poet there is a residual fear that if you lose the self you will lose your art. Gradually, however (for me it took fifteen years!), you discover that what you thought was the self had little to do with your own true nature. Or your art, for that matter.

When I learned this I began to understand that the period of zazen that lays the foundation of the day is meant to grow until it swallows both the day and night. Time viewed as periods of practice and nonpractice is as fanciful a duality as the notion that Zen is Oriental. The kapok in the *zafu* beneath your ass is without nationality.

I was wondering the other day about this body that wakes up to a cold rain from an instructive dream, takes its coffee out to the granary to sit on a red cushion. The body sees the totems of consolation hanging around the room: animal skins, a heron wing, malformed antlers, crow and peregrine feathers, a Sioux-painted coyote skull, a grizzly turd, a sea-lion's caudal bone, a wild-turkey foot, favored stones, a brass Bureau of Indian Affairs body tag from Wyoming Territory, a bear claw, a prehistoric grizzly tooth. These are familiar, beloved objects of earth, but the day is not familiar because it is a new one. The bird that passes across the window is a reminder of the shortness of life, but it is mostly a bird flying past the window.

"The days are stacked against what we think we are," I wrote in a poem. The point here, albeit blunt, is that when you forget what you are, you truly "see" the day. The man who howls in anger on the phone, because he has been crossed, an hour later is a comic figure dog-paddling in a sump of pride. He isn't conscious enough at the moment to realize that there is evil afloat in the land, within and without. This condition can be called "self-sunken." A little later, when he takes a walk on the shores of the lake, he does himself a favor by becoming nothing. He forgets being "right" or "wrong," which enables him to watch time herself flickering across the water. This is delightful illusion.

The hardest thing for me to accept was that my life was what it was every day. This seemed to negate notions of grandeur necessary for an interest in survival. The turnaround came when an interviewer asked me about the discipline that I use to be productive. It occurred to me at that moment that discipline was what you are every day, how conscious you are willing to be. In the *Tao Te Ching* it says, "Act without doing; work without effort." So you write to express your true nature, part of which is an aesthetic sense that reflects the intricacies of life rather than the short-circuits devised by the ego. Assuming the technique of the art has been learned, it can then arrive out of silence rather than by the self-administered cattle prod to the temples that is postmodernism.

After this body eats a tad too much for lunch it returns to the granary, stokes the fire, and takes a nap with its beloved dog, who, at eleven, is in the winter of her life. A distinct lump of sorrow forms, which, on being observed, reminds the body of the Protestant hymn "Fly, Fly Away," and we are returned to the fragility of birds. The sense of transience is then embraced. When the dead sister reappears in dreams she is always a bird.

On waking with a start, because it is the dog's nature to bark on occasion at nothing in particular, the work is resumed. There has been an exhausting effort in recent years through the form of poetry and novels to understand native cultures. The study of native cultures tends to lead you far afield from all you have learned, including much that you have perceived and assumed was reality. At first this is disconcerting, but there are many benefits to letting the world fall apart. I find that I have to spend a great deal of time alone in the natural world to be of use to anyone else. Above my desk there is a wonderfully comic reproduction of Hokusai's blind men leading each other across a stream.

Whatever I have learned I owe largely to others. It was back in

1967 that I met Peter Matthiessen and Deborah Love, then Gary Snyder, though in both cases I had read the work. But in these formative stages of practice the Sangha is especially important. George Quash introduced me to the work of Trungpa—*Cutting Through Spiritual Materialism* is an improbably vital book. Shortly thereafter I met Bob Watkins, a true Zen man, who had studied with Suzuki Roshi and Kobun Chino Sensei. The work of Lucien Stryk has been critical to me though I have never met him. Then, through Dan Gerber, I met Kobun himself, who has revived me a number of times. Through all of this I had the steadying companionship of Dan Gerber, who is presently my teacher. Without this succession (or modest lineage!) I'd be dead as a doornail since I have been a man, at times, of intemperate habits. I'm still amazed how the world, with my cooperation, can knock me off Achala's log back into the fire. There is something here of the child who, upon waking, thinks he can fly, even though he failed badly the day before.

There is an urge to keep everything secret. But this is what Protestants call the sin of pride, also greed. They have another notion relevant here, that of the "stumbling block," wherein the mature in the faith behave in such a way as to impede the neophyte. There is, sadly, a lot of this among Buddhists, the spiritual materialism that infers that I have lived in this town a long time and you are only a newcomer. This is like shouting at a child that he is only three years old. It is also the kind of terrifying bullshit that has permanently enfeebled Christianity. Disregarding an afterlife, he who would be first will be last.

We should sit after the fashion of Dogen or Suzuki Roshi: as a river within its banks, the night sky in the heavens, the earth turning easily with her burden. We must practice like John Muir's bears: "Bears are made of the same dust as we and breathe the same winds and drink the same waters, his life not long, not short, knows no beginning, no ending, to him life unstinted, unplanned, is above the accident of time, and his years, markless, boundless, equal eternity."

This is all peculiar but quite unremarkable. It is night now and the snow is falling. I go outside and my warm slippers melt a track for a few moments. To the east there is a break in the clouds and I feel attended to by the stars and the blackness above the clouds, the endless blessed night that cushions us.

✦

If you don't already practice meditation, Jim Harrison's red-cushion route in his granary perpetuates the unpleasant image of sitting uncomfortably, your back aching, your mind racing ahead to all the things you need to be doing, and hyperventilating because now you are concentrating on whether or not you're breathing. As far as I'm concerned, you're a better man than I am, Gunga Jim.

Having failed miserably at this technique, I've discovered there are many ways to meditate. Folding laundry, for instance. Concentrating on completing one task at a time. Gardening, cutting the grass, washing the dishes. Meditation can be both secular and spiritual. There are many paths to the present moment. I share my favorite path with Joan Borysenko: "a small, moist piece of chocolate cake eaten with exquisite attention and tremendous gratitude." You might like to start there, too.

—SBB

SOLITUDE

The tarpaper shack is set back from the road about twenty feet; immediately behind it, a hardscrabble hillside rises at an angle negotiable only by an expert climber. The windows are dark, menacing, lined with old newspapers and blankets. A wisp of smoke rises from the cinder-block chimney, as it does year-round. Blocking access to the dirt driveway is a heavy metal chain; in case it's not clear that the owner really doesn't want you turning around on his property, a hand-scrawled sign on it reads "Keep Out." Inside the shack is Jake, doing whatever a hermit does all day long.

In the twenty-five years I've owned a summer house in the Catskill Mountains, Jake has been one of my closest neighbors—which is to say, in this poor, sparsely populated little corner of the earth, that he lives about five miles away. Driving by, I would often see him puttering around his cabin or standing at the edge of the woods just staring, listening, sniffing. During the first few years I was around, Jake, an expert fly tier, sold lures to local fishermen, although if he didn't approve of their look he wouldn't sell them the fly. Eventually, he approved of no one, and kept the flies for himself. Many years went by before I mustered the courage to stop and introduce myself—after parking way down the road, of course. The very thought of Jake aroused in me some primitive fear from my childhood about scary bad men. Every kid's neighborhood has its hermit; mine had three. What had they done that caused them to shut themselves off from the rest of the world—from friends, colleagues, women? What did they fear they would do if they remained part of it?

The inside of Jake's hermitage looks very much like the images I had concocted in my childish imagination: well-chewed linoleum floors; crude handmade furniture of two-by-fours and plywood; low, dull lighting; ominous-looking tools everywhere; a musky odor; a woodstove *crackling and spitting noisily. As a kid in the presence of this large, scrofulous man in his small, primitive lair I would have been scared witless. Now Jake, his forearms heavily tattooed, a Pall Mall dangling from his lips, his cap pulled low over his forehead, points to a faded picture on the wall. It could be Robert Mitchum; it's Jake, fifty years ago. He pulls a huge trunk from beneath his bed—filled with little boys' bones! I once would have thought—opens it, and shows me dozens of compartments filled with literally thousands of nymphs, wet flies, dry flies, stone flies, caddis flies, terrestrial flies, streamers. He points to his workbench, right next to his bed, where he constructs these tiny works of art from the materials in a dozen glass jars—deer hair, porcupine quills, hawk feathers, snakeskin, nylon filaments, shreds of colorful party favors.*

Suddenly, Jake's life looks pretty good, free of professional obligation, family responsibility, love's heartbreak—of the frustration, hard work, and disappointments of communal living. What man hasn't fantasized about chucking it all and retreating to some outback bunker to live by his own wits and brawn, totally off the grid? Most of us weigh the trade-off and pull back. Some men take the path.

The Hermit

Jake Jacobsen

True solitude is a ding of birdsong, seething leaves, whirling colors or a clamour of tracks in the snow.

EDWARD HOAGLAND

I don't know when I moved up here; it was a long time ago. Thirty, forty years ago, maybe longer. You lose track of time in the woods, you think in terms of cycles and seasons. I've gotten by doing a little carpentry, plumbing, odd jobs, shingling, but I spend most of my time in the woods with the animals. People up here don't have much to do with me and I don't want much to do with them. They think I'm a weirdo, the mountain man, a crazy, so they leave me alone. They go, Hey, there's the hermit. But I don't care what the locals think of me. Some of these guys in the nice houses got no life. They just lay around, doing nothing. Some of the men can't drive a nail straight. You feel sorry for them.

I've always loved water, so now I've got Basket Brook out front of me and the Big D—the Delaware River—a half mile down the road. I was born on the water, on a coal barge, March 11, 1925, and I've loved it ever since. My father was a barge captain, delivered coal up and down the East River in New York. We lived in the cabin on the barge, no bigger than this room here. My father had a rope going all around the barge on a pulley, so when we wanted to run around he'd hook us up to a homemade harness. If we fell off at least he knew we wouldn't drown. Sometimes he'd come around looking for us, find us dangling off the side of the boat on the harness, our feet kicking at the surface of the water like we were walking on it.

I went in the navy when I was seventeen and a half on a minority hitch, which let you go in six months early. That was 1942. I was a first-class seaman, a boatswain's mate, and went all over the Pacific and North Atlantic for six years. I saw some of the war, not much. I loved the navy—best years of my life. But then my wife filed the papers to get me home on a dependency discharge. I had a son and she wanted me home, so I was automatically cut loose. I took a bus from California all the way back to Brooklyn, and the first night I was home my wife says she's going to the movies with her girlfriend because they're giving away free dinner plates. I told her I'd buy her the damn plate, but she went anyway. That was the last time I ever saw her. Never saw my son again, either, but I heard he went in the navy. Biggest mistake I ever made in my life, getting married. But I learned my lesson. Never again.

After that I lived with a woman named Pearl Dougherty for six years and we had three sons. But I wouldn't marry her. I'd learned my lesson. One day she says she's going to take the kids to live with her mother in the South. I never saw them again, either. That's when I said, No more women. I gave them all up, I lost my faith in them. I got away, moved up here next to the brook, which was the smartest thing I ever did.

Sometimes you reminisce, you get to thinking it would be nice to have a family, some grandkids. It bugs you. I used to miss my boys. I'd come in the house and walk upstairs and look around the banister to see who was hiding. Half the time all three of them would jump me, get me on the floor and start beating on me. But I never laid a finger on them. I often wonder what happened to them, if they're still alive, what they're doing. The oldest would be about fifty now.

Every now and then I miss the company of women. I've got a hernia so I don't miss the sex. I don't even think about it anymore. I could have got it fixed up, but I said, The hell with it. I'm too old. At times I get lonely, but it's not like I want anyone else around. So I take a walk and forget about it. If I see a beaver or a muskrat or a fish it helps put that stuff out of my mind. That's it, it's over. Gone. Forgotten. I walk across the road and listen to the sound of the brook. It peace-ifies me.

When I first got up here I could make a good living as a trapper. I used to get a lot of beaver from the river; foxes, raccoons, a couple coyotes from the woods. I made a quill call from the wing of a duck to call in deer. Then I figured I'd copy animal sounds into a tape recorder and play them back to call the animals in. It worked beautifully, especially with fox. They'd hear their own bark and come running. I had a green plastic funnel I'd put up to my ear and I'd sit in the woods all day, wearing camouflage, identifying animal sounds. *There's a fox. There's a porcupine.* I'd hear something gnawing away on a bone. *What's that?*

THE HERMIT

When you're concentrating in the woods, you don't have to think about anything else. You see footprints, you leave them alone, don't step on them, and put a trap there. You've got that animal. Put it there a week and you'll get four or five. I used to have books in my pocket to keep track of where my traps were. You learn to read the signs, look for where the bark is gnawed, the ferns flattened. I'd put dirt with raccoon's urine next to a trap, hide behind a tree and watch an animal walk right up to it. You've got that animal. You dissect him and take the glands out and pretty soon you've got scent for fifty traps.

You have to be careful about your own scent, too. A lot of these so-called hunters around here don't understand that and wonder why they can spend a week in the woods and not see one animal. If you've got aftershave or hair lotion on they'll pick up that smell and they're gone. I take ordinary water from the brook to wash my face and hands. I rinse my hands in the brook. You spend that kind of time in the woods, pretty soon you start to think like an animal.

I've always felt responsible for the nature around here. The animals don't have anybody else to look out for them. Even when I was trapping a lot, I had great respect for them. You don't ever want to take a whole family; you've got to leave seeds for the little ones. If you get one that's immature, you put a board over it, hold it down with your foot, and release the trap. You think, Okay, you son of a bitch, don't squirt me. Just walk away. Some of them will charge you a little, just to spook you. You go, Come on now, I was nice to you, now get the hell out of here.

One time this 'coon came around and had these stickers all over him. I felt sorry for him, so I put a rubber hose around his mouth so he wouldn't bite me and took the stickers off. Don't you know the thing came around for a week just to say hello? A few weeks later he comes back, covered with stickers. I took a furring stick, pinnned him down, and took the stickers off again.

Now when I go out I just like to look, make sure everything's

okay. My trapping and fishing days are over. There's peace and contentment for me to go up and sit in the woods for a couple hours.
The animals talk to you in their own way to let you know, Don't
come too close. But they'll let you look. Every once in a while when
I'm up in the woods I'll say a prayer. I used to thank Him, you
know, for letting me have that beaver, that muskrat. Now I thank
Him for just letting me *see* the beaver. It never took much to make
me happy, and it takes even less now.

People say you're wacky or you're a hermit or you're this or that.
I say good, let them think. I got peace with myself. I think I'm a
good man. I didn't make much of a husband or father, but I try to
take care of things around here, right in this little part of the world.
I'd like to be buried right up in the woods. Or better yet, you could
just throw my body in the river. Hell, that's where I came from in
the first place.

✦

*Surely one of the joys of reading is the moment a sentence
leaps off the page and straight into your heart. That happened for me when Jake Jacobsen mentioned his prayer these
days is gratitude for being able just to* see *the beaver. "It never
took much to make me happy, and it takes even less now."
Recently I was reminded of just how little I need to make me
happy, and it occurred during a solitary walk in the woods. I
was alone. But I wasn't lonely. I was complete.*

*A day off or an hour of solitude doesn't sound like a lot, but
it sure would make a lot of men and women I know happy.
Too many of us approach time alone—solitude—as if it were
a frivolous, expendable luxury, rather than a spiritual, creative, and psychological necessity. Why should this be so?*

*Could it be that by shortchanging ourselves, the only thing
impoverished is our inner life? And after all, if the lack
doesn't show on the surface, if we can pull it off one more time*

with smoke and mirrors, why, of course it doesn't count. Oh, yes, it does.

"It is a difficult lesson to learn today—to leave one's friends and family and deliberately practice the art of solitude for an hour or a day or a week," the writer Anne Morrow Lindbergh observed a half century ago. "And yet, once it is done, I find there is a quality to being alone that is incredibly precious. Life rushes back into the void, richer, more vivid, fuller than before."

The soulcraft of devoutly caring for our authentic selves as well as we care for others rarely comes naturally or easily. But with practice, with patience, with perseverance, and occasional solitary walks in the woods, it does come.

—SBB

THOUGHTS FOR THE ROAD

Ten Things Every Man Worth His Salt Should Know How to Do

Jake Morrissey

1. Sweep a woman off her feet.
2. Calm a fear.
3. Make a wish come true—for someone else.
4. Keep a promise.
5. Motivate a peer.
6. Make a child giggle.
7. Tell a ghost story.
8. Change a tire.
9. Write a love letter.
10. Ask for directions.

PART THREE

RULES OF THE ROAD

Not I—nor anyone else, can travel that road for you.
You must travel it yourself.

WALT WHITMAN

HEROES

How do you account for bravery, for one man laying his life down for another, for a stranger, even? Experts weigh in with a variety of explanations. Acts of altruism are part of our species-preserving behavior, a happy result of our complex evolutionary history. Or: men are impulsive risk takers and rarely think before acting, a gender-wide personality flaw that often results in benefit to the commonweal. Or: society expects men to be protectors, so men have no choice.

All of these explanations are doubtless true, although they don't figure in the way that the writer Larry Brown approaches the subject. But maybe the question is just a koan, the simple answer hidden within it. Men are brave because they are men. Because they are heroes.

The Chief

Larry Brown

In our world of big names, curiously, our true Heroes tend to be anonymous.

Daniel J. Boorstein

Once when I was a rookie, I rolled out on a call to a car that was on fire. That became a common thing pretty quickly, but the first one was scary. The back end of the car was blazing, pretty close to the gas tank, it was at night, and I didn't really want to walk up to it, even though I had a hose in my hands, but the guy who had driven the truck out there and was in fact training me just grabbed me by the shoulder and dragged me right up into the middle of it and made me put it out, which I did. There was nothing to it. I was just afraid of the fire. I also thought that maybe the tank would blow and shower me with burning gas. We didn't discuss any of that. He just shoved me up in it and I had no choice but to pull on the handle on the nozzle and let the water out on it. Later on, I realized that it was a good thing he did for me, because later on I saw firefighters who worked for my department who were afraid to get close to a fire. They were in the wrong line of work, of course, and eventually got out of it.

It's only later on that the fear leaves for the most part and the adrenaline rush takes its place. Young men are real good at getting it. A fire becomes a living thing to them, which it is, a thing that can fight back and will, despite your best efforts—a thing that will burn your ass severely every time you let your exposed skin get too close to it. Firemen have to be careful but that doesn't keep them from getting killed.

One night fifteen years later I was with the same guy again, at Holly Springs, Mississippi, where the state fire academy was conducting an LP-gas seminar. Every one I ever went to was pretty much the same: pretty goddamn scary. But it wasn't particularly dangerous if every man did his part. All it was was a system of pipes with a bunch of holes bored in them. Christmas tree, that's what we called it. We'd been to Christmas trees in Oxford, in Greenwood, and the boys from the academy went all over the state with this rig, letting every department get a shot at letting their boys at it. It's an exercise that's hairy the very first time you try it.

The pipes were hooked to a gas truck through a hose. Everybody backed off while a kerosene-soaked rag was laid on a pipe about five feet off the ground and lit. Then the guy at the truck turned the gas on and flames started coming out of all the holes when the fumes hit the burning rag. Firefighters were waiting with two charged hoses, inch-and-a-half lines, three men on each line, one man holding the shoulders of the inside men, one man waiting back about ten or fifteen feet since he had no hose. Neither did the man in the middle. He was depending on the two teams to keep him from getting burned horribly or to death.

The ball of blue-white flame lit the lowered face shields and threw an image of its own rising, exposing their unsmiling faces and shining eyes as the guy at the truck turned up the volume on the gas. It got bigger and bigger and began to roar, and the electricity that is in the air when a group of men have to face something that frightens them was there because they knew how it would char skin black if they got too close to it.

There's always a lot of people around to watch something like that. Anybody driving by is probably going to stop and watch it, all these firetrucks out there, all those men, this ball of flame almost twenty feet around lighting up the buildings and the cars and the groups of people standing around watching, wondering what the hell's going on.

The idea is to turn the fog nozzles on, which throw a wide pattern of tiny droplets under tremendous pressure, about one hundred pounds per square inch. It's like a big umbrella of water ten feet wide and you hold it in your hand and the other men hold it with you. It'll whip a little skinny guy's ass like mine and is tough for even a big man to hold by himself if the correct pressure is coming through it from the truck. The idea is for the two teams to walk up to the fire together, fog streams flowing, the officer in the middle of them saying, Steady, steady, and walking them closer, behind a solid wall of water, two big umbrellas out in front whose edges were meshed solidly together. They are so steady and operating so smoothly as a team that the pressure of the water forces the fire back upon itself, and even though across that short distance of five feet or so it is somewhere in excess of 1,500 degrees, on their side it is cool and wet, the air stirred by the water that is streaming from the hoses. When they have pushed the fire back successfully and are standing there, holding it at bay, proving to themselves that they can, only then does the officer, who is standing in that bright and brilliant light with them, agreeing that they have done what is required of them in this training seminar, that they have passed, and will get another certification, only then does he turn his head to the man behind him, who comes up and gets down on his hands and knees and crawls between his legs and shuts off a valve down there, one that's been waiting for him. He, too, is depending on the men above him to protect him from harm.

I'd already had my run at it. It was old hat, I'd done it before, and even though I was off duty I'd ridden up with my turnouts and helmet with Jerry, the guy who shoved me up in my first car fire. He was an assistant chief by then, but I don't think I'd made captain yet. We had some cold beer in the back of that nice red pickup. I just went for the fun of it, to be with the men who were on duty, so that they would know that I was a part of them. So my buddies and I who had already taken our turns were back in the dark sipping on cool ones, watching the action, just waiting to ride back to Oxford. Jerry was the officer holding the two teams together. They did it just like they were supposed to, meshed the streams, pushed the fire back, were making steady progress.

Then somebody on the right side tried to run. Or jerked back, or did not press forward with his team, because the fan on the right side wavered and the big blue ball of flame shot through it immediately and engulfed Jerry's arm until he yelled at them and steadied them and made them hold. He turned his head for the man behind him to come up and he held them steady. By then we were all walking forward quickly and pulling our turnout coats back on and starting to fasten snaps, put on helmets. But the Christmas tree went black prematurely. Maybe the man at the gas truck saw it. Maybe somebody signaled him with a radio. I don't know. It's been so long ago.

Jerry was burned very badly. When they got the coat off his sleeve there was already a cooked patch of meat on his forearm, probably a little smaller than one of those Nerf footballs, but about the same shape. Huddles were being had. Some people were led away. There were murderous looks given in the direction of the man who had failed.

Jerry still wears the scar from that night, will always wear it, the burn was so bad. I remember standing in the parking lot, infuriated at the man who had done this to my friend, a man I had gone to school with, whose father had fought beside mine in World War II. But it wouldn't have done any good for somebody to whip his ass. He had shamed himself in front of his own department, and he was not one of ours. There were three or four different departments there that night, and six or eight trucks. I don't remember what city he was from, or everything that was said. And I'm sure now that he had more on his mind than he could bear that night, and I can't imagine what the ride back to his own town was like for him. Did they refuse to speak to him or were they sympathetic? Did they say, "Aw, man, it could have happened to anybody, it doesn't mean anything"? Did they tell other men in their own department about it? How great, do you suppose, was his shame?

Some men are made of different stuff from others. Firefighting for them is something that gets into their blood, like bird hunting, and it simply becomes a way of life. I could have stayed there until I retired, but I wanted to write. There would have been no shame in it whatsoever. It is an honorable and noble profession—the business of helping people. It is also sometimes a fearsome occupation. To go into a burning building is always an act of insanity to some of the public, who stand on the sidewalk gawking as the smoke pours from an upper window and the trucks run in howling in their gleaming red paint. And soon hoses are put out and pumps begin to throb and the hoses swell and harden like bricks. And men rush about and yell things and it seems like organized hysteria until you become one of those men and know what a supply line is and how to figure friction loss and operate a relief valve, understand the relationship of pump to engine and the difference between volume and pressure.

But facing a real fire never gets any easier. Sometimes it takes all the balls you've got to go up to one, because it's always hot, and it's always smoky, and it always chokes the living life right out of your throat unless you're down low or wearing a breathing apparatus. And it burns all kinds of other things—plastics, fabric, paint, wood. But after you go in enough times, you learn to touch a door with the back of your hand since it's more sensitive than the palm, that the fog nozzle will put it out if you can get close enough to it. The fear is something that you learn to try and control, and you try always to keep your head about you, because losing it in a bad situation might mean losing your life or the lives of your partners.

I was only in a few incidents where I thought I might be killed. I got my ears singed a few times, but that's to be expected in this line of business. You have to be careful not to get electrocuted or fall off a ladder or run over somebody with a firetruck. Driving to a fire in the truck for the first time is a pretty scary thing. Your legs shake while you're working the clutch and pressing down on the gas.

And walking up to a couple of smashed cars with trapped occupants on a highway littered with broken glass and thrown dirt and pieces of taillight lenses is something you never get used to. There may be people screaming. Lots of times there are. But you get trained on how to get them out and you just do what you've learned at the state fire academy, sometimes with doctors teaching you.

I don't know if any of it has anything to do with bravery. To me it was always a deal—the city was paying me to do this job and I had to do it just like the one I'd had before, which was driving a forklift around the stockroom and out on the loading dock, and driving a truck to Nashville every weekend to pick up a load of plated parts. It was just another job, albeit an infinitely more interesting one than the one I'd been doing. There wasn't any other place I knew of where you got to wear a uniform with a badge and ride around in a shiny red truck and have all the kids look at you. But the bad things that went along with it sometimes made it a hard job and by that I mean blood and death and dangerous conditions. In truth there was a lot of sitting around and boredom. But I never found anything I loved to do better.

Jerry's the chief of the Oxford, Mississippi, fire department now, has been for about a year and a half. He was there when I got there and he stayed on and rose through the ranks and now is the man at Fire Station 1. I don't see him much anymore because I don't go by and sit the way I used to when I worked there. I admire him for sticking to it, for handling all the crap calls in the rain or snow, all the false alarms the kids out on the campus pull, the wrecks and bad fires he's now having to direct. I can't think of anybody I'd rather have with me if I ever had to take a charged line and run into a burning building again.

A man like him is somebody I think of as a hero, a man who goes, not quietly about his job, but often in the dead of night, when the yellow traffic lights are blinking and most of the citizens of Oxford are asleep. They never hear his roaring siren or see his flashing red lights throw a brief spot of color on their bedroom blinds as he passes. But he is always there for them, with the men he now leads, even if they know nothing of the things he sees and protects them from. He's not in the paper a lot and plenty of people don't know his name. But if you need somebody to save you in the dead of night, he's your man. Fire man.

Order

If one man embodies the manly fascination with how things work, it's Charles Simonyi. The Microsoft programmer, who directed the teams that wrote Excel and Word and just finished something called Intentional Programming, shares the title of chief architect with Bill Gates. Hanging around him—in his airplane hangar at Boeing Airfield, say—you get the impression there is virtually no mechanical device he can't look at for a minute or two and figure out. In fact, as he surveys his stable of helicopters and airplanes, including a luxurious Falcon 50, he can't help but play the game. "What do you think that does?" he asks as he walks under one of his airplanes and points at an array of hydraulic devices deep within the open landing-gear bay. "Let's see if we can figure it out." It's no contest. I like to spend an afternoon figuring out how to yank the starter motor from my old truck, but this is mechanical aptitude of a whole other dimension.

I've asked Charles to share his thoughts on how things work, hoping they might illuminate the core need we all have to understand—and control, of course—our environment and grasp the order that governs the physical world. Boyishly handsome, with a flop of dark hair across his forehead, lively blue eyes, and a charming Hungarian accent, Charles is delighted to ruminate on his lifelong love affair with things mechanical, but is less sure he can contribute anything useful about the concept of order. It turns out, of course, that he knows plenty about order—particularly its role in helping men center their lives.

Order, at least at its simplest level, certainly rules Charles's domestic life. His extraordinary 22,000-square-foot house, which stretches across five and a half lots of shorefront on Seattle's Lake Washington, is virtually bereft of furniture. The postmodern mansion, "version 3.0," is constructed of glass and silver metals—mostly brushed stainless steel and brushed chrome—and teak, the only visible wood. Every piece of

162

hardware, every electronic component, every fixture is of the highest quality. A three-room library, replete with stacks and a librarian, houses tens of thousands of books reflecting his varied interests: chemical engineering, aviation, human biology, nuclear submarines, to name a few. The south end of the house is devoted to a conference center and a "museum room," which features the foremost collection of Lichtensteins in the world, as well as the work of Vasarely (an order freak) and Jasper Johns. There's a pool, sauna, game room with helicopter and fighter-jet simulators, a gym with virtual-reality step climbers and bikes, and a sprawling workshop—my first stop on the extended tour. The room fairly pulses with bridled energy—a lathe and drill press stand idle; various other power tools hang from the walls. Charles begins riffling through tool drawers, finally finding what he wants to show me—a small measuring instrument of the finest precision. "The most disorderly part of this instrument is the human holding it," he says.

How Things Work

Charles Simonyi

Order is not pressure which is imposed on from without but an equilibrium which is set up from within.

JOSÉ ORTEGA Y GASSET

For as long as I can remember I've been obsessed with knowing how things work. I found childhood incredibly upsetting and frustrating because every day I had new questions, I would see new problems, new conundrums, and I couldn't come up with answers fast enough to satisfy my need to know. I began life surrounded by all this random information I couldn't process, and ever since then

I've been trying to bring some kind of order to it—or at least to the questions that swirl in my mind.

I learned to speak very late, when I was about four, and then learned to read very soon after that, so by the time I went to school I was reading like crazy—books about the future, space travel, rockets, machines. I discovered that after I read a book I was able to conjure up the mechanics of things in my mind in incredible detail. That was because I *had* to know how things worked. After I read Jules Verne's *20,000 Leagues Under the Sea* I tried to rebuild in my head Captain Nemo's submarine. There were very few hints in the book you could use, so I had to interpolate. I read the books over and over to find new morsels of information. In one scene, Captain Nemo pushes a gray button to slow down the sub. Where was that button? What other buttons were there? The goal was to get a perfect mental image of the submarine, and now I could add the gray button to the schematic. I didn't see any of the Disney movies then, which helped, I think. In fact, later on when I did see some interpretations of Captain Nemo's equipment, they weren't as good as mine.

I soon realized that the only way to really learn how something works is hands-on. I began to acquire things and take them apart—several clocks, to start with. Then I went through my chemistry phase—that was horrible. I blew up a lot of stuff. If I'd had American-style materials I would have been very dangerous. I took apart every toy I owned. Socially, I was kind of a weird nerd, just full of endless questions and problems. It was the postwar era and there were soldiers everywhere. I'd look at a rifle and wonder, If there is a spring in the magazine, how come the cartridges are not pushed out when the magazine is detached? I had this infinite frustration and desperately wanted to be an adult. When I was grown up, I thought, I would be able to understand everything.

When I was about eight or nine, my father gave me a prewar German Erector set of very high quality, which marked the passage from my destruction to my building phase. When people play with

Erector sets they usually build cars, planes, combines—models of things. But I had no interest in modeling things. I was interested in function only. I built things that modeled an operation, not a shape. I was interested in building a clutch, brakes, a centrifugal regulator—things that had a legitimate function.

The best thing I built when I was a boy was a gearbox that shifted gears after reading commands from a paper tape. I used scissors to cut little pulses in the edge of the paper tape (I used dry packing tape), which were read by a contact, which closed a relay to a servomotor that shifted the gears. The interesting thing was that the Erector set came with very few screws and I had to learn how to optimize my design. If I were going to use a screw to hold something together, it had to do more than one job. This notion of optimization and multiple use gave me a fantastic advantage later when I began thinking about and working with computers.

The other thing was that I invented a new way to build gearboxes. A typical gearbox has two gears for every speed, so if you had a four-speed transmission it would have eight gears in it. I built a gearbox that needed only two more gears than the total number of speeds. So a normal ten-speed gearbox had twenty gears, but my scheme required only twelve. Many years later, I got interested in working with lathes. A lathe has to turn screws of many different pitches, so a good one has a very big gearbox in it with maybe twenty or thirty speeds. Guess what? It uses the mechanism I came across independently as a kid. It had been around long before I came across it.

Even though I was learning these fantastic things, I rarely felt gratified because more and more problems kept coming at me. But I learned two skills that still serve me well. The first was how to do a mental emulation and a mental search for information—create the vivid mental image of the inner workings of Captain Nemo's sub. The second was how to optimize—build within the limited resources that I had. Still, these skills met an enormous challenge when I was fourteen and saw my first computer at a trade show in Hungary. A sign said that it had 2K of memory of 36-bit words. I thought, What is a computer? What's a word? A bit? Is 2K a lot, a little? I looked at this box sitting on a pedestal and it gave no hint to any of these questions. What was it? I had read a little about computers. People were always talking about how you could feed music scores into the machine and a completely new one would come out. I had a very healthy skepticism about this, which was completely justified. But I also wondered, What does it mean to "feed" material into the computer? What form does the feedstock take? Does the computer have a mouth? I was upset, but it was intriguing because it was special and expensive and mysterious. It was like Captain Nemo's submarine without any buttons, not even one gray button. I asked my dad to help me learn everything about them. I read articles that didn't really answer my questions and just made me more eager to get more information. I got a job around computers and managed to understand some parts, but not the whole.

Then, one day, six months into my investigations, an epiphany: Oh, there's this register thing that shows where you fetch the next instruction and some instructions are jumps and the address is writtten into this register and then the flow of control changes and you can do this conditionally. Wow! And I realized I was learning in precisely the way I had learned about Captain Nemo's submarine. I was pretending to understand, playing at understanding, before I actually understood. It's how I've learned everything. Before I could read, my mother would recite poems to me from books, then I would parrot the poems while holding the book. Everyone thought I was reading, but I had just memorized the poem and was pretending. Then one day I recognized the actual words. I could read! I was good at math as a child, could do calculus in elementary school. And in every case I can remember how I played the game of knowing, pretending to understand—being able to memorize and apply a complex mathematical formula but not really comprehending it until much later.

Today, my style of learning is a little different. All the pretending in the world couldn't help me understand how a modern computer works. When I was a boy, if I looked at a clock for a month I could understand the clock. Today's computer is a billion times more complex than a clock. The information is completely hidden. You would need the best microscope in the world to understand from scratch how a chip works and you'd need a thousand scientists working a thousand years to figure out from the little traces what's going on.

So I've learned to appreciate the beauty and utility of user manuals. Now I can have the manuals for fighter jets, helicopters, submarines. I have an operations manual for the Gemini spacecraft that has annotations in it made by Neil Armstrong. It was his copy. Someone once asked me if I knew how the astronauts peed in the spacecraft. I said, Let's look it up. In the manual there's even a checklist for peeing; it's actually quite complex. The urine had to be heated or it would freeze and there was a special way to dispose of it. The astronaut had to wear something on his penis called a uriceptacle. But I couldn't actually find a definition of what it was anywhere.

By my childhood standards, I guess, consulting a manual is like cheating. But today I don't have time to figure things out for myself. The manual satisfies me and enables me to think above that level. I don't have to worry about how *that* particular thing works anymore; I can read about it and then worry about the next thing. The way you think about new things is to absorb as much knowledge about the current ones as possible.

In the last thirty years, the mechanical view—the inquisitive view, the computing view—has been vindicated. We've taken apart many things in life and found them to be mechanical. DNA, for instance—we've taken that clock apart. DNA is a little machine, more like a memory, with a partner called a ribosome—a protein that turns the DNA into structures that become the organism. Years ago, people metaphorically referred to the cell as a factory. Today we know what's in the factory, who's the supervisor, and where the manuals are located, which is in the DNA. It turns out to be a precise metaphor. The question of whether machines acquire personality is no longer a frivolous one. The answer is, Yes, we do.

For me the big question in life has never been why, but how. I feel comfortable with my process of discovery being just what it is. I've never had the urge to find something "larger." I think it's already pretty large and it's pretty wonderful and if somebody wants to see even larger meaning—the hand of God—that's fine. I'm skeptical about getting too far ahead of myself. I need to learn all the hard answers, all the information, before I can go further. Answers bring meaning and order to my life.

Of course, *order* is a funny word and a not entirely desirable goal. When you have complete order, like the perfect grid of a chessboard, or a perfectly ordered life, or a long string of zeros, it's boring. You have no information, no value. The other extreme, complete disorder, is the same—meaningless. Only when you mix the two, when you superimpose disorder upon order—when you introduce a flaw to the perfect grid, spontaneity to a perfectly planned day, or a one to all those zeros—do you create the kind of tension, twists, exceptions, and quirks that are interesting and valuable.

That is where the most useful information lies, right along that nexus of order and disorder, knowing and not knowing—any two extremes, in fact. If you understand that, you have a great advantage in life. If you forget where you are, just look at the extremes. They're fixed reference points for navigation. They're not where you want to be, but they'll tell you exactly where you are.

✦

Like Charles Simonyi, when I was young I also fervently believed that the answer to life's mysteries would be revealed to me when I grew up. This has not been the case.
But there is one fascinating bit of information I've stum-

bled upon in my travails that might come in handy. It's the real difference between men and women: the way in which they order the universe.

Case in point: user manuals. Men want knowledge and so, as Charles pointed out, they have a higher appreciation for the beauty and utility of user manuals. Before a new product is even taken out of the box, the man of the house will sit down and he shall not be moved until every instructional word has been reviewed, commented upon under his breath, and memorized.

For men, life's essential question is How? *As in,* How *can I fix it?* How *was I supposed to know that, if you didn't tell me?*

But in a woman's universe, needs (usually other people's) take priority over her wants. Her thirst for knowledge is quenched by the silent observation of unspoken signals, information that crystallizes into clarity when her intuition is applied. What a woman needs—day in, day out—is understanding. To give it and to get it.

For women, the only answer worth waiting for comes from asking Why? *As in,* Why *would you want to?* Why *did you do that?*

It can be frustrating not speaking the language of your traveling companion. So the next time he wants to read the user manual, don't even try to offer an opinion. Instead, why not offer to turn the page? "Men and women are like right and left hands," the American suffragette Jeannette Rankin observed, "it doesn't make sense not to use both."

—SBB

PATRIOTISM

Cut to the summer of 1969. The day has been like every other day of the summer: eight hours of labor for a construction company, a quick dinner, then a drive to a Minneapolis suburb, where I play in a league from which the '72 Olympic hockey team will be culled. It's a blissful life for an eighteen-year-old between college semesters—nothing but work and play—but tonight an uneasy air fills the rink. This evening, the draft board will conduct its annual lottery, selecting at random eighty dates from the calendar year. If my birthday or that of many of the other young men I'm playing with falls on one of those dates, I and they will be conscripted into the army.

Unless, of course, we have a good excuse as to why we shouldn't serve our country the way our fathers and grandfathers did. Fortunately, just attending college is good enough for a temporary exemption, and even were I to drop out my mother has vowed to spirit me away to Canada. But I'm uncomfortable with all the protectiveness and privilege. I don't agree with the American administration's policy in Vietnam, but I also don't want to feel like a shirker, like someone else should fulfill my duty and obligation to my country. I don't need a surrogate to undergo what has long been considered a necessary rite of passage into manhood. I've decided that I want to be drafted, because I want to find out what I'll do.

When I get home later on, my father gives me the news: not even close. My draft number is three hundred forty-something. I still wonder what I would have done. For James Jones, a four-star general in the Marine Corps, there was never even a shred of doubt.

A Higher Calling

General James Jones

The private conscience is the last and only protection of the civilized world.

MARTHA GELLHORN

Patriotism is devotion to one's country. You don't have to be a professional military officer, as I've been for the past thirty-four years, to feel a deep sense of obligation toward your country. There are many people who are just as patriotic and feel just as strongly about their nation as I do. Being a Marine is just my way of expressing it.

A proud family legacy helped me, very early in life, to formulate a powerful desire to serve my country. When I was born in 1943 in Kansas City, Missouri, my father was a major in the Marine Corps, an infantry officer stationed in the Pacific. His brother, at the age of twenty-eight, was one of the youngest battalion commanders in the Corps. Name any island battle in the Pacific and one of them was probably there. My uncle was awarded a Navy Cross, and both he and my father received a Silver Star, a Bronze Star medal, and a Purple Heart.

After the war, my father went to work for International Harvester. In 1947, he was assigned to Paris, and for the next fifteen years, I lived in France. U.S. military forces were visible in France during that time—entire American military communities were being built, with houses, commissaries, and schools. My parents' social life mainly revolved around the American Marines, and, by extension, I associated myself with them as well.

Oddly, during that period, even though I clearly identified

myself as an American, I knew more about French culture than my own. I always felt caught between two worlds, being able to negotiate my way in each, but also seeing myself as different and slightly apart from both. Every three years, we traveled back to the United States and would spend two months with both sets of my grandparents in Joplin, Missouri. The contrast in quality of life between France and the United States during the postwar years was stark. France took a long time to dig out from the war. Air-raid sirens were still being tested regularly, and much of the country was without gas or electricity. However, the French had regained an essential element of their lifestyle that was lost during the war: their freedom. I understood that this freedom had been won through the sacrifices of selfless and dedicated people: people like my father and my uncle, and my mother and aunt who supported them.

Growing up in a postwar environment gave me a tremendous sense of pride and appreciation for America's contributions during the war. My father was a history buff and always pointed out the broader issues involving America's role in the world. Every third year when we came back to the States, as the ocean liner steamed into New York Harbor, he'd awaken us at five o'clock to ensure that we saw the Statue of Liberty and that we understood what it represented.

I entered the Marine Corps in 1967 to fulfill a sense of duty, obligation, and family honor. I wanted to belong to the military society that had shaped my father's and my uncle's values. Sadly, my career began at a time when public support and the sense of national prestige that had long sustained the U.S. Armed Forces had eroded. Unlike during World War II, the war in Vietnam was not a catalyst for national pride or military duty. The widespread antimilitary fervor was unsettling for me, as I was convinced that serving my country was absolutely the right thing to do.

The experience of wearing your country's uniform in combat is the ultimate expression of patriotism; it alters forever what it means to make a commitment. Noble abstractions collapse in the face of the hard reality that the choices you make can cost lives. In Vietnam, I quickly learned that combat leadership is the highest form of responsibility and the ultimate test of one's mettle.

In 1970, my initial service obligation was complete. Antimilitary feelings ran strong in much of the country, and it seemed that most of my peers planned to leave the Corps. There was a prevailing mind-set that only those who couldn't make it in the civilian world would stay in the military. I found a job, but five days before I was to start, I expressed to my wife, Diane, my strong reservations about leaving the Marine Corps. Diane helped me sort through it, and together, we decided to stay with the Corps. It's a decision we have never regretted.

One of the great satisfactions of being a Marine is the privilege of associating with people who share common purposes and values, and have a strong desire to serve their country. I consider the Marine Corps to be a society, not a bureaucracy. As a society, we focus on the well-being of our members. The rank insignia we wear can be considered, among other things, an expression of experience. The four stars on my collar represent a basis of that experience and, after thirty-four years of service, it is incumbent upon me to share my experiences with newer members of our Marine Corps. I like to think that the Corps offers an exemplary model to the larger society we serve. Putting the achievements of the group ahead of individual glory— that's a pretty good message.

Being a Marine involves commitment. I liken it to a calling for the priesthood: a lifelong contract, whether you wear the uniform for three years or three decades. The only thing asked of you is that you serve honorably, that you don't embarrass the nation, your fellow Marines, or yourself, and that you leave a positive legacy for those who follow you. It's a privilege to be a member of the finest fighting military organization the world has ever known.

Some people ask whether being a Marine requires sacrifice. Certainly, the lifestyle is challenging, but it's so fulfilling that Marines don't think of it as sacrifice, though our spouses rightfully do! In

1991, for example, I had the privilege of commanding the Marine portion of an operation that rescued half a million Kurds in the mountains of northern Iraq. It was difficult to be separated from my family for eight months, but mission accomplishment and the satisfaction of helping people in need were a form of reward for us all. It was a great feeling. I saw a seventeen-year-old Marine from the streets of Chicago, who had tears running down his face because he was so overwhelmed with the impact of our mission. That Marine knew he was doing something important . . . probably one of the most significant things he'd ever done or will ever do. Until then, he'd never left Chicago, but he shared my feelings about what we were doing. Such an experience is something that money will never buy.

One of my greatest concerns is that patriotism, as it is expressed by men in uniform, is undervalued during this time of economic prosperity and relative stability. The lessons of the twentieth century must not be forgotten. We must strive to foster a lasting understanding of the role that national security plays in the development of democratic values, freedom, and our expanding economic well-being. Unfortunately, it sometimes takes a catastrophe to draw sufficient attention to the value of national security. What will be the Pearl Harbor of the twenty-first century?

To me, patriotism encompasses duty, allegiance, honor, and trust in your country and your countrymen. That's a profoundly internal feeling; you can't fabricate it. Someone or some set of experiences, has to put it there. In my case, it was both: my unique boyhood perspective on America and the impact my country had on other people's lives, as well as the values I inherited from the two men I admire most, my father and my uncle. The ultimate expression of patriotism is to extend your country's values and potential for good into the world, to set good examples, to be the light on the hill for people who want to be free—the people who want to provide for their children and families, and make the world better. But it all begins with the individual, a single man with his own sense of duty.

RISK

When I conceived of A Man's Journey, *my thought was to invite some of the most exciting, fascinating, compelling, passionate, and soulful men in the world to contribute their thoughts on what it means to live authentically.*

Sting headed my list.

Yes, yes, yes. Being the sexiest man alive did have a little something to do with it, I'll admit. But what topic suited him best?

The American novelist Willa Cather insisted that there are only two human stories, "and they go on repeating themselves as fiercely as if they had never happened before." Of course, she was right, which is why every raconteur tells them over and over, and every lyricist puts them to song. From the Old Testament to Every Breath You Take, *the two stories that keep our souls enthralled are passion and betrayal.*

I thought Sting could help us return passion to its rightful place in our lives. I knew that he wouldn't continue to perpetuate the narrow, bodice-ripping, clichéd smear job that's given passion a bad rap. The soul and breadth of meaning buried within Sting's lyrics and vocal interpretations; the style and dedication with which he tackles the projects he takes on, whether it's scoring a movie, learning a new instrument, song, or mastering a new yoga posture; the great love he has for his family; his sense of humor; his loyalty to his friends, colleagues, and causes—all of this is what passion is to me.

So I was very surprised when he gently declined. He was willing to participate in the book, but expressing passion on the page wasn't a comfortable fit for him. He didn't see himself as a passionate man.

I asked him if he'd listened to his own music. Sting laughed heartily. Then he asked if he could write instead about a friend of his? Could he write about risk?

—SBB

Let Your Soul Be Your Bookie

Sting

You can make a fresh start with your final breath.

BERTOLT BRECHT

One man's risk is another's sure bet. I may have the reputation for being a risk taker, but when I look back, I wasn't always conscious of taking them. At least, not at the time. It might have appeared that way to outsiders. But to me, at the crossroads, there weren't really two divergent paths for me to consider, two stark but equally compelling choices. There was a dead end and the edge of a cliff. So if it's die or jump, is it risk or destiny? Maybe it doesn't matter. Maybe risk *is* destiny.

I suppose the first big risk I ever took was to leave my "profession," which was teaching. I was twenty-four, had a wife, a baby, a dog, a little car. My foot was on the first rung of the ladder, but I wasn't going up; I had one boot in the grave. I knew that for sure the minute the head teacher warned me in horror that if I left, I'd lose my pension.

Pension? Didn't know I had one. All I did know was that I didn't want a life with a pension plan waiting at the end of it. I know that attitude was arrogant. I was born into a working-class family and, for us, pensions were the reward for hard, honest toil. But it wasn't going to be *my* reward. Arrogance is a highly underappreciated character trait. In fact, arrogance fuels risk.

My former wife was an actress pursuing a career in London and I knew that if I was going to make it as a musician, I had to be in London, too. So we packed up all our belongings, which besides the baby and the dog was a rocking chair, and set off in our bat-

tered Citroën toward the living-room floor of a friend. I really had
no prospects. What was I thinking? Well, I wasn't. There seems to
be very little cognitive process associated with risks. But it was also
strangely joyous—like you're about to dive into some very cold
water and the minute before you hit the water you think, "There's
no turning back now. I've done this." And there's a great freedom
in knowing that there aren't any safety nets.

Whenever you change the direction of your life, it's going to
scare the people around you. That's a given. But if it doesn't scare
the daylights out of *you,* it's not a real risk. Very often the fear comes
only after you're well into it. Those early days were both debilitating and frightening for me because the only way I could support
my family was to go on the dole. Turn up on Wednesday afternoon,
sign your name, and say you're available for work. I never felt I
should be there, doing that, but I was grateful for it each week
because during the day I could practice my music. That's when I
met Stuart Copeland, who would later be the drummer of the
Police, and he had this idea of forming a band. He said he liked my
playing and singing and wondered if I wanted to risk tagging along
to see how it might go. Was there a choice? It didn't seem like it at
the time, it just seemed like the answer to my prayers. So again the
paradox: If you've got no choice, how can you call it a risk?

I've never believed there's anything to be gained from an edu-
cated risk, where you weigh all the consequences and then take your
chances and hope you chose the best possible outcome. Usually we
take on well-thought-out wagers for practical reasons, like for
money. But more often than not they backfire. Even the most brilliant strategy, the most reasonable plan can morph overnight into a
leech, sucking the integrity out of you, until you're barely able to say
"Never again." That is, until the next reasonably profitable, well-
thought-out devil's IOU presents itself.

Sometimes people mix up thrill seeking and risk taking, but I
think they're totally different experiences, with different motivations

and outcomes. Thrill seeking is flirting with danger, taunting the fates. Thrill seeking seems to be a particularly male endeavor; it's probably encoded in our DNA. It's speeding motorcycles, parachute jumping, mountain climbing, drug taking, and adultery when you've got a great wife and a beautiful family. My perverse enjoyment of rough plane rides brings out the thrill seeker in me. I was once in a near-crash in a small plane flying over Venezuela. When I walked away from it, surviving was one of the best feelings I'd had for a long time. Surviving. What a rush. Women understand this wild streak in their sons, but barely tolerate it in their men. Perhaps external thrills are most seductive when our daily lives disappoint us. I sometimes think that we men seek thrills because we don't always have the courage to take real risks, whether they're the emotional risks necessary in successful personal relationships, or practical ones, as in changing jobs.

True risk, that sudden leap into cold water, can carry you into a state of grace. Coincidences, synchronicity, chance, karmic charm, it doesn't matter what you call it, there's a positive force that intervenes to cover your back. Things click. It makes sense because true risk is the only thing that forces spiritual and emotional growth so immediately, so dramatically.

In my life there's always been a connection between risk and luck. A lot of people approach risk as if it's the enemy, when it's really fortune's accomplice. A risk you take may seem ridiculous to other people, but risk isn't random or rash when it's a necessity. The night I decided to walk away from the Police, I felt I'd reached the summit. We were being hailed as the hottest band of the decade. In barely five years we'd gone from playing for a handful of people in bars to 67,000 fans in Shea Stadium. We'd sold forty million records. I had more money than I knew what to do with. But I was miserable. I was out of control and so was my life. Everything was falling apart—my first marriage was breaking up, my relationships with the other guys in the band were horrendous, yet I had the world envying me. As I walked off the stage, I knew I had to make a change. Everybody thought I was certifiable. But I was joyous, relieved. Risk had given me back my soul.

As one grows older, one has more to lose and the risks loom larger. I'm halfway through my life. How do I become the old man that I could admire now, a wise elder? How do I grow old gracefully, especially in my profession, which glorifies youth so aggressively? How do I become useful to the people around me and my society as an older person? I think it's crucial to start fresh, take a blank canvas, do things that defy logic, whether it's introducing an audience who's used to listening to music in four-four time to a more complex meter, or making a movie that's unconventional, or popularizing somewhat unfamiliar topics such as rain forest issues or meditation or whatever. What's disconcerting or unexpected often pleases me, especially if it takes my audience and me in a new direction. In the end I know I won't find it personally rewarding just to toe the line, stick to the formula. I've got to progress more as a person than as a personality.

What's my biggest risk now? How about being happy? I used to subscribe to the theory that in order to write anything worthwhile, you needed to be in some sort of turmoil. And I wasn't alone in that belief. I would manufacture all sorts of problems in order to be able to create. But in the last few years I've made a conscious decision to create from a profound depth of happiness, and no one is more amazed than I am that some of the best work of the deposed "King of Pain" was inspired by joy.

It always has impressed me that the Chinese pictogram for *crisis* is identical to the one for *opportunity*. I'm convinced that taking risks redeems, restores, and reinvents. So the next time you're overwhelmed by curiosity, or the prospect of change makes your stomach heave and the ground beneath your feet rumble, my advice is, don't look back. Risk is sitting on your shoulder, my friend. Nothing in your life is beyond redemption. Dive into that cold water. All bets are off.

RESILIENCE

A terrible thing has happened. No one has died, but the blow is severe. How do you break the news to your loved ones? What sort of model of behavior should you, the "man of the house," present to them? Should you be stoic or desolated? Raging or sanguine? Philosophical? In retaliation mode?

Perhaps our most important job is to search the aftermath for nuggets of preserved goodness—as my daughter once wrote to me on a birthday card when she was six, we must "take a look at all we have." This is what writer Bill Klaber did after a tragedy beset his family.

Love Among the Ruins

William Klaber

After the earthquake and the fire comes the still, small voice.
DOROTHY THOMPSON

People began arriving at nine in the morning wearing boots and old clothes. They brought their own shovels, rakes, and wheelbarrows. Many brought food. The bright sun promised a warm day, and soon the air was filled with the sounds of cheerful greetings and communal labor. The scene was reminiscent of a barn raising, but the task before us was actually more like its opposite. We were there to pick through piles of charred rubble—the remains of what had once been our house.

We were on vacation in North Carolina when we got the news. It was our sixth trip as a family to the Outer Banks, and our first

180

stay in Journey's End, an unassuming cottage that sat snugly behind the first dune, its roof steeply pitched to deflect the wind coming off the water. This seemed like a prudent design, for on our five previous trips to the Carolina coast we had encountered four hurricanes. Now there would be a fifth.

Two days into our stay a tight Category II named Dennis appeared in the eastern Caribbean and began marching in our direction. A few days later the surf began to boil and the island was put on evacuation alert. Tom and Greta, our two teenagers, and Siena, our three-year-old, were caught in the excitement. Jean was not. Just two weeks before, her mother, Erika, had died unexpectedly. Jean had not yet had time to honor her grief and was in no mood to be uprooted. When the telephone rang late in the afternoon I picked it up, assuming it was a friend looking for a storm report. It was Karen, Jean's sister. "I have some terrible news," she said, sobbing, barely able to speak. "It's your house . . . there was a fire . . . there's nothing left."

There was a flash in which I briefly saw my reflection. I was in the house furiously fighting the fire—as though I could change events simply by wishing hard enough. When the vision passed, I called everyone inside and repeated the news. There were tears and cries of disbelief. I stifled my own welling emotions by reminding myself that I was a grown-up, but secretly I took solace in the tears of my family. I also felt challenged as a father to show the children, then and in the months to come, how to stand up again when life delivers a big hit.

We had planned to leave for home the next day, but by morning our sturdy beach house was shaking. Dennis had arrived sooner than expected and we were trapped. We fought 75-mile-per-hour winds as we bolted the shutters, retreating inside as the sea surged to the base of the first dune. But it never threatened to overtake it, and for all its roar the hurricane provided an odd, welcome sanctuary—a place, cut off from the world, in which we could face our inner turmoil and comfort one another. We played cards, worked a puzzle, and occasionally ventured outside. For amusement we walked from the calm lee of the house into the fierce wind, which would tumble us back. It was crude comedy, and it felt good to hear the kids laugh.

In moments of reversal I think it is not uncommon to look for life lessons as compensation for pain and loss. Almost immediately I began to kindle the hope that through our ordeal I would grow, in some way, wiser. I even began deciding what my lesson would be. It seemed obvious. I had lost all my things, yet I still needed to be content. Thus, it appeared, I was to learn that we place too much importance upon our possessions.

We first saw the house twenty years ago when Jean and I, living together in New York, were searching for a weekend place along the upper Delaware River. It was a three-story fixer-upper with peeling paint and a pronounced lean to the south. Inside, copper plumbing was strapped to the ceilings and luan paneling was nailed over broken plaster. But our hearts had been won. The crooked house stood atop a hill with a stunning view, and the porches spoke of happy times.

The hundred-acre farm had been settled in 1860 by Patrick O'Meara. Using axes, mules, and pulleys, he cleared the land and yanked stumps from the hardscrabble hillsides. The largest trees were hewn square with an adze and fastened with wood pegs to become the timber frames of the barn and the small house that would stand nearby. The buildings sat on foundations of bluestone that O'Meara cut by hand from a small quarry at the back of the property. As the farm prospered and children arrived, a larger house was built around the first.

Although I spent many an afternoon in the early years sweating pipes and patching roof leaks, it was a fun place. There were gatherings and visits from friends, usually accompanied by music and dancing. Most of all, it seemed a stage set begging for children. One weekend, while standing in front of the house, I proposed to Jean and she accepted. When Tom was born, we drove through a March blizzard to sit by the woodstove and watch the snow fall with our new son. When Greta came a few years later, we left the city and moved in full-time.

And so our children grew up in the old house that bore witness to its moments. There were the sounds of babies crying, kittens being born, laughter at the kitchen table, fiddle music on the stereo, and Thanksgiving prayers. There were birthday parties, blizzard parties, chess games in front of the fire, and dinners by oil lamp on the porch. The echoes of these fine times fused with the walls, melded with those of the first settlers, and then radiated their warmth back into the rooms. Everyone felt it. Despite twenty years of renovations we had not been able to remove the funk. In the house there was the sense that life was good, but very imperfect. Now it was gone.

And so were all our things. At some point in life most of us experience the violation of being robbed: a car, locker, or house broken into. Rarely do we encounter the felon who puts a gun to our back and demands our every possession. Even the most diligent thief doesn't bother with the family portraits or the angel atop the Christmas tree. When we arrived back upstate there was an outpouring of heartfelt concern. We were offered half a dozen homes as shelter and took up residence in the house of a friend who was away for a few months. School was to begin in a week and we had a lot to do to get ready.

The school and its future had dominated our activities the past year, culminating in a recent referendum. After a bitter campaign, those favoring merging our district with that of our neighbors and accepting state aid to build a new high school won a clear victory over those who wanted things to remain the way they were. Both Jean and I were active on the merger side. To nonresidents, it might seem inconceivable that someone would torch a house over a school vote, but the campaign pushed well beyond the rational. After the vote our opponents charged that "massive voter fraud" had taken place, and in a letter circulated around town, Jean and I were identified as the "ringleaders."

That was two weeks before we left for North Carolina. The moment we heard the house had burned, arson leapt into our minds. It was a repugnant thought, and we felt no desire to be victims or martyrs. "We'll never know," I said to Jean early on, "but I do know I can't pretend it isn't a possibility." At the same time we knew we couldn't have that thought eating away at us. So not only did we have to cope with the loss of our home, we had to live with the idea that someone may have set the fire, and somehow, on some level, that had to be okay. This bit of emotional jujitsu was not easy, especially at four in the morning, but during the day we managed. We didn't pretend the situation was otherwise, nor did we dwell on it. It was rarely spoken of, and then only to close friends.

Humor became our comfort. When a friend asked how things were going and I told her that I felt a little worn, she rejoined, "Well, I guess after the euphoria of losing all your possessions wears off, there's bound to be a letdown." Upon driving by a house under construction in which steel framing was used instead of wood, another friend remarked, "They're having great success marketing this model to people active in school politics." A cohort in the merger campaign began humming an updated B-52s song, "Living in Your Own Private Kosovo."

The tune was funny, strangely comforting, but, of course, off the mark. Even if our worst fears were true, neither the Serb army nor the Hutu militia was after us. We had lost our possessions but we had insurance, savings, friends and family. Compared with most villagers who make the front page, we were living in a marshmallow world.

After the fire I became acutely aware of people who were in the midst of personal difficulties, many of them far more severe than my own. I considered this new awareness desirable personal growth, and it was oddly humbling. I was making tragedy comparisons that led to feelings of embarrassment—the chunk of the sky that had fallen upon my head had really not been so very large. After all, I had lost only things.

Women are better than men, I think, at honoring loss. The explanation may have to do with genetics, but men seem to pay less attention to their wounds, a helpful trait, perhaps, when one is fighting off the Visigoths, but somewhat less useful in modern life. Now only occasionally vulnerable to waves of sadness, I thought I was "recovering." On hearing myself laugh, I would congratulate myself on my apparent progress toward the thing-free satori we jokingly referred to as "the incredible lightness of being." I was, I thought, learning my catechism—personal possessions aren't all that important.

But over time I began to feel oddly detached. I wasn't in pain, but I was flat. I was living in attractive surroundings, but it was as though my life was, in some way, taking place in a motel room. I felt a loss of magic.

Slowly it occurred to me that I'd got my lesson wrong. Things actually mattered more than I thought. My assignment was not to understand that the human spirit is superior to possessions, but rather to discover for myself the way objects have meaning in our lives, the manner in which they are sacred or become so. As we began our insurance inventories we noticed that the things that commanded little or no replacement value were often the things we most wanted back—the door frame in the upstairs hall where Jean had marked the children's height each year, for example. Worthless to the world, precious to us.

My personal list included the chair my father used when he was the editor of our town newspaper, the table my grandmother got as a wedding gift a century earlier, and the ice ax I used while climbing Mount McKinley. There were slides of a solo journey on the upper Amazon when I was nineteen, photos of a midlife walkabout in Nepal, and a video of Tom and me walking across a field when he was only a year old. There were photographs of my father as a boy, and one of his father as a young man, and one of his father and his wife (my great-grandparents) seated in a carriage.

There was a quilt made by my mother, a book of poems written by her mother, and a silver cup won by my father's mother in a New York tennis tournament in 1905. And there were our wedding photographs and all the photographs of the children taken in the past fifteen years.

Jean's inventory included personal journals going back twenty-five years, paintings by some close friends, one of whom was no longer alive, a doll she got in an Easter basket when she was two, a flute she carried as a young woman to Majorca and the Baja, and the slides of those journeys. And, of course, photographs of her mother.

As the sharp pain of loss became the dull ache of loss, I began to understand in a new way how objects carry the souls of those who have come before and how they surround us with their energy. I also started feeling better about feeling bad about losing my things. And I learned that precious objects, most particularly a house, should be properly mourned, like people, with gatherings and ceremonies.

And so it was that on a brisk autumn morning people began arriving with shovels, rakes, and wheelbarrows. We were there to view the body and say good-bye. Getting dirty together would be our communion. Also, like those who had raised the timbers on the same spot a hundred and forty years earlier, we were there to celebrate a new beginning. The day's demolition would be the first step in reconstruction. In the swirl of anguish after losing our home, we had discovered the real depth of our affection for our town, despite what may have happened. And if there was something we wanted our children to gain from the loss, it was a sense of regeneration.

We hadn't expected to recover much that day, but hoped there were objects we would see again, things made of metal or stone. Neither, however, had fared well in the intense heat of the fire. Even the cast-iron fry pans did not come out intact. As the work went on, it became apparent that very little was going to emerge from the ashes.

But then there was a cry. Someone had pulled a charred glob from the mess and, just before discarding it, had pried it apart to discover that it was a photo album. The heat of the fire had fused the pages, and although many of the photos had damage on the edges, the central images were intact. It seemed impossible that perishable photographs could have survived such an inferno, but here they were. A little while later another shout, another glob, a second photo album. Then a third.

It was a small miracle. Jean said that it felt as though the spirit of the house, in a last gesture, had somehow wrapped itself around these images. There were photographs of our wedding, and of the early days of the house. Pictures of the kids when they were little, and trips we had taken as a family. There was a photo of the house in which the heat and the water had caused the chemicals to bleed through yellow and orange, a bizarre but strangely beautiful representation of the house in flames. And there was another in which the fire damage had made an intimate frame—a portrait of Jean's mother. These unlikely survivors were carried to the garage and laid out on a large table. There, in their distress, they seemed to speak for all that was lost, and, at the same time, signal the precious moments of life yet to come.

✦

We see the images on the nightly news so frequently, but the enormity of the human drama and sorrow rarely registers: homes burned to the ground by flash fires, or submerged by rushing water. Houses ripped asunder by earthquakes, tornadoes, hurricanes. The survivors stand near the wreckage of their lives and say with gratitude and disbelief, "Thank God, no one was killed. It was only things we lost."

Then the news crew moves on to the next disaster and the camera isn't there to bear witness to the shattering moment they realize that the things they lost weren't just knickknacks but talismans. Irreplaceable. Precious. To anyone else, it might just look like what's left of a pair of salt and pepper shakers from the Grand Canyon being swept into the garbage can. But to a couple who first met at the Grand Canyon, who recently celebrated their fiftieth wedding anniversary there, and lovingly displayed them on their dining room sideboard, these were sacred memory vessels.

I was so moved by Bill Klaber's epiphany about personal possessions because he's expressing a truth many of us believe but feel uncomfortable defending. We're allowed to love our possessions.

I believe cherished objects can be very revealing, offering insights into our personalities in intimate and illuminating ways. Surrounding ourselves with objects that speak to our souls brings us authentic moments of pleasure. Still, a lot of us have become numb to the objects that surround us; dust gathers from past marriages and previous incarnations that have little relevance to our present lives.

After I finished Bill Klaber's essay, I was possessed with a desire to sweep through the rooms of my house and edit my possessions once again. I want to make sure that each item displayed is there because of the special smile or tear it evokes in my heart. I also plan to make a list of the things that I would deeply mourn if they went missing tomorrow. Not so that I can hoard them by the front door in case of a fire, God forbid, but so that I can remember why they mean so much to me and give thanks—right now—for the priceless memories they represent.

Mark Twain believed that beloved houses are spiritually living entities meant to cherish their inhabitants. He described his family's home as having "a heart and a soul, and eyes to see with; and approvals and solicitudes and deep sympathies; it was of us, and we were in its confidence and lived in its grace and the peace of its benedictions." I believe the last gesture of Bill and Jean Klaber's House of Belonging was meant to remind them that the love that found shelter within their walls is stronger than the death of a dwelling.

—SBB

FAITH

How do you pray? What do you pray for? Is it crass to ask for special consideration, foolish to ask for too little? Is anyone listening? It would be comforting to think that priests and rabbis and imams have a hot line to God. You'd certainly think Burt Visotzky would. He's a professor of biblical studies at Union Theological Seminary, author of seven books, recipient of many prestigious grants and awards—even a consultant on the Dreamworks movie Prince of Egypt.

Plus he's a really good guy. But Burt is often plagued by doubts. And oddly, like Robert Browning—"I show you doubt, to prove that faith exists"—he ends up strengthened by his uncertainty.

My Problem with Prayer

Burt Visotzky

More things are wrought by prayer than this world dreams of.

ALFRED, LORD TENNYSON

Prayer, we are taught, actually helps. Jews are enjoined by tradition to pray three times daily. The fact of the matter is that observant Jews, who care about such matters, pray all the time. There is a prayer to be said before taking a sip of water at the cooler. There is a prayer to be said upon exiting the men's room. There is a prayer to be said at sighting a beautiful woman. There is a prayer before meals and a prayer for after meals. There is a prayer to be said for just about every event that daily life throws at you.

In theory, this is good. It makes the mundane moments somehow special, sacred. If we thank God for every blade of grass, then we are aware of God's presence in our lives. Holiness pervades our daily round. Prayer elevates us from drudgery to a state of grace. My teacher, Rabbi Abraham Joshua Heschel, explained that prayer helped ensure our sense of "radical amazement" at the world God created.

In Jewish prayer there is not only the opportunity to thank God for daily fortune, for the minor miracles that get us through the dark hours, but there is structured time to make requests of God. The daily liturgy allows one to pray and petition for the necessary wisdom to succeed, for the strength to change, for forgiveness, for good health, for a good harvest, for justice and rule of law to prevail, even for the downfall of our enemies. It all sounds pretty in theory, more so in practice since most of Jewish prayer is delivered in Hebrew song.

Of course, all of this prayer assumes that there is a God who listens. That God cares. That God responds to human need. That God is fair and good. Much as I like all of the traditional theory about prayer, I find it problematic when I stop to give it thought. I have a problem with prayer because I have a problem with God, or at least with the notion of God that such prayer may presume. Not every rabbi has problems with God or with praying to God. But I do.

My problem is cancer. I offer it as an example because it is a problem that many people share. Moreover, it's an apt metaphor for all that is wrong with the world. It might be cancer in my family, AIDS in yours, joblessness in another, depression in yet another, even earthquakes. Prayer works better when life seems fair. Yet no one afflicted with cancer seems to deserve it. So how can I pray for just rewards or even a fair meting of punishments when life doesn't seem to be fair at all?

The woman I am married to, whom I love very much, is a cancer survivor. When I met her just over five years ago, she had already survived a bout of breast cancer. Early on in our dating, when we were still at the getting-to-know-you stage, she revealed this life-defining fact. Sandy had endured surgery, radiation treatments—all the anguish and torture that goes with cancer. When I met her she had been cancer-free for two years. I assimilated this news with only vague awareness of what it really meant for her health then or for our future together. It didn't matter. I fell in love.

We married a year later. Six months following our wedding my wife, always a quick study, decided to have an adult bat mitzvah. It was something she had missed as a young teenager and wanted to make up for now. In an astonishingly brief time she learned to read Hebrew, chant the blessings, read from the Torah scroll, and recite a portion of the Prophets. On the Sabbath of Passover, which marked her fortieth birthday, she stood before the congregation and read from Ezekiel's vision of the Valley of the Dry Bones. The prophet tells us that "the bones are the whole house of Israel" and asks, "Son of Man, can these bones live?" For Sandy, having suffered cancer, the resounding answer was, "Yes, these bones live!" The prayer Jews recite three times daily seemed apposite: Praised be God who restores the dead to life.

Six months later, just before our first wedding anniversary, my wife's cancer returned. More surgery, a long recovery period, more scars. I learned that the invisible scars healed more slowly than those made by the knife upon her body. In the period between those two cancer attacks, my wife had spent her spare time visiting an elderly shut-in, learning to read Hebrew and chant from the Torah, and, for what it was worth, had cast her lot with God by marrying a rabbi. In the interests of full disclosure I should reveal that my wife is a lawyer, a litigator, no less. But all the nasty lawyer jokes aside, I think my wife is righteous, upright, good, and loving.

So how do I pray to the God who sends my wife cancer? How do I pray when an earthquake claims tens of thousands of innocent lives? How do I pray when I am not at all sure God hears me and if so whether God cares at all? What good is prayer to me if I think the universe is a place of random cruelty devoid of God, or worse, a universe where God acts capriciously and perhaps even cruelly? None of these questions is new. The Jewish community has asked them in abundance since the Holocaust and, in fact, for millennia before that.

The question of God goes all the way back to the book of Job. There, the answer offered is pale and unsatisfying, even if true: we mere humans cannot know God. In any case, here is not the place to engage in theology. Instead, I want to focus on the value of prayer—no matter what one may think about God.

I happen to think that prayer still helps when we are indubitably confronted with the excruciating fact of our mortal existence. I believe that prayer offers relief: a way to start the day, a way to end the day, a way to get through the day. No matter what one thinks of God, I think prayer has its place. Let me try to explain what it can do, God or not.

First, prayer offers us the opportunity to kvetch. We can, in full view of our congregation or in the privacy of our own home, pour out our hearts to God. We can whine, wheedle, cajole, be pathetic. It is wonderfully cathartic. We can tell God the secrets we hide from our spouses. We can confess to God fears that we hide even from our therapists. We can be as weak as we wish without embarrassing our children. God can be a listening ear.

And while we presume to have God's attention, we can vent our anger at our human condition. We can rage against God for the cancer, the pain, the sickness, the poverty, the very mortality that is our condition. God will bear our fury. It is better to shout at God than at our children. It is better to rage at God than at our spouse. It is better to act out with God than with our friends and community. God will endure it.

There is yet another value to prayer. Much of it is done in community. When the severity of the decree seems too much to bear alone, we can stand surrounded by friends. We can accept the support of our community. We can find comfort in the very regularity of the service, the mundane repetitions. The very familiarity of the surroundings offers solace.

And let us not forget that often when we pray, we sing. We gain strength from music and song. We gather power from voices lifted in unison. Whether on key or off, we sing with others in the knowledge that they, too, bear their burdens. They have their moments, their troubles. Yet we unite to join in song and praise for what we share—that we are all but frail, mortal creatures.

Prayer, we learn, actually helps.

It is now two years and more that my wife is free of cancer, thank God. I do not have any illusions at all that our prayers were directly answered. To think that would be hubris—too much pride to think that we might have been rewarded while so many others seemed to have been ignored by God. In fact, I'm still angry at God. I know my issues with God will be a long, long time in finding their resolution. Meanwhile, I do volunteer work at Cancer-Care, Inc. My wife, for her part, continues her exemplary good works. She now serves on the board of directors of the organization that first matched her up with her elderly shut-in years ago. And each week, early in the morning, my wife and I go to the synagogue. Together, we pray.

✦

I am always deeply moved by the reverence of observant Jews and the different form of prayers they offer. How exquisite the prayer spoken upon sighting a beautiful woman must be!

When our prayers give thanks for the bounty of life's small wonders—the simple abundance—that surrounds us all each day, the unexpected feeling of radical amazement can fill us with awe. So why do we sometimes feel so empty when we pray the most common kind—those of petition and requests for help?

Perhaps it's because secretly we believe God won't hear or help us.

I know that this is true for me because for a long time I also had a problem with prayer. I couldn't understand why some of my prayers were answered almost instantly, while other, more urgent pleas seemed to fall on deaf ears even before the words left my lips.

Because my relationship to the Divine has been the most passionate one I have experienced on this earth, the sense of estrangement I imagined was crushing. My prayers were reasonable, I was a good woman, I did good in the world; why should they not be answered according to my heart's desires? But they weren't and so I stopped praying.

Then one lonely day I came across the sign that Carl Jung had in his home: "Bidden or not bidden, God is Present." This was an amazing epiphany for me. Whether I realized it or not, with every breath, with every heartbeat, I was praying. My desires were prayers; so were my unfulfilled longings, holy hungers and thirst, sighs, remorse, regrets.

When I was disappointed, I prayed with my discouragement and tears. When I was angry, I prayed with my rage, jealousy, envy, or whatever dark emotion was keeping me company. When I experienced a few moments of contentment, I prayed with my pleasure and appreciation. I realized that human beings pray when we laugh, when we cry. We pray when we work, when we play. We pray when we make love or make a meal.

One way or another, from our first breath to our last, we pray. Some people, like Burt Visotzky, know when they pray. Other people think they, too, have a problem with prayer, and so they aren't down on their knees in the morning or in church or in synagogue once a week. But they're up in the dark with sick children, visiting elderly shut-ins on their lunch hour, supporting the dreams of those they love with their work, helping a friend through a crisis. This, too, is prayer.

—SBB

COURAGE

The crossroads Mel White encountered in the middle of his life must have seemed more like the opening of a labyrinth than a fork in the road. Long married with children, he decided to openly acknowledge his homosexuality. A ghostwriter for right-wing Christian organizations, he decided to detail his anguish in an autobiography, Stranger at the Gate: To Be Gay and Christian in America. *And he decided to challenge head-on the most vocal antigay religious leaders, many of whom used to be his employers and friends. Along the way, he felt his religious beliefs challenged, shaken, and ultimately revivified by his experience.*

There are crossroads, and then there are crossroads.

To Thine Own Self

Mel White

In true courage there is always an element of choice, of an ethical choice, and of anguish, and also of action and deed. There is always a flame of spirit in it, a vision of some necessity higher than oneself.

BRENDA UELAND

I am a homosexual. For thirty-five years I thought homosexuality was a sickness and a sin. As a victim of those tragic untruths, I lived my life in a closet, pursued by guilt, fear, and anger. Finally, the truth set me free. Now I can say without hesitation, "I am gay, I am proud, and God loves me without reservation!" But getting to that

197

happy place, which involved rejecting the negative, restrictive understanding of my religion and replacing it with a positive, life-affirming one, was a long and painful journey.

I discovered my same-sex orientation at the International Boy Scout Jamboree in 1953, when I was thirteen. I suddenly fell head-over-heels in love with Darrell, my thirteen-year-old tentmate. Growing up in a conservative Christian family, I immediately assumed that my attraction to Darrell was very wrong.

I didn't want to be homosexual. I hadn't chosen homosexuality as a "lifestyle." In fact, I spent the next three and a half decades trying to overcome my "sickness" and to seek God's forgiveness for my sin. I read the Bible and prayed frantically. I married and had children. I confessed my struggle to my young bride and for twenty-three years we spent more than $100,000 on Christian therapy to help me get over being a homosexual.

I didn't act on my homosexual feelings. In fact I confessed my "temptation" to a variety of pastors, teachers, counselors, and therapists who assured me that if I prayed hard enough, God would heal me or give me the power to "overcome." I practiced meditation, biofeedback, and daily spiritual discipline. I underwent electric-shock therapy. I was even exorcised. Finally, desperate and depressed, I slashed my wrists and hoped to die.

At that point, Lyla, my wonderful wife, intervened. "I like gay people," she said. "I just didn't want you to be one. But you are and I have to accept that. You've been a good husband and father. Now, I want you to be free to experience life as an equally good gay man." We both wept as I packed my suitcase and moved from our family home.

We were honest with our two children and tried to answer every question they asked. But, even as we both assured them that we would always be a family, we could see their hurt and confusion. I moved into an apartment, just blocks away from our home in Pasadena. Because my schedule left me more free time than Lyla's work as a high school teacher, I fixed breakfast for our children and drove them to and from school. Though separated and eventually divorced, Lyla and I coparented our children, went to church on Sunday, and spent weekends and vacations together as a family.

At All Saints Episcopal Church, I fell in love with Gary Nixon, a handsome baritone in the Coventry Choir. We've been together in a loving, committed relationship for fifteen years. Lyla and the children have welcomed Gary into our extended family. Obviously, everyone has struggled and suffered in the process. There is no way to describe adequately what we all went through to reach this place of healing and reconciliation. But, thank God, we made it. We are a family still.

In 1993, hoping to help others avoid the mistakes I had made, I wrote my autobiography, *Stranger at the Gate: To Be Gay and Christian in America*. In the book, I detailed my experiences as a ghostwriter for many prominent Christian leaders who had no idea that I was struggling with my homosexual identity. Suddenly, I found myself on *60 Minutes* and *Larry King Live* debating antigay religious leaders who believed (as I once had) that my homosexuality was a depravity. Almost invariably they condemned me to death (citing a passage in Leviticus) and declared me "abandoned by God" (invoking a passage in Romans). In defending myself against these attacks, I became a gay activist almost accidentally.

The sudden, unexpected media interest in my story catapulted me into the front lines of a war being waged against homosexuality by the same powerful men who had been my friends and clients. While I was ghostwriting their autobiographies, they were raising money and mobilizing volunteers by promoting fear of the "evil Soviet Empire." When the Soviet Union collapsed, they began using the fear of an imaginary "gay agenda" in the very same way.

In 1993, I was installed as dean of the Cathedral of Hope Metropolitan Community Church, a primarily lesbian and gay congregation in Dallas, Texas. Serving more than ten thousand people,

Cathedral of Hope is the world's largest Christian church with a primary ministry to sexual minorities. As the number of gay men murdered in Texas by gay bashers increased, so did my anger and frustration. I struggled with an unsettling reality. The primary sources fueling the violence and hatred of these children of God were other Christians, many of them my old friends.

For two years, I tried to establish a dialogue with Christians whose antigay rhetoric sanctioned and led (directly and indirectly) to the suffering and death of God's lesbian, gay, bisexual, and transgendered children. Among these Christian leaders were people I knew well, many of them former clients—Billy Graham, Pat Robertson, Jerry Falwell, D. James Kennedy. I wanted these preachers, who had powerful media ministries, to understand the terrible human consequences of the war they were waging against sexual minorities. Careers were being destroyed, lives wasted, children discarded, homes broken, churches divided. Something had to be done to end the division and devastation.

Finally, in a moment of extreme frustration, I wrote to my friends in 1994, "It's hopeless. I'm not even going to try to get through to them anymore." One week later, Lynn Cothren, Coretta Scott King's personal assistant, warned me in a letter from the King Center in Atlanta that I had broken a primary rule for pursuing justice nonviolently. To give up on one's adversary, she wrote, itself was "an act of violence."

When I admitted that I wasn't aware of such rules, Lynn pointed me gently to the teachings of Martin Luther King, Jr. King in turn directed me to Gandhi, and Gandhi and King both referred me back to Jesus. Through these activist giants of nonviolent civil rights movements in the past, I discovered the principles of nonviolent warfare established in the heat of battle. I never imagined that my pursuit of justice for sexual minorities would collapse my old faith system and launch me on a whole new spiritual journey, the journey into "soul force."

During his early years as an attorney in South Africa, M. K. Gandhi, a Hindu, was deeply moved by the teachings of Jesus. "The Sermon on the Mount," says Gandhi, "went straight to my heart." Determined to reduce "principles into practice," Gandhi created Satyagraha: a plan of action that developed inner lives while working to transform society. Gandhi refined his "truth force" or "soul force" principles while leading justice movements in South Africa and then India.

While a student at Crozier Theological Seminary, Dr. Martin Luther King, Jr., discovered Gandhi's soul force principles and used them to shape the nonviolent civil rights movement in the United States. "While the Montgomery boycott was going on," King wrote, "India's Gandhi was the guiding light of our technique of nonviolent social change. Nonviolent resistance had emerged as the technique of the movement, while love stood as the regulating ideal. In other words, Christ furnished the spirit and motivation, while Gandhi furnished the method."

Now, my partner, Gary Nixon, and I are searching the lives and teachings of Gandhi and King to see how their soul force principles apply to our current struggle for justice—a struggle not just for sexual minorities but for all who suffer injustice. In the study and practice of soul force our own spirits are being redirected and renewed.

Frankly, the Christian faith as I once knew it—the harsh, judgmental, sin-oriented version—is gone from my life forever. But from the ruins, I am piecing together a whole new picture of Jesus. Thanks to soul force, I am beginning to hear and understand the words and actions of that first-century Jewish carpenter in a whole new way. This new take on Jesus is undermining many of my old Christian assumptions about God and making some serious changes in the way I see myself, my allies, and my adversaries.

To seek truth and to confront untruth wherever we find it is one of three primary soul force mandates. For Gandhi, who titled his autobiography *My Experiment with Truth,* God has many names, but

God's ultimate name is Truth. Jesus identified himself with "Truth," naming God's Spirit "the Spirit of Truth." In the Gospels he says, "Know [believe in, seek, hunger for] the Truth and the Truth will set you free."

For Gandhi, the struggle to know truth is the struggle to know God. And because untruth invariably causes God's children to suffer, the struggle to confront untruth is the struggle to do God's will in the world. Therefore, as an activist, one determined to help relieve the suffering of my sisters and brothers who are victims of the war being waged against sexual minorities, I am called to seek truth and to confront relentlessly the untruth that is used to justify their suffering.

Love (nonviolence) is the second of the primary soul force mandates. In reading Gandhi and King, I met Jesus for the second time. In their soul force principles, Jesus' words about love took on new substance. "Love your enemies" was transformed by soul force from a bumper sticker slogan to a plan of action that would lead to the transformation of society and to the renewal of my own soul. "Your enemies are just victims of misinformation as you have been," Gandhi advised. "Don't kill, hate, or abandon them. Bring them truth in love relentlessly. And in the process," Gandhi promises, "your own soul will be ennobled and enlarged."

To take on the suffering of my enemy is the third soul force mandate. It is far too early in my own soul force journey to know anything about voluntary, redemptive suffering, but the lives of the martyrs and the saints make it clear that when our confrontation with untruth is guided by love, we go on loving our enemies, even if they kill us.

Gandhi's call to absorb the suffering of those who confront or condemn me has given me a whole new picture of Jesus, "the suffering servant," who accepted suffering without comment or complaint and in the process helped redefine the human spirit. In fact, the more I read Gandhi and King and all the other justice heroes and "sheroes" we admire, the more I see how voluntary self-suffering became the key to their success at ending the suffering of others. "Greater love has no person than this," Jesus said, "than to lay down one's life for one's friend."

Three soul force mandates: truth, love, and voluntary redemptive suffering. Out of those three mandates flow hundreds of other soul force rules or principles to guide us in our attempts to resolve our conflicts nonviolently. I have only begun to experiment with the principles as an agent of social change, but already I am beginning to notice the changes they are making in me. In applying the principles of truth, love, and self-suffering, I am beginning to experience the presence of God in my life in whole new ways.

The soul force principles work. For seven years I had pursued Jerry Falwell as "an enemy of truth." In August 1999, I wrote Jerry in the spirit of soul force to apologize for my attacks and asked him, once again, to meet with me to discuss "our mutual concerns." On October 23, two hundred of my friends and colleagues sat down with Reverend Falwell and two hundred of his coworkers to begin working together to end the violent words from both sides that lead to violent actions against us all. The world's media celebrated this Anti-Violence Summit as a rapprochement by gay people of faith with Jerry Falwell and the Christian right. In fact, it was only the first baby step in that direction. But I'm convinced that the Spirit of Truth, God's Spirit, will use the principles of soul force to strengthen and to guide us for the rest of the journey and renew our spirits along the way.

LOYALTY

Why do middle-aged men leave? An answer of sorts may be found among our primate cousins. Depressed old monkeys show a rise in all sorts of physiological measurements when surrounded by young female monkeys. Otherwise moribund parts of their anatomy look up, too. Studies of May-December affairs reveal that formerly impotent older men, too, recover, if only temporarily, a sexual vigor they haven't known since their youth when they become involved with younger women. A middle-aged man who leaves his marriage isn't just abandoning his middle-aged wife, he's trying to flee his own ineluctable mortality.

As a psychiatrist, Peter Kramer, author of Listening to Prozac *and* Should You Leave? *has listened to many men and women discuss their impending breakups. It's not his position to judge, but he does find himself wondering about the meaning of a word that seems to have lost its place in marriage: loyalty.*

Coffee and Sympathy

Peter D. Kramer

However often marriage is dissolved, it remains indissoluble. Real divorce, the divorce of the heart and nerve and fiber, does not exist, since there is no divorce from memory.

VIRGILIA PETERSON

Over lunch, a colleague tells me he is leaving his wife. His marriage is not the subject we are here to discuss, not the ostensible subject. Nor has he asked my opinion. But he has put the topic on the table, and from the length of the silence that follows, I understand that he expects a response.

My assigned role, I believe, is that of the quiz-show host who asks, "Final answer?" I play that part sometimes. Three years ago, a woman I had just met told me of her plans to leave her dull and reliable husband for a stimulating younger man. She asked what I thought. As psychotherapists are said to do, I posed a question in return: How prone are you to regret? I heard later from a friend that the woman considered the conversation helpful and that she did not leave her husband, not then. I believe she left later. If I were brave, I would phone and find out what she thinks now of the conversation.

Advice is difficult. How skilled are we at predicting the course of human affairs? And then there is the matter of rhetoric, how to give advice that is perturbing but not coercive. Because I have written a book about marriage and divorce, I worry that what I say will be taken too seriously.

I do have an opinion about my lunchmate's announcement, or something less than an opinion: a feeling, a slight revulsion. So far as I can tell, the response is based on the length of his marriage, twenty-odd years, and his wife's age, which is my age, early fifties. I do not like to see men walk away from women in late middle age.

I know they should sometimes. There are abusive marriages, there are marriages that run out of gas. There are wives who do terrible things. An opinion worth owning will not be based on demographics alone. Advice must be handcrafted. And yet here it is, unignorable, the queasiness in the gut.

They come to see me in my office, deserted women in their fifties and sixties. I suspect it's because I work in a university community, a town that supports half a dozen colleges. Or I see them at seminars, or cocktail parties. They befriend one another, single women of a certain age. They are wonderful, wonderful in the manner of all bright, creative, productive people.

Which is to say they are difficult. If I provide an opening, my luncheon companion will tell me his wife is difficult. A word that does not elicit from me the compassion it might. Is he not difficult? And who are they, the easygoing women? I mistrust easy. It makes me question the balance of power. Besides, so much of change is mere oscillation. Fleeing the complex mate, we seek the transparent one—until that one seems bland, and we yearn for complexity.

His wife is difficult, he is about to say, and she looks a bit the worse for wear. Which he will not say, though it is true. I want to ask, who put on those miles? I am glad he still looks so good, but looking good is a function of social perception, how we value older men. Perception and genetic happenstance—the luck of the draw.

These thoughts are cynical, I know, and one-sided. I want to claim I am not a judgmental guy. Every day I hear about extramarital affairs, and I think, hey, we're all primates here. We're not operating on cortex only, not every minute. I know, too, that there's old hash to settle in every marriage, and an unrealized dream or two. Go at it, I say. Go at it and go for it.

Here before me is a man deserving of sympathy, and sympathy is my business, more or less. It is only that I am thinking of the women at those cocktail parties, how much I like them, how much they like and help one another, how lovely they are. Smart, accomplished, graceful—my colleague's wife has always struck me that way. And he's a bit of a Neanderthal; lovable in that fashion, but only because we define boyishness as lovable in older men.

They do not need my help, do not need my sentiment, the women. The men who leave have done them a favor, inspiring them to turn to one another, emotional and intellectual helpmeets. Much good will come of the leaving—much elegant research and writing. Mankind will benefit. No need for self-righteousness here.

Though to justify this crochet, this hobbyhorse of mine, I might say a word about the self. Poorly bounded, the self, in the view of psychotherapists today. Here is the common metaphor: Imagine a child learning to skate. She teeters, except when her mother is on the ice beside her. How can that be? The external mother seems to serve a function internal to the daughter—her confidence, even her coordination. We are all of us like that, different people altogether when supported emotionally. To end a relationship is to tear away part of the self.

And with such ease. That's what gets to me. Not that I favor covenant marriage, not that I want to make it hard for people to escape trouble. It's not the process that has me worried. It's the lack of apparent consequence for men, the difference in the prices that he and his wife will pay. The leaving, whatever the details, is too concordant with the American attention to value. His value in the social marketplace has increased over the years, while hers has declined. He knows it. That's the basis of the culture, a price for everything.

My colleague will remarry, if he wishes. The odds are in his favor. Ten years ago, which is as far as the government analyses go, a divorced man in his early fifties was three times as likely to remarry as a same-aged woman; for men and women in their late fifties, the ratio was four to one. In their sixties, forget about it—each year, two women in a thousand will marry. Experts believe that since those data were collected, the discrepancies have widened. And women live longer than men.

I am raising an issue of fairness, one that goes beyond the division of assets, beyond the widely recognized outcome of divorce, that however punitive the settlement seems to the husband, a few years down the road he will be better off financially and his wife worse off than each is now. My concern is that my colleague's difficult, worse-for-wear wife is being deprived of a social good, of the intimate companionship that is part of the solid, supported self.

Fairness may seem an odd consideration for a psychotherapist. A theorist I admire, Ivan Boszormenyi-Nagy, has built a career on the study of give-and-take in relationships. He believes that justice done is a psychic good, that earned entitlement—fairness—is something like an effective antidepressant, conferring zest and confidence. Nagy is right, no doubt. We are animals primed to thrive on our own altruism. A skill, giving—a satisfying one to learn, even late on. But we thrive also on trophy wives and on vengeance and self-righteousness; my unscientific assessment is that there's an edgy stimulation—maybe amphetamine rather than Prozac—in take-and-take.

If I were honest, I would admit that my preference for staying is aesthetic. Don't you love the couples who battle into old age? I mean, they've already done all the damage they're going to do to the kids. Might as well have it out. This is their story, and they're in it to the denouement. Which will include grudging respect, if the fight goes well, and the scarring over of an old wound or two. Memory is failing anyway—good to be with someone who's been through a few things with you. I'm not just saying this, I like working with old warring couples. If they're not outright paranoid, if they have a sense of humor. And the couples who have merely hit a bump in the road, the ones who know at some level that they have no business pulling apart—what could be more satisfying than helping them sit together?

Entropy—isn't that the issue? Everything's falling apart at such a rate on this planet, rain forests shrinking, polar caps melting, the seas rising. You'd think we could manage to maintain a little complexity in our private lives. To work a few kinks out of the narrative before it all ends. I mean, come on, guys. This is where the fun is, right here at home.

Easy for me to say. My parents are still married after half a century. Their parents died married, and theirs, and so on as far back as anyone can remember. It's harder for some people, I know that. Loyalty doesn't come naturally to them. Or they've been unlucky. So much perturbs marriages. Illness. Money troubles. Loss. It helps to have stable moods, it helps to have had good judgment when young.

My colleague's been married two decades; he gets credit for that.

We live too long, that's the problem. He's fifty-three, he's been in the same fight forever. You only go around once. The world looks good out there, him on his own with every possibility open. I can see it his way.

So I will set aside the crochet, the hobbyhorse. I will call for the coffee and tell my colleague, I didn't see it coming. Or, I'm not surprised.

It hardly matters which. I will show myself open to hearing the particulars, try not to take them with too many grains of salt. We are not reforming a culture here. I am listening to a man in crisis, a man I have liked well enough. A fellow I wish well.

How about dessert? I signal to the waiter that I'll pick up the check, slipping him my card. This one's on me. Saying, Yes, I know, she can be difficult.

That is my skill, the one my colleague expects me to exercise: sitting beside him, metaphorically, and looking out on the world as he does. That's what my training has prepared me to do—set aside preconceptions and see matters afresh. Though I doubt I will drop my prejudice in favor of continuity, not entirely. I'm not sure I would be doing my colleague a favor if I did. Better perhaps when the moment is right to allude to my leanings, in the interest (as they say) of full disclosure. Meanwhile, I will try to sit beside him and look out, past the baklava we will share, or the flan, to the future. I will have his interests at heart. Balancing earned entitlement and shared memories against those great American desiderata, the main chance and the fresh start.

✦

As we were putting this book together, there were a few topics I considered essential. I wanted a man's perspective on adultery, divorce, and the difference between sex and love. But none of the authors we approached wanted to tackle these issues, even though all of them were candid in conversations about the affairs that led to their own divorces. Some of those affairs, they'd confessed over a few drinks, were more about sex than love. The affairs that were about love (especially if the man was over forty-five) led to his being reunited with his "soul mate." Other times the marriage stayed together, even though the end of the affair was deeply mourned every day.

So much insight, such reluctance to share it.

Being a woman who has endured the heartbreak of ending a long-standing marriage, I wasn't asking these men to write about their former spouses, any more than I could do so; as a writer, I wanted them to write about their own emotions. But still, they declined and then I realized why. No matter how bitter the partings had been, all of these men still felt a sense of some kind of loyalty, reflecting in their reticence what they couldn't give in their marriages. The writer Helen Rowland observed that "when two people decide to get a divorce, it isn't a sign that they 'don't understand' one another, but a sign that they have, at last, begun to."

So I was very appreciative of Peter Kramer's provocative essay, which brushed ever so slightly on these subjects. But as a woman reader, I was disappointed by Peter's reluctance to speak his true feelings to his colleague, even though he was willing to write about them. I wanted Peter to end the encounter (as well as the essay) with something like this: "It's really too bad about you and your wife. I always thought she was an extraordinary woman." I did ask him if he would be willing to rethink the ending; he did, but didn't want to change it.

So I can't script other people's conversations any more than I can script my own life. Still, for a woman of a certain age who has been left behind, the hardest thing to imagine is that she doesn't deserve it. "You don't deserve this," her friends will insist. But the paradox is, of course, that she does deserve more love, more happiness, more loyalty. And so Life has the courage to intervene for us. You may be as reluctant to believe this as I once was, but what we won't consciously deal with in our relationships will arrive someday on our doorstep as fate. (Thank you, Dr. Jung.)

I always loved Lyndon Baines Johnson's definition of fealty. "I don't want loyalty. I want loyalty. *I want him to kiss my ass in Macy's window at high noon and tell me it smells like roses." It's crass, but then sometimes so is life.*

—SBB

Boundaries

Eddie Staton is a man of many faces. The one he's wearing at the moment is relaxed and jolly. As he picks at his food in an Omaha diner, he's interrupted every few minutes by friends and acquaintances who stop to say hello and shake his hand. Eddie kindly thanks them, asks after their families, and wishes them all the best. Then he returns to his food and the topic at hand and his face grows taut. He looks like a man you would not want to go up against, which is pretty much what you'd expect a guy who almost single-handedly took on the youth gangs of Omaha to look like.

Eddie is a director of MADDADS—Men Against Destruction Defending Against Drugs and Social Disorder. Since 1986, when he and a friend put together a neighborhood patrol to chase drug dealers and thugs from their street corners, the organization has grown to include fifty-seven chapters around the country with 55,000 members—all of them devoted to exercising righteous male power to protect their communities.

Now fifty-two, a recently ordained minister after a long career in municipal government and the father of six grown children, Eddie looks back on that first patrol as an epiphany in his understanding of what a father's responsibilities are to his children and his community. "I used to think it was just all about love," he says. "But then I realized it was about tough love."

Fathers to the Community

Eddie Staton

The art of leadership is saying no, not yes. It is very easy to say yes.
Tony Blair

I always vowed that, when it came to being a father, I wouldn't be anything like mine. The last time I saw him, I was eleven and living in Pueblo, Colorado. My parents were separated and he brought me a little Brownie camera on Easter Sunday. Then he disappeared. Not long after, my mother remarried—a combat engineer in the air force who adopted us, a good man who took care of my mother but had little to do with my sister, brother, and me. When I was in ninth grade we moved to Germany and I remember going off by myself a lot and thinking, I wish my stepfather would sit down and just talk to me. I decided then that when I had kids I was always going to be there, I didn't care what happened. Something stuck with me then about what a father's real responsibilities are, and it sticks with me now.

And when I had kids, a lot did happen. I got married when I was in the air force, and my wife and I had three kids just like that. But then I messed up: I fell in love with a woman in my church. My wife let me have the kids, who were then eight, seven, and six. I remarried and had two more children with my next wife, and she had one from her previous marriage, so we now had six kids. But she got mixed up with drugs. After putting her in rehab four times, I finally decided I'd had enough. I raised the kids and they were pretty well launched. But I felt a real sense of failure about not being able to help my wife.

When my kids were born, I thought of them as a real accomplishment. Of course, the idea of a black man being available and nurturing and responsible to his family is kind of an anomaly, at least among the popular media. I used to discuss that very issue with a friend of mine, John Foster. John had five daughters and one son and was vice president of the municipal employees union of the city of Omaha. I was then the director of the human relations department. We'd talk about how we had to get a message out to the media that not all black dads were irresponsible deadbeats, that there were men out there doing the hard work of fatherhood. We knew there were other men who felt the way we did about their kids. But we didn't know how to go about it.

Then a catalytic event occurred that changed everything. One night John called me up and said his son had been beaten up by some gang members. This was in 1986, when the gang problem hit Omaha like a sledgehammer. The police and mayor were in denial, but in the black community we knew we had a major problem. John's son was home from college over a holiday and some gang members tried to take his Jeep at a gas station. He fought them off, but five guys ended up beating him pretty badly.

John said he was lying on his bed when his son came in the door, and John jumped up like somebody had shot him out of a gun. His son was all bloody, his clothes torn up. John went to his closet, loaded a .357 Magnum and a .44 Magnum, put on his coat, got into his car, and went after those people. He went into fast-food restaurants, back alleys, housing developments, looked for them everywhere. He said to me later, "That's when I knew I was a mad dad." I said, "John, we've got to remember that. That anger is what's got to propel us into action."

We decided first to go to our ministers, because we knew it was going to take God's hand to help with this one. We were outraged that this could happen—a good kid comes back from college and gets beaten up in his own neighborhood. We called a press conference with the ministers behind us and asked for another fifty black men to meet with us, to stand with us and stop this violence that had our kids shooting and killing one another. We've got to stand up and be men in this community, we said. Two hundred and fifty men showed up.

The first thing we did was go out and clean up graffiti. We painted over an old building. Now, any time you get more than five black men on any corner who are not singing doo-wop or throwing dice, the media are going to be there. I think we stunned a lot of people. That was something the community had not been seeing from black men. I remember one interviewer asking me, What took you black men so long to stand up and do what you're doing? And my response was, What took you so long to recognize us?

But we decided we weren't getting to the kids who needed to be gotten to. So one night after church service I said to John, Let's go home, go to bed early, get up at midnight, and see what's going on out there. We parked off Thirtieth Street right behind McDonald's. The parking lot was packed with kids, the music blowing loud, gunshots going off in the air. I said, John, what are we getting ourselves into? We walked right into the crowd—we were wearing these black T-shirts that said, "Mad Dads Are Coming Together." Some of the kids had seen us on TV. Some said, All right! Here come the Mad Dads. We ran into so many kids we knew. The ones smoking marijuana just snuck off.

What we found that night was that we needed street patrols dealing with these kids on a regular basis, so we organized another group of men, borrowed some walkie-talkies, and spread up and down the streets of our neighborhood. We could call on the walkie-talkie and a group of men would come running. We found our presence made a difference: we did crowd control, broke up all kinds of fights, worked with the police—we began then to feel like fathers to the community. It didn't make a difference who the kid was; good or bad, he was still a kid who needed a man. I can't tell you how many times we put our arms around kids and had to push the Uzi out of the way to hug him.

A lot of people ask me how I define honorable masculinity. Love and tenderness, that's the first requisite of a good father. A father has to plant a voice inside his kid's head that tells him when he's wrong. A lot of black men today have found other ways to express masculinity—by carrying a gun, having a baby out of wedlock, or being in a gang. Our perspective of what's right and wrong has gotten screwed up. So many people accept the dope selling because it's a kind of providing. The little kid sees his father doesn't work but he's always got money. Now what does that say to the guy who gets an education and goes to college? These things have got to be turned around, not by what we say but what we do. An example has to be set.

That's why I have a fit with these men sitting quietly in the pews in church. *What is wrong with you all? It's time to make some noise! If you're a good man, stand up and let the whole community know, let our kids see you.* If you go to most churches, they're full of women and the few men are preachers because there's no role for just the average man in church. We ought to have tutoring programs, support groups. I think we work out our soul's salvation by what we do with and for each other, not by how many times we go to church and praise God.

More than anything, it's important for a black man to be a *visible* man in his community, so that our kids have something to look to aside from the pimp, hustler, dope dealer, and gangbanger—the hypersexual man who likes to make babies but won't take care of them. We need a highly visible image of the strong black man who loves his kids, community, family, and his God. If we can show that, then our kids have a choice, and that choice will turn our communities around.

A couple of years ago, I was about to leave to give a speech in Utah when my uncle called. He told me that my father lived in

Utah and that I should look him up. I said I didn't know whether I'd have the time, but I knew I was going to see him. When I got to the house, he was standing on the front porch and he ran down to greet me. We just hugged and hugged. I hadn't seen him in almost forty years. He said, I saw you on the news, I know what you've been doing. And I said, Why the hell ain't you called? He went through this long litany of lies, but I didn't care. I thought I'd be mad at him, but I wasn't.

But I also felt his blessing, however long it took to get it. I think God just had a different plan for me. He wanted me to see that the choices we make can alter our destinies. When it comes to their kids, men have to be careful with their choices. You make the right decision, and your child could be the answer to some big social problem. You make the wrong one, and the kid is just another part of the problem itself.

Mentoring

The late psychologist Erik Erikson theorized that at a certain age, sometime between thirty-five and fifty-five, men begin to show concern for the generation nipping at their heels, particularly for young adults and children who are not their own. This "generative" stage of life, in which men feel an obligation to act as caretakers for the larger culture, is the capstone of Erikson's three-stage model of human development and central to achieving a sense of fulfillment. It follows biological generativity (having a child) and parental generativity (raising him).

It's easy to see the truth and wisdom of Erikson's life model. Yet it ignores a large segment of men who never have children. Having skipped the first two stages, does this mean they will never feel the desire to be mentors—to be generative?

Hardly. Keith Johnson, a longtime magazine writer and editor, first sensed the urge right about when Erikson said he should, in early middle age. He has now helped usher into adulthood several fortunate young men, in some cases paying their way through expensive colleges. Keith, who is gay, was always aware that his concern for the young men he chose to help might seem suspect. So watching them evolve into successful, productive adults was just that much more gratifying.

In loco parentis

Keith Johnson

*I always pass on good advice. It is the only thing to do with it.
It is never of any use to oneself.*

OSCAR WILDE

Surely the mentoring urge is primal. It struck me around age forty, a result of midlife intimations of mortality: I am going to die, but if I share with younger people some of what I have learned, part of me will live on. I have now reached my mid-sixties, and nothing has brought me more pleasure than seeing half a dozen young people through adolescence into adulthood. One young man who has sought me out for honest feedback and reassurance says the experience has been rare and valuable, "like finding a banister in the dark."

In *The Seasons of a Man's Life,* his classic analysis of the stages of male psychological development, Daniel J. Levinson concludes that in early adulthood, relationships with older mentors are often "the most complex, and developmentally important, a man can have." Nearly all of his subjects' mentors were men. "A good mentor is an admixture of good father and good friend," Levinson writes. "He serves as guide, teacher and sponsor. He represents skill, knowledge, virtue, accomplishment—the superior qualities a young man hopes someday to acquire." Most significant, says Levinson, the mentor shares in "the youthful Dream, . . . giving it his blessing, helping to define the newly emerging self in its newly discovered world."

Two factors heightened the mentoring impulse in my case. I come from a family of teachers. And I am gay, without biological offspring. With young men who are straight, my relationships have been what those of a straight man would be. Other young men have turned out to be gay, although I had no inkling of that at the outset. In their case, I have played a special role. I have shown them that an adult gay man whom they know leads a life that is stable, successful, useful, dignified, and blessed not infrequently with joy.

I was lucky enough to have two loving and reasonably competent parents who stayed married to each other and lived into their eighties, so—unlike most of those I have mentored—I have been spared parental inadequacy or loss. But I came of age in the 1950s, a thoroughly repressive time well evoked in Calvin Trilling's haunting memoir, *Remembering Denny*. To my best recollection, the subject of homosexuality arose seriously just once in my four years of college, when a roommate was reading *Death in Venice* for a senior literature course and we discussed it—briefly.

I never had an older gay man as a mentor and role model. If I had, accepting my sexuality and its consequences could have been a lot less painful and drawn out. My own mentors helped in other ways, however. They honored and developed my intellectual gifts, valued my thoughts and feelings. A history professor and a college chaplain guided me over intellectual and spiritual terrain largely unfamiliar to my parents and helped me form an independent identity. That's partly why I, in turn, have encouraged separation and autonomy in the young men I have mentored.

I got into the mentoring business almost by accident. A love of Anglican church music, acquired when I lived in London, led me on my return to New York to a parish that maintains a superb English-cathedral-style choir of men and boys. The boy choristers, ages ten to fourteen, attend a small boarding school maintained by the church. The school's headmaster, fiercely protective of his young charges, encouraged me to get to know one vastly gifted eighth-grader whose father was unsuccessfully fighting alcoholism and would soon be divorced. We hit it off wonderfully from the start—among many other things, we both savor bad puns—and I offered him an emotional haven from the tensions of a dysfunctional family. He was nearly thirty before he had the courage to accept his homosexuality. Today, nearly twenty-five years after we met, he is an accomplished musician and remains a close friend. He told me recently that throughout his prep school and college years, my Manhattan apartment was the only place he felt he could relax and be himself. He found my friendship supportive, accepting, available but not pushy.

That early connection led to others. One of his choir school classmates, whose father had died and whose mother was about to divorce his stepfather, needed help with his prep school fees. I provided that. His mother soon moved to France, so my home became his and I eventually adopted him. We share interests in everything from medieval architecture to French food, and enjoy an easy camaraderie. At my urging, rather than study only music in college, he took on a demanding five-year program that combined conservatory training with a liberal arts major in religion. He continues to pursue both tracks as an organist, choirmaster, and Nietzsche scholar.

In late adolescence, one of my son's prep school classmates had serious problems dealing with his sexuality; over the years I have been a role model and counselor for him. This young man reminded me recently of something else I had done for him that I had nearly forgotten. Mentoring is a form of teaching, and a teacher soon learns that there is no telling what a student will take away from the classroom. In this case, I once told him that I make certain to prepare a decent dinner every day; if you don't take care of yourself, I said, you can't expect anyone else to. That spoke to him of the importance of self-respect for its own sake and for earning the respect of others. We are good friends; I have relied on his historian's expertise for a major research project, and on his judgment as an editor.

My most recent mentoring relationships began in 1997, when a prep school classmate of mine died unexpectedly. He left a widow and two teenaged sons, both graduates of the choir school. After the older boy started there, I had become a family friend. Once the younger boy went on to prep school, I had sometimes joined his parents on visits to their sons for crew races, concerts, and family weekends. Both parents were obviously devoted to their sons; the family exuded love and intimacy.

Just days before his father died, the older boy had enrolled at a major private university. His younger brother, a prep school senior, would do so a year later. I knew their father had had financial problems, so as soon as I learned of his death I offered to make sure the boys could complete their education. That led to increasingly close involvement as a loco parent, in a friend's wry phrase. I could in no way replace the boys' father in their lives, but I could help shore them up emotionally as well as financially at a difficult time.

For the first year or more, their mother made sure I was on hand for school and college visits and that I saw the boys regularly during their holidays. I made myself available to them, reading the books they were reading, discussing their courses with them, attending their performances, arranging interviews about possible careers, loaning them my apartment for the summer, and doing everything else I could to assure them that an adult under no obligation to them loved them unconditionally and cherished their company. The summer after their father's death, I spent a week as Mr. Mom, looking after the boys while their grandmother took their mother on a well-deserved trip to Europe. That September, in one hectic weekend, we installed the younger boy at his college and celebrated his brother's twentieth birthday with a bang-up dinner at a famous restaurant.

Anyone seeing the four of us together would have taken us for a family, which in a sense we had become. However, I grew concerned about concealing my sexuality from the boys and their mother. I worried that if I came out to them, they might all misunderstand my interest in the boys, who in any case are straight, but that if I did not the mother might misconstrue my interest in her.

Because I respected the older boy's judgment, and because I wanted him to know that I did, I informed him and asked his advice about the other two. He reacted sympathetically, but thought that neither his mother nor his brother was quite ready to deal with the subject. Some time later, he found an appropriate moment to tell his mother, and soon told his brother as well. I hadn't asked him to do that—I thought the news should come from me directly—but his initiative made it easier for me. I then talked one-on-one with both mother and younger son. The process was surprisingly painless, and deepened our friendships.

To address their loss and other issues, all three undertook psychotherapy with my encouragement. We now do fewer things together, but that's inevitable, even desirable. Their grief seems less omnipresent, their need for me less pressing. The mother, a strong and handsome woman, dates other men and will almost certainly remarry. The boys are busy with their college lives and well launched toward the increased separation from family that is psychologically necessary to reaching adulthood. We continue to talk openly and often about our lives, but our relations are increasingly (and gratifyingly) adult to adult.

What have I learned from my experience as a loco parent? First, it has brought home to me vividly that some biological parents—though decidedly not those of the two boys I've just described—are ill-fitted to their responsibilities or unwilling to assume them. In a toast at my sixtieth birthday party, my son noted that I take young people seriously. I was genuinely surprised that he found this worth remarking, since vast numbers of parents and teachers do exactly that. He insisted otherwise, obviously from experience.

I have also come to wonder why so many would-be parents go to such extraordinary trouble and expense to overcome their difficulties with having children of their own. For me, at least, the satisfaction I have found in the friendships I have described more than suffices. Isn't conveying some of what you have learned of life—your intellectual and emotional DNA, if you will—more to the point than passing along a bunch of chromosomes? That seems trivial by comparison, especially given the huge number of children who desperately need a caring home.

Johnson's Law says that the best way to do something for yourself is to do something for someone else. When I talk with friends or acquaintances about my various in-loco sons, they often respond with polite remarks about my generosity. That of course misses the point of Johnson's Law. I genuinely enjoy these guys, so there's nothing particularly unselfish about what I do for them. Besides, I can think of little better use of my time and money.

Johnson's Law has a corollary, however: it is easier to give than to receive. Acknowledging your dependence on someone else's generosity can be tough. There are other hazards: A mentor risks taking on a controlling role, inadvertently or not, creating understandable resentment. Conversely, you can delude yourself that you are more important to the other person than you really are, and you can become emotionally dependent on the relationship.

All mentorships come to an end, sometimes badly, though so far mine have turned out well. To become mature adults, young people must separate from mentors as well as from parents. In *The Seasons of a Man's Life,* Levinson writes that much of the value of mentoring comes after it is over. "Following the separation," he says, "the younger man may take the admired qualities of the mentor more fully into himself. . . . His personality is enriched as he makes the mentor a more intrinsic part of himself." For the older man, that seems as good a way as any to defy mortality.

THOUGHTS FOR THE ROAD

Ten Things I Hope My Kids Learn
Sooner Than I Did

Greg Bestick

1. The amazing amount of "anything and everything" that's out of your hands.
2. The pleasures of pausing somewhere you shouldn't at two in the afternoon.
3. How money works.
4. It's the small moments that make it worthwhile.
5. How to dance.
6. Success in life is how well you deal with Plan C.
7. Admitting you don't have all the answers produces remarkable results.
8. Don't tell someone who knows how to do his job how to do his job.
9. Figure out who the important people are; make sure they know you know.
10. Where the clitoris is.

PART FOUR

ISLANDS OF FAME AND FORTUNE

Blessings on Him who invented sleep, the mantle that covers all human thoughts, the food that satisfies hunger, the drink that slakes thirst, the fire that warms cold, the cold that moderates heat, and lastly, the common currency that buys all things, the balance and weight that equalizes the shepherd and the king, the simpleton and the sage.

CERVANTES IN *Don Quixote*

MONEY

Money means different things to different men—status, freedom, achievement, social mobility, moral obligation, among other things. Having too little or too much can be equally devastating, as Nelson W. Aldrich, Jr., whose parents managed to liquidate a substantial family fortune, knows only too well. Now Aldrich, editor of The American Benefactor *and author of* Old Money: The Mythology of America's Upper Class, *is working on leaving his own legacy regarding all things financial: complete indifference.*

You Can Never Lose Enough

Nelson W. Aldrich, Jr.

Money is better than poverty, if only for financial reasons.
WOODY ALLEN

This story is as accurate as I can make it, but that's not saying very much. Few topics demand more creative accounting than one's wealth and one's parents. Gratitude, self-pity, resentment, modesty—whatever circumstances seem to call for, my story will bend to it. Plus, I've told these anecdotes so often, to so many different people, that their truth value by now may be entirely mythical—a compromise between perverted memories and the prejudices of the age.

Mythification was in the air the first time I recall money being discussed in my family. It was around 1950, or five years after my father came home from the war. He was an architect, a "name" partner in his firm; I was about fifteen and trying, perhaps, to test the war hero's prowess in another sort of struggle. I asked him, "So how much do you make, Daddy?"

My question was certainly not motivated by anxiety over our standard of living. We lived in a large shingled house, inherited from my great-grandparents, in a tiny gated community tightly knit by cousinage, education, class, and wealth. The house was on a knoll (indeed, it was called "The Knoll" on our stationery) overlooking the ocean north of Boston, and nothing deemed necessary to the upbringing of a proper little Brahmin—sailboats, tennis courts, tutors, trips to Europe, country day and boarding schools, certain admission to Harvard College, debutante parties, etc.—was unavailable to us.

Daddy thought the question impertinent, of course, though not for the reason usually given in stories like this. My parents did discuss money, and especially in front of the children. Weighing the moral-financial worth of a thing was a discipline incumbent on these descendants of Puritans. What was unmentionable in their view was the social power of money: money as a stratifier, money as a source of anxiety, money as an object of predation, money as a measure of success, and so on. It was the invidious power of the stuff that my father sensed I was probing for with my question, and it shook him.

It shook him all the more because it raised an issue painfully endemic to his class—the issue of earned versus inherited money. The distinction didn't matter much to his forebears. They were aware—as who wasn't in America, storied land of equal opportunity and the self-made man—that inherited wealth counted for less on one's moral ledger than the money one made. But before World War II the moral ledger had lines for other values—ancestry, taste, class affiliation, and community loyalty and service—which somewhat counterbalanced, not least in the eyes of self-made men, the vague taint of shame attached to wealth that was just there, without expenditure of effort, intelligence, or prowess, by accident of birth.

But those values had grown faint during the war, the greatest democratizing experience of the century. People like us (OCD, as my grandmother would sometimes say: "our class, dear") had always been sensitive to the ancient cry of class resentment, "I'm as good as you, any day!" but after the war the best of them were far readier to reply, with varying degrees of astonishment, "Why, you're as good as I am!" Thus the question of how much he made posed an impossible dilemma to my father. Architects seldom earn a lot of money under any circumstances; architects just starting out, as he was, earn very little. So whether he took my question to be getting at his earned income or his combined earned and unearned income, either way he risked diminishing his manly stature in my eyes.

The earned figure, besides being literally responsive to my question, must also have seemed the safer risk. "About ten thousand dollars," he said.

Safer than he knew. Ultimately, the social power of money depends on its purchasing power, and at fifteen I had little or no sense of what $10,000 might buy. All those family discussions of the moral-financial worth of a thing had affected me oddly. Unlike, say, the nouveaux riches who were even then clamoring to get into the Eastern Yacht Club—people, that is, who knew the price of everything and the value of nothing—I knew the value of everything and the price of nothing. The same, as I look back on it, was true of my father—and indeed of his father, and his father's father.

The trait would prove financially disastrous to all of us. For the value that trumped price in this male line was aesthetic; all that glittered—beautifully, of course—was worth any amount of gold. Great-grandfather Aldrich was bedazzled first by fine furniture and carpets, then, spectacularly, by houses. He built his last one himself: a walled estate in Rhode Island, with its own soaring water tower, Romanesque barns, and elaborate boathouse, all three designed by my Beaux Arts–trained grandfather. The nicest touch was in the barns, which were connected by underground railway to the main house, a formidable pile of local granite arranged, as elegantly as one can with granite, into ninety-nine rooms. Grandfather Aldrich was equally taken with houses, but, being an architect, he built most of them for others, only two for himself. What he found irresistible were yachts and cars and a life of intellectual and aesthetic appreciation; he was a trustee, it seemed to me, of every noteworthy institution in Beantown.

My father's case was different only in that he had fewer resources. Necessarily: the granite pile had absorbed a good bit of the family fortune, but fetched almost nothing when it was sold during the Depression to the Catholic Church. His father's preference for fiduciary service over crass moneymaking was also costly. Still, there was a good deal left for my father to finish off—along with his mother's money as well.

How he did it I might have foretold myself. One of his many concerns about me was my lack of ambition; yet there was one obvious form of it that he never failed, in his many lectures on my "future," to warn me against: "I don't care what you do," he would say (always with the lethal *sous-entendue*: as long as you do your damnedest at it). "But don't, for God's sake, become a businessman."

Ah, well, it so happened that in the early seventies my father was persuaded by his financial advisor to became a businessman himself—in, specifically, the shopping mall business. Worse, he was persuaded not only to finance one with his own money, but also to design it. Lawyers are wisely warned against taking themselves as clients, on pain of losing the case; architects, whose cost to the client rises in direct proportion to their aesthetic ambition, are also warned against it, on pain of losing all their money. And so he did.

On my mother's side of the family, meanwhile, a similar sort of folly was afoot. They, too, neglected to count the cost, but the aesthetic that beguiled them was romantic love. My grandmother made a very respectable marriage to my mother's father, had two girls, then ran off with an impecunious Hungarian count whose

Schloss in the Carpathian Mountains needed a new roof. My grandfather was then smitten by a high-maintenance monologuist and a sizable chunk of his inheritance vanished in the divorce. My mother outdid them both in careless cost accounting. She can be excused for marrying my father, as she was barely eighteen at the time, but her three subsequent marriages were ardent impulses of the heart. So were the subsequent divorces, since she gallantly spared all four ex-husbands any expense of alimony or settlement. She also spared herself, however, the expense and care of motherhood, cheerfully abandoning those duties to the fathers of her two children. She lacked the instinct, she told me.

Her supreme act of carelessness, however, was to disinherit me and my half-sister (by husband number three). She was living on an island at the time; husband number four had been dismissed but not divorced; and she was quietly, at the insistence of her own peculiar *amor fati,* drinking herself to death. In this she was assisted, possibly inadvertently, by her housekeeper: not an "old family retainer" but a local woman whom she had employed at the suggestion of the woman's son, the liquor store delivery boy, a year or so before her death. In her will much of her estate (reduced but substantial enough to have been of great help to careless me) went to this woman and some friends; a few thousand dollars went to her children (to show she hadn't forgotten she had children); and the remainder, by far the greatest portion, went to a local charity. I would commend her generosity for this except that she probably doesn't deserve it. There's evidence that in totting up who should get what, she had underestimated her capital by a multiple of ten or so: another accounting error, in this case redounding tenfold to the benefit of the remainderman.

Not that it would have made any difference to me or my half-sister if she'd got it right. We contested the will, arguing that she was of unsound mind. In her last years (her early fifties) she was not only drinking heavily but taking tranquilizers as well. One mid-

233

winter evening she had been seen walking through the village in her nightie; she had tried to drown herself off the beach in front of her house. We showed the court a painting she'd done, a New England graveyard in which every headstone had her name on it.

We lost. The trial was instructive. I learned that in law there's no such thing as "family money"—money, I mean, that follows the genes. Indeed, American individualism might be said to begin and end on the deathbed, with our last will and testament. Napoleon's Code forbids disinheritance of the children. In that tradition, a parent's wealth is not considered wholly his or hers: posterity has a claim on it. As Americans, however, we own our money, individually, free and clear. We can do exactly as we wish with it: we have no obligation to our descendants, just as our forbears had no obligation to us. We do of course have various trust mechanisms by which money can be tied to a family—or "tied up," as glum inheritors often put it. But the knot is optional and tied, if at all, by the will of the individual possessor, not by law or widespread custom (like primogeniture).

But there is a myth of family money and many Americans do believe in it. One of my stepfathers did. He was husband number three, and the father of my half-sister. About a year after our mother's funeral, my half-sister was killed in a car wreck. She had inherited about $60,000, as I did, from a trust fund established by one of our mother's grandfathers and "triggered" by her death. My half-sister left no will, of course (she was only twenty-one when she died), and the money went to her nearest living relative, her father. He was a doctor, prosperous but by no means rich, yet he decided, on family money principles, to shunt her inheritance over to me.

What else have I learned from my family's carelessness about money? To be careless, is the short answer. All the financially consequential choices I've made in life—career(s), marriages, jobs, number of children, insurance purchases, stock market investments, retirement plans, real estate purchases—I've made without regard to the present or future plumpness of my wallet. You might suppose that my mother's disinheritance of me, followed by my father's bankruptcy, would concentrate my mind on lower things, but they didn't. The coming of Reaganism didn't, either. I noted that something called "the entrepreneur" had become America's new ideal type, and that CEOs and investment bankers had joined the ranks of celebrities. I heard that there was no such thing as a free lunch, that the free-lunch class into which I was born was only slightly better (because a lot less dangerous) than the welfare class, and that I, indeed, was a sort of welfare prince.

Reaganism also taught me how deeply sinister is the conjunction of our "land of the free" and "home of the brave." Thanks to the generous "Daddy state" in which I'd grown up, I had always thought that freedom was a dubious good anyway: freedom to go sleep under a bridge. This was the ethos of Reaganism exactly, and I knew I wasn't brave enough to bear it.

But I could, as they say, "care less" about it. And I did, and still do. Moreover, I'm not sure that money-careless people like me aren't a good sort to have around in a country like this. Certainly my carelessness has had about it the necessary measure of negligence, as my wife and children will testify. But I like to think that negligence, at least in my case, comes into the world of appearances as something finer, perhaps even more beautiful—negligence edging into insouciance, nonchalance, *sprezzatura,* a casual grace. Cool, in a word: the best mask of terror available to the insecure man. Besides, who, in this aggregation of rich and would-be rich people that we call a society, is secure? Maybe only those who were brought up to think they were.

✦

Like Nelson Aldrich, I grew up in a family of big spenders. However, my parents didn't have a family fortune to squander, only Dad's weekly paycheck. But on some unconscious level, I knew that even if I wasn't "to the manner born," or manor, then at least I'd be living in one someday. (Those were the days, however, when middle-class young ladies believed the only route to the Big House was by "marrying well." But that, as they say, is another essay for another book.)

Although my parents didn't have any money, they did possess a wealth of what I now recognize as priceless: abundant consciousness. They were generous, taught four little children good manners at great restaurants every Sunday, entertained lavishly, and shared their good fortune with everyone who crossed their paths. My father was the biggest tipper since Diamond Jim Brady; I thought all the waiters and porters fussed over him and us because Dad was such a big shot (and in their/our eyes, he sure was). My mother doubled every recipe she ever made because someone down the street or in the parish "might need it" (and they always did). I don't think I even realized we didn't have any "real" money until I was a freshman in a private Catholic high school and started to hear the word debutante. *When I asked my parents when was I going to have my coming-out party, they laughed and told me, I'd already made my debut—on the day I was born. And it was a great party.*

But the downside of all this largesse was that my parents were so carefree with money that they never saved a dime. So when the time came for my hardworking father to retire, there wasn't a nest egg; he continued working in a series of ever-diminishing menial jobs until the bitter end. After he died, my mother lived the next five years of her life riddled with fear, burdened with debt and guilt because she relied on the slender checks her children (who were all struggling on their own) sent every month to supplement her Social Security. After her funeral, when I was going through her papers, I discovered a slim red ledger in which she kept track of her *accounts. The pain evidenced in the penciled figures and era-sures still haunts me. It's one of life's ironies that although nei-ther of my parents lived to bask in the ease of my financial success, the small insurance policy premium that my mother paid each month with her widow's mite (before even heat, light, and food bills) eventually blessed me with one of the biggest financial miracles of my life: the $1,250 with which I started the Simple Abundance Charitable Fund the summer before* Simple Abundance *was published. By then I was a student of the spiritual laws of money and tithing my way to financial serenity.*

Coming from a family of spenders, it was shocking (but not too surprising) when I married into a family of savers. My husband and I were the yin and yang of money handlers, which was a source of constant distress. But saving out of fear rather than prudence becomes hoarding, just as insidiously as spending out of denial becomes irresponsibility. Living as if the wolf is banging down the door, even when the pantry is well stocked, is as soul crushing as spending as if you have all the money in the world when you don't.

We're zealots at pursuing financial security, when what we really should be doing is praying for financial serenity. The financial security illusion is based on man-made laws of money: buy low, sell high, Roth IRA, mutual funds, money markets, long-term investments, high-end yield. Do all this and you'll never have another worry because you've accumu-lated all you'll ever need. Ha! And how long do you think it takes to lose it? Try twenty-four hours.

Financial serenity is based on the spiritual laws of money, and like natural laws such as gravity and relativity, these are constant and immutable, come bull or bear. Spiritual law, no matter of which path, tells us that as we give, so shall we receive. Money is energy, and as we evolve the energy changes form. The green paper and plastic cards in your wallet are only contemporary representations of this energy. If you do your banking on the Internet, you don't even see the energy shift accounts. Five thousand years ago, the common currency was sheep and shells. I have a special gold ring made from one of the earliest forms of coin currency dating back to the Byzantine Empire, but I couldn't ride the bus or buy a cup of coffee with it today. I wear it to remind me of money's true nature: ever-transforming energy.

But if there's one lesson I learned well from my parents, it's that true wealth is a state of mind. It's never the amount of money one has, or hasn't, it's the amount of faith. Abundance and lack are parallel realities and each day we choose which one we'll inhabit, regardless of whether or not there's a comma in your checking account balance.

"Guard me against the arrogance of privilege, against the indulgence of feeling that I don't have enough, and the poverty of spirit that refuses to acknowledge what is daily given me," Gunilla Norris writes in a beautiful meditation, "Paying Bills," from her modern book of hours, Being Home.

"Instruct me in judicious spending and in gratitude with no holds barred."

Or as my Dad would tell you, "Always remember, if you take care of the Red Caps, the Red Caps will take care of you."

—SBB

HARMONY

*Now in his eighties, the eminent religious scholar Huston Smith,
author of* The World's Religions *and other books, is skilled at giving
voice and language to big questions. I once heard him liken the human
ability to understand and communicate with God to a dog's ability to
know its owner. By comprehending a few of its owner's commands,
and by sensing his presence even when it cannot see him, the dog has a
real, if very limited connection with the human world. We, too, can
periodically sense the presence of something larger, but are about as
capable of communicating with it as a dog is with us. Just to know the
little we know, we have to stop, listen, and watch or we'll miss the miracle, however fleetingly it may occur.*

*I also heard Smith say once that as a spiritual human being he felt
he had a responsibility to the past, present, and future. He never mentioned how he managed to fulfill that obligation, to find a harmony
among all three states in a single gesture, so recently I asked him. His
wise, touching response reveals how all of us, no matter how remote we
may feel from cosmic truth, are capable of investing the simplest rituals
and duties of our daily lives with eternal significance.*

Making Perfect Dirt

Huston Smith

The loss of wealth is loss of dirt,
As sages in all times assert;
The happy man's without a shirt.
JOHN HEYWOOD

It began nineteen years ago when a six-year-old granddaughter paid us a week's visit in Syracuse. Some six-year-olds are content to watch television, but not this self-starter. She wanted *projects*. Some were quickly dispatched—an hour here, a half day there—but this is the story of one that has lasted nineteen years thus far and has affected my spiritual journey.

At one end of our vegetable garden there was a compost heap. For the most part it enjoyed benign neglect, as the saying goes, but occasionally I would poke at it indifferently. One brisk morning we vigorously attacked it together and turned the whole heap over, whereupon her active mind wanted to know why we were doing that. What was the purpose? What did our shoveling accomplish? That extracted from me a short lecture on composting. Vegetation decays to become once again the earth from which it sprang, I explained. The cycle repeats itself and is, biologically speaking, everlasting. Air—scientists call it oxygen—speeds up the process, which was why we were turning the pile over: to work more air into the moldering grass, leaves, and vegetable matter and accelerate its turning into humus.

She was fascinated. Part of the heap was ripe, but it contained stones and various kinds of bric-a-brac, so we seized on a wooden crate that was lying around, covered it with chicken wire, and sifted out the intruders. The result was, well, remarkable. I didn't

240

know what the word *friable* meant until I ran my hands through that pure, black dirt, felt it crumble in my hands and then sift through my fingers when I spread them apart. A product of this order called for a name, and one was soon forthcoming: Perfect Dirt. It turned into a trade name, and much of the rest of the week was spent packaging Perfect Dirt in plastic bags, which we hand-delivered to friends I knew to be fellow gardeners—office secretaries, neighbors, and (on the last afternoon of my granddaughter's visit) passersby who took us up on our sidewalk poster, "Free Perfect Dirt." The project was a smashing success—she, totally absorbed in the project itself, and I absorbed in the pleasure of working alongside my visiting granddaughter.

She went on to greater things, among them becoming a marine biologist, but the project she set in motion survived her departure. Nineteen years and three geographical moves later, I am still making Perfect Dirt. With unexpected, life-enhancing consequences, it turns out, which is the point of this story.

The consequences crept up on me. At first I sensed only that I was riding the wake that she had set in motion; the day wasn't quite complete without my taking a look at our compost pile and seeing if it needed a bit of attention. But then it started to feel as if the project was assuming the initiative and drawing me into its act. I remembered Woody Guthrie's song that begins, "All my life is turning, sunup and sundown," and every turn of my spading fork phased me into nature's untiring gyrations—the wheeling of its planets, the circling seasons, the rhythms of its daily round.

And in time a second realization dawned. In retrospect I realize that I had been experiencing this second entry for quite a while before words took shape to give it a voice.

The first word that came to mind was *participation*—in composting I was participating in nature's rounds. Then, though, an adjective moved in to underscore that word. I was *consciously* participating in nature's rounds. Willy-nilly, everything participates in nature's gyrations—"ashes to ashes, dust to dust"—but we human beings are the only creatures that can choose either to enter the feedback loops intentionally or sit back and freeload on the ride.

That realization takes me from my garden to my study, where hangs one of the most treasured artifacts that I have gleaned from the world.

It is a bark painting of an emu that I acquired while I was spending a summer—its winter—in Australia. It was found discarded in the bush, but was in such good condition that it made its way into the hands of an anthropologist at the University of Melbourne who—I gasped at his generosity—gave it to me. In doing so he explained its history.

The artist belonged to the emu clan, and was about to set forth to hunt down an emu, who, at his approach, would voluntarily sacrifice its life to provide the sustenance that the members of the clan needed. But not if the hunter had not assured its replacement by painting its successor. Painting equaled creating. That there are still people on our planet whose minds work that way, I find one of the most astonishing (and moving) facts of our times, but my reason for mentioning the anecdote is this: it shows us active, intentional participation with nature at its zenith—the most vivid instance of such participation I have encountered. To our way of thinking, Mother Nature creates the emu that will replace the sacrificial victim. Not so with the aboriginal hunter. Nature required that he get into the act.

The more I reflect on that aboriginal mind-set, the more I find myself envying it, for it has things exactly right. All life has its active and passive poles, and by painting/creating his emu the hunter was giving rein to his active side. Nature needed him, and that need built him into its picture decisively and increased his sense of belonging.

That is why, in an act of imitation, every afternoon that I am at home finds me in my backyard for fifteen minutes tending to what has become the fourth component of my daily spiritual practice. For as long as I can remember that practice begins, on arising, with hatha yoga for the body, a reading from a religious classic for my mind, and a blend of prayer and meditation for my spirit. Those three practices remain in place, but it helps to have them grounded, and that is what the addition of composting accomplishes. Being physically anchored to the earth helps to keep my ego from bobbing along mindlessly on the sea of life. In Kyoto there is a bridge named the Half-dipper Bridge. Its name derives from a practice of the thirteenth-century Zen master Dogen. As an act of gratitude, whenever he would drink from the river the bridge spans, he would pour back half of the dipper of water he scooped from it for his needs. That gratitude is half the story, but composting adds to it the element of creating what you return.

There are some who will want to raise the issue of quantity. Of what account are my wheelbarrows of perfect dirt in the face of the global ecological crisis that threatens to extinguish life on this planet? They miss the point, as this next Buddhist reference attests.

Alarmed by the thousands of sentient beings that a raging forest fire was killing, a tiny bird flew some distance to a neighboring lake, scooped up a beakful of water, and emptied it on the flame. It kept shuttling back and forth between the lake and the fire until it collapsed from exhaustion. It knew how little its ministrations would accomplish. Still, it continued to the end because it found that that was the only thing it wanted to do.

To conclude my own story, it helps to set it in perspective if I add that I am married to an avid gardener. The arrangement is that I create the dirt—with a little help from above, to be sure—and she can then do with it as she pleases.

There are feebler contracts on which to prolong a marriage.

✦

How many times have you wondered about some aspect of your life that ended in bitter disappointment despite all your best efforts: What was the purpose of that? And what exactly did all that shoveling accomplish? *Diddly, that's what. Squat. Thanks very much . . .*

What I loved about Huston Smith's gently provocative essay was that he finally answered questions I've asked of heaven many times, only to come to think of them as rhetorical. But with the idea of composting as a spiritual metaphor, as well as a practice, then the shoveling starts to make sense. All of those mysterious times when we seem stuck, we're meant to just gently turn the pile (pain, remorse, regret, guilt) over, work a little more Spirit into the moldering parts of our broken dreams. Next, with a little loving attention, carefully pick out the stones and bric-a-brac no longer necessary. And then wait. The season will come to sow again, but this time, instead of our seeds falling onto rocky soil, they will find their home in perfect dirt. The most that we can do, then, when we are emotionally, creatively, or spiritually stuck, is all Nature asks of herself: participate in the regeneration of our own destiny.

—SBB

RECRUITMENT

My junior year in college took a long time to complete. Disgusted with just about everything in my personal universe, I left after the first semester, traveled around the country, then spent six months driving a concrete-mixer truck in Oregon. I was happy, independent, making good money, but promised my parents I would finish my degree. A year after I left I returned, hoping to struggle through a few more courses to satisfy the requirements for a major in English literature and then get back to my alternative-lifestyle career as a truck driver.

In the first class of my nineteenth-century literature course, a tall, skinny, boyishly handsome man paced behind a lectern and pummeled students with personal questions. In no time, all dozen or so of us were engaged in a lively debate—I forget the topic—while the professor, Bob ("Call me Bob") Bell, newly degreed from Harvard and in his first year as a teacher, smiled broadly. Within a week, I was deeply, joyfully into Middlemarch *and a regular, highly competitive tennis game with the young prof, after which we discussed the tragic relationship between Dorothea and Ladislaw over a couple of beers. I took three more courses with Bob, including an independent study, and managed to complete my major and earn a degree with some measure of distinction. But not without the help and inspiration of the man who, though only a few years older, had become my mentor, good friend, and role model.*

Bob has gotten only better with time. He now holds the William R. Kenan chair at Williams College and, in 1998, was named recipient of the Robert Foster Cherry Award for Great Teachers by Baylor University. A prolific author, he also founded the Project for Effective Teaching at Williams to mentor young faculty. He can't imagine a more gratifying life, he says. Every day is filled with the "double pleasure" of teaching and learning.

A Professor for All Seasons

Robert H. Bell

I have ceased to question stars and books; I have begun to listen to the teaching my blood whispers to me.

HERMAN HESSE

Teaching my first freshman English class at Williams College in 1972, I began with Robert Frost's "Once by the Pacific." Gingerly, I asked, "What is this poem about?" Ted smirked, tossed his blond ponytail, and said, "It's about pink elephants." I believed then that no matter how mistaken or impertinent a student's response, the teacher must take it seriously. I asked Ted, "What do you mean?"

"It's about pink elephants," repeated Ted. "It means whatever you want it to mean."

"I don't think so," I said. "When a pickpocket looks at a saint, he sees a pocket. That doesn't mean the saint is just a pocket."

The class uttered a collective "Whoa!" Ted cocked his head and said, "Hmmm." An initiation for Ted, and an early lesson for the young professor: maybe not *everything* a student says is sacred, or even serious. Soon Ted and I were playing basketball together, still friendly combatants; his smart-aleck skepticism became a positive element in our class discussions.

I loved being a young teacher. When I began teaching at twenty-six, I couldn't imagine anything more fun than discussing a Yeats poem or lecturing on *Tom Jones*. What I lacked in experience, dignity, and wisdom, I made up in energy and bravado. Usually my momentum carried me—even rescued me from a few crash-and-burn situations.

Although sometimes I was less than triumphant. In a Shakespeare class, Jenny asked why Banquo's ghost carries a glass. "Ah yes, good question, Jenny," I said in my professorial tone, pointing my teacher finger. "Banquo's glass is an important symbol. A glass, or what we'd call an hourglass, represents time, and Macbeth is the enemy of time."

Jenny was shaking her head slowly. "Professor, my footnote says glass is not an hourglass but a mirror."

"Really?" I said cavalierly. "Well, Jenny, I guess you can't believe everything you read."

The class was chuckling. Pleased that humor had saved me, I was enjoying a quiet sigh of relief, when Jenny rejoined: "Or hear." Another early lesson: Let the class enjoy a big laugh at my expense; not everything the teacher utters is sacred.

The two primary qualities of any teacher are dedicated love of the material and affectionate respect for the students. I genuinely liked my students and enjoyed their companionship. I ate meals with them at the house where I was faculty associate while debating politics and comparing favorite rock bands. I played intramural basketball and softball and, with fellow Bostonian students, lived and died with the Red Sox and Celtics. Ray Cox and I were jubilant when the Celts beat Phoenix in triple overtime in 1974.

I played bit parts in two Williams theater productions: a solid debut as the Wall in *A Midsummer Night's Dream,* and a brief turn as the priest in *Twelfth Night.* The priest has one speech of eight goofy lines, each of which in our production cued elaborate stage movement. Afraid I'd confuse the couplets, I wrote the first syllable of each line on my fingers. The director spotted them and chewed me out as though I were cheating on an exam. By the time I had my moment in the spotlight, perspiration had smudged the Magic Marker clues—I didn't know fingers could sweat—but I did deliver the eight lines in order.

The teaching life was rich with material, I found. In my thirties, I enjoyed a minor second career as a humorist, publishing pieces in magazines, broadcasting shorts on NPR stations. Much of my material was autobiographical, worked up in class. There were moments, candor compels me to confess, when "Introduction to the Novel" became "The Bob Bell Show." Looking back, I realize my tendency to perform both energized and limited my early teaching. Still, I'd maintain that part of teaching, or one kind of good teaching, is performance: if you're dramatizing a character in Shakespeare or a humorous episode in Dickens, a little theatricality can't hurt. A vivid presence helps an English teacher bear witness to the power of glorious language and the value of critical inquiry. Students are a captive audience, and like most people they respond more willingly to personality than to complexity, more readily to autobiography than to abstraction. I overflowed with anecdotes and jokes. The trick is to put personal experience to educational use. Trouble was, even very smart Williams students seemed to remember my incidental one-liners or autobiographical anecdotes better than my meticulous analysis of Faulkner's characterization.

I may have had the fundamental skills of a teacher, but I needed to mature beyond boyish egocentricity. If my students were to develop, I had to develop with them. I was too focused on performance to imagine what students might need and use. Occasionally, I would reflect on real-life subjects—career or marriage. But I was self-conscious about seeming pompous or paternal and would hasten "home" to the text: "Well, that's enough of Life 101—let's look more closely at Cleopatra's next speech." I was wrong: students wrote on course evaluations, "Give us more Life 101—we need it!"

While my priorities were academic and intellectual and I never saw myself as a minister or counselor, as a first child I played the role of big brother instinctively. I was on a 10K run with Troy when he informed me he'd been accepted at medical school and shooting hoops with Randy when he told me he'd been turned down everywhere. After a class on Cleopatra's suicide, Priscilla confided that her father had killed himself. Teachers can only imagine the fears and horrors students bring with them: Marcia grieving for a beloved brother killed in a freak accident. Sometimes I could comfort; occasionally I could help.

As I grew older, I found more opportunities to offer support or guidance to students. A few years ago my senior honors student was a young woman of extraordinary benevolence—she cared for a homeless man, Big-Sistered two local girls, tutored disadvantaged children, and hoped to teach in Africa. I suggested that she also apply to seminary. "Oh, I don't think I have the calling!" she replied. One afternoon, instead of talking about biblical imagery in *The Sound and the Fury,* we talked about her spiritual doubts and longings. I persuaded her to apply to Yale Divinity School, where she met and married a man with the same calling; when they finished, they took a parish together.

Not all encounters with students are sanguine. Once, playing basketball, I lined up against a student who murmured darkly, "Two years ago you made me read *Middlemarch.* Tonight you're gonna pay." Relations between teachers and students can magnify ordinary human confusion, stress, and miscommunication. Naturally students resist being evaluated and graded; a few resent the professor for his judgments. Some students (some teachers, too) are troubled, disturbed, inordinately needy, fantasizing, or projecting. I've had students send me suggestive valentines. One graduate wanted me to intervene with her parents, who were "plotting to send her to a mental asylum." It was evident she was on drugs, distraught, perhaps psychotic, but what could I do and why had she called *me?* Because, she said, in that large lecture class three years earlier she knew I was talking "directly" to her, that I "really understood" her. Well, I understood Faulkner and Austen, but not what to do in such a highly charged, potentially life-threatening situation.

Students may be smitten with their professors, and vice versa. The young, in a high state of alert and ardent aspiration, caught up in that sensual music, can be disconcertingly attractive. The teacher must recognize the proper boundaries—not always an easy thing to do. When I was in my late thirties, I taught a beautiful, gifted, but tortured young woman who monopolized discussions in class, as though she were taking an individual tutorial with me. After one class, when I gently urged her to leave more space for her less confident classmates, she burst into bitter tears. Later she dropped out of school and wrote me long, intimate letters. I liked and admired her enormously, found her fascinating—worried about her.

When she was preparing to return to college, she asked me to select her courses and register for her. She approached me while I was conversing with several colleagues—the first time I had seen her in over a year. I said, "Great to see you—come by my office soon!" The next morning I received an angry, pathetic letter: *How could you be so callous? How could you treat me that way?* Anybody reading the letter, stuck in my faculty mail slot without an envelope, would have assumed that I was intimate with an undergraduate. Now I was alarmed that I was too close to her but frightened that withdrawal could do real harm: She had been talking regularly about suicide. What is the role of a teacher who cares for a student in trouble?

I've learned that teaching requires both firm boundaries and fluid connections, intellectual authority and personal contact. Education is communication. (*Teach:* an active verb, requires a subject and an object.) But higher education is not personal therapy. It can be dangerous for a teacher to be an intimate confidante. As I've grown older, I've learned that a professor can demonstrate the opposite possibility, the value of less intimacy and subjectivity. College students don't necessarily need a professorial pal or a drinking companion, but they may well value an older counselor, someone definitely not Dad but interested, concerned, willing to listen and advise.

After thirty years of teaching, I've discovered so many more things I need to say about *King Lear* or *Tom Jones* that I have less time for contemporary allusions and amusing digressions. I've deliberately subordinated myself more rigorously to my authors. I once heard a world-renowned musicologist lecture on Handel. Applauded enthusiastically, the lecturer held up a recording and pointed emphatically to the image of the composer. That's now my ideal of teacherly advocacy: the object of veneration is not the lecturer but the work of art. Blessedly, getting older, I care less, or at least not nearly so much, about appearing cool, funny, or attractive; teaching *Tristram Shandy* or *Song of Solomon,* I'll be the Geek of the Week. He who abaseth himself exalteth the Lord.

The passage of time has necessarily altered my relationships with students. While we no longer like the same music, wear similar clothes (what twenty-year-old wears "relaxed fit"?), speak a common idiom, I've gained both greater authority and richer connections with students. A teacher needs to be able to hear himself as well as students. At a certain point in this life's odyssey—around the time one starts using phrases like "at a certain point in this life's odyssey"—students stopped calling me by my first name. By the time I was forty I was gray-haired and unmistakably professorial. When I invited my thesis student in 1986 to call me by my first name, she continued to address me as Professor Bell. I repeated the invitation. The next week she wrote me an abashed confession: *Dear Professor Bell—I'm sorry, I can't call you by your first name. You just don't seem like a "Bob" to me.* Today, if I am ever tempted to "be a Bob," I have two teenage daughters to remind me that I'm not.

Significant moments in education, I've learned, may be conspicuously undramatic. Last year, when I was teaching Richard Wilbur's poem "The Writer," I asked my first-year students what was appealing about the speaker's attitude toward his daughter. Anne Dwyer said softly, "His respect for her." Respectfulness also characterizes the teacher's attitude toward the material and his students. Simone Weil says, "Attention is the rarest and purest form of generosity." I want to demonstrate the efficacy and pleasure of generous attention to literature, to encourage disciplined, imaginative responses to language, and to give pure, sustained attention to the student's reading and writing. The hardest part, where I really earn the big bucks, is grading students' essays—lots of them. It's grueling but gratifying, for it verifies the importance of critical thinking. If an eighteen-year-old is to take very seriously words and ideas, she must perceive that the teacher, her reader, is responding thoughtfully to every idea she has—and to the words she uses to express it.

Education should be challenging, demanding, even painful. Learning is disorienting, frightening, and overwhelming. This makes teaching seem awfully somber. It's not. For me teaching is anything but dutiful: it's joyful. I have boundless fun talking about *King Henry IV* or Eudora Welty. I've never had to contrive enthusiasm. And demonstrating it is almost a sacrament—one of the English teacher's means of bearing witness to the value of literature. The word *enthusiasm* comes from the Greek for "filled with the gods." A word invented by James Joyce, *joyicity*, identifies the author himself with pleasure. I experience joyicity quoting poetry, watching plays, analyzing texts, reveling in felicities of language. I want to convey the fun of reading, thinking, dramatizing, revising, correcting, speculating. I enjoy it every bit as much now as I did in 1972, when I would finish one class and immediately begin daydreaming about the next. Next month I turn fifty-four, and I will enter another classroom, meet twenty-five eager English majors, and distribute three passages, the opening lines of Chaucer's "General Prologue," Milton's "Paradise Lost," and Eliot's "The Waste Land." For me it is like another visit to Narnia, except that grown-ups can return, perhaps less intoxicated, histrionic, and humorous but more productive, happier, and wiser.

Like an athlete, a teacher must adapt, refine his craft, compensate for attributes that diminish or disappear. My boyhood hero, Ted Williams, wanted to be the greatest hitter who ever lived. If he wasn't, he came damn close, second only to Babe Ruth. But without a doubt Ted Williams was the greatest *old* hitter in baseball history. Batting .388 in 1957 was even more amazing than hitting .406 in 1941. I'd love to be known as one of Williams College's great old teachers. It's something to shoot for.

⟡

Every person I know who considers herself lucky can usually trace her luck back to one special teacher. From Plato and Aristotle (who taught Alexander the Great) to Helen Keller and Annie Sullivan, every day teachers from grade to graduate school change the course of world history.

William James described religion as "the attempt to be in harmony with an unseen order of things." That's my description of teaching. In every spiritual tradition, teachers of truth known as Masters are honored and held in higher esteem than kings. However, next to politicians, teachers are the most maligned public servants in our culture because we take them for granted. Revere them? We barely pay them a living wage. And in these troubling times when the miserable and misbegotten seek to disrupt the natural order of life with lead bullets, why would any sane person want to put himself at risk each morning by walking into a classroom? This is a question a friend of mine who has been a teacher in New York public schools for sixteen years is asking himself right now, as is his wife.

Why, indeed? I suppose because next to the religious life, teaching is a divine calling that simply cannot be ignored because Love is the recruiter. It is said that the three most difficult karmas are beauty, fame, and wealth. I'd add being a teacher. I know from teaching workshops how much the teacher must give away of his own psychic energy and emotion to create a safe haven for the students, because as Bob Bell so rightly observes, "learning is disorienting, frightening, and overwhelming." And the only power that can overcome fear on that level is love. At its purest form teaching is cosmic communion and connection. Vital information for the survival of the species is being entrusted to those who will need it. We can only pray that it will continue to be passed on.

We are all called to teach others at some point in our lives; it doesn't have to be in a classroom setting. Teachers are Spirit's agents provocateurs. Toward the end of his life, after passionately and persistently exploring the origins of the universe, Albert Einstein came to know that "Something deeply hidden had to be behind things." He was right. It was a teacher.

—SBB

WORK

Today will be a great day. Dave, the largest man I know, has pulled down half a dozen enormous maple trees next to my summer house with his skidder, a fat-tired Colossus of brute machinery that's a perfect character match for its owner. The maples, in combination with a windstorm, have been threatening to reduce the house to matchsticks—or so I rationalized the tree-clearing project to my skeptical wife. While there was some justification to my paranoia, we both knew I really wanted the trees felled so I could spend a blissful week or so cutting, splitting, hauling, and stacking them in neat piles around the property.

That's what I call fun, work that combines a cool tool of destruction—in this case, a chain saw—with gulaglike labor and produces a large result, like a perfectly constructed woodpile. The power saw is my only concession to modern convenience. I split the rounds with a maul and wedge, heft the sections by hand to the edge of a field, where I stack them to dry, and drag the brush deep into the woods. It's dirty, plodding, scratchy, backbreaking work—and I love it. A couple hours into the toil a peace and calm settles over me that I'm unable to achieve through any other activity. At the end of the day I'm whipped but buzzed, and in my euphoria wonder whether my need for hard, physical work is a vestigial endowment, a throwback to a time when it was absolutely essential to the survival of my unique strand of DNA. Maybe I still belong on the savannah with a loincloth and spear, a pregnant mate and a couple of nippers at my side, cultivating a dusty patch of soil when I'm not stalking the local protein supply.

Whatever. All I know is that I find righteous pleasure in sheer toil, and I'm not alone in feeling that way. I belong to a huge fraternity of men who like to sweat blood. Former Big Ten football player and novelist Elwood Reid is one of the more prominent physical specimens among us.

255

Blood, Sweat, and Cheers

Elwood Reid

*Far and away the best prize that life offers is the chance to
work hard at work worth doing.*

THEODORE ROOSEVELT

There was no way around it. At the age of thirty-three I had
become an outsized marshmallow—a sallow guy who spent his
days writing in a basement. My hands were uncallused and weak. I
had a gut and could barely eke out ten push-ups. I became easily
winded and broke into a furious sweat with the slightest exertion.
It didn't take long for my solid Midwestern work ethic to begin
screaming at me, telling me I had to get unsoft or else.

I suppose this sudden and drastic appraisal had been a long time
coming. I was, after all, a coach's son, a wrestler and former Big Ten
college football player who'd spent nearly a decade trying to ignore
the old working-class jock lurking inside.

As a young football recruit I looked the part, six feet six, two
hundred and eighty-five pounds—muscle and more muscle. I was
good. I liked to hit, but I didn't love football, not with that full-
throttle intensity the game required. No, I had a secret—I loved
books, and even though I'd never met a writer (born and raised in
that literary hotbed, Cleveland), I wanted to be one. In other
words I was in trouble—stuck between two worlds, the blunt and
physical realm of football and the foreign world of books and literary salons. But my job was football, a job I'd been preparing for
my whole life. So I played the game and toiled for the coaches, my
days evenly divided between lifting, running, and hitting. I kept
hoping that I'd snap out of my literary daydreams and go back to

being just another kid who wanted to play in the NFL and all that other Wheaties-box crap.

After a year at the University of Michigan, my dream of becoming a writer began to flicker and fade as I sculpted myself into a scowling, thick-necked guy who thought only of the next practice the way a lion anticipates its next kill. Of course the steady stream of novels I sat up nights reading, sore from practice, were doing their best to take me away to places I'd never been before. The books helped me put the strange business of big-time college ball in perspective. Try strapping on the pads after reading *Portnoy's Complaint* or listening to a coach scream in your earhole to hit harder after reading *Survival in Auschwitz*. But in the morning when my feet hit the cold tile floor, the aches and pains of the previous day's practice came swirling back and I knew I had a job. And that job was football. I'd grown up in the Rustbelt, where the job defined the man even if the job was only something to be endured—assembly-line zombie, punch-press operator, whatever.

Being able to endure any job bestowed on one a strange form of heroism in a town seemingly devoid of the usual heroes—our baseball team, the Indians, was a perennial basement dweller. And the Browns were good but not great, losing year after year to Denver and breaking the city's heart. So Cleveland relied on its working-class Joes to take their daily beatings and stand tall for the city, working long and hard even as the river burned, the mayor's hair caught fire, and Cleveland became a national put-down, a punch line for how bad things could get.

My father showed me how sport and work devolved from the same ethic. Memories of the afternoons spent tossing a baseball or practicing a double-leg takedown with him are as vivid as those of the days learning to run a rototiller or fell a tulip tree without collateral damage. At first I chafed against the long hours of hauling firewood, weeding, painting houses, and mowing lawns, but I endured and learned to give in to the work until it became a sort of meditation. I took the same approach to football and wrestling practices. When my teammates complained about a particularly long or brutal practice, I hunkered down and got to work. For me the greatest satisfaction was the walk back to the locker room, sweaty and tired, knowing that I'd given it my all and that tomorrow the same would be asked of me again.

They say athletes die twice, but when you are nineteen, fast, strong, and like to hit, the fact that your playing days can end with a simple twist of the knee or a vicious, brain-dampening tackle only spurs you to lay it down and burn it up before your ability fades away.

In my case it was a neck injury that ended my playing days. In an instant I became a former player. All that had seemed unattainable before—the literature and writing classes I was never able to take because they conflicted with practice—were suddenly within reach. The problem was that I still had the body of an athlete and when I looked in the mirror, the muscles jumped to attention, ready and willing to hit. I didn't look like a guy who wanted to write or spend his days with his nose in a book, so I vowed to let my body wither. Athletes didn't write novels and the people who talked about books (skinny, cool, lots of black, knew all the right bands) grew uncomfortable when I would amble into class, squeeze behind a desk, and try to contribute to the discussion of *Crime and Punishment*. I grew my hair long and quit all athletic activity except for the occasional guilt-fueled run around the block. And it worked for a little while—the literati let me hang around and butcher their academic lingo. I felt less and less like a jock as my body softened and my world expanded.

After college I headed for Alaska, hoping to get as far away from my ex–football player identity as I could. I was eager to have adventures I would be able to write about. My money quickly ran out, but instead of running back to the Midwest I held my ground and took a job as a frame carpenter. The paycheck was good and I liked the work—the way it left me feeling used up at the end of a twelve-hour day spent pounding nails and lifting beams. I learned how to shut my brain off and lay it down. Years passed and whether I knew it or not, I was still trying to blunt the jock in me with physical labor, because it was the only way I could justify the few hours a week I spent sitting at a desk and writing, an activity I still deemed soft and suspicious.

The jobs came and went, but they all had one thing in common—I used my body and not my brain. All those reflexes that had made me a good athlete were still there, waiting to be challenged. I even found a way to channel the aggression and sheer physical abandon that had served me so well on the football field. After work I bounced in a scruffy bar (punk rock upstairs, liver beaters and gin hounds downstairs), fighting when I had to, head-butting rowdy drunks to the tiled floor, or on a good night, tossing cocky frat boys against the Dumpsters in the back alley. I was good at it and took pride in what my body was still capable of.

I wrote on the sly, punching out stories that were rejected dozens of times before being abandoned to a drawer, where they were forgotten. My physical work became both a crutch and a cross. It allowed me to pursue writing part-time and keep my body happy. But I feared becoming forever a carpenter who wanted to be a writer, and then finally just a bitter guy swinging a hammer. I began hoping for the carpentry equivalent of a sudden neck injury to force me out of the rut I'd seemed to have worked my way into.

Then, after years of rejection, my life took a pleasant swerve. A major magazine wanted to publish a story of mine. Editors and agents began calling, but more important, my daughter was born. I remember walking out of the hospital, past a bookstore and a group of men in dirty work clothes on lunch break. The exhilaration of watching my daughter's entry into the world quickly wore off as I studied the working men—the way they looked at their shoes when men in suits passed or hid their hands when a pretty girl walked by. I saw the way people looked right through them as if they were members of some invisible army—necessary, but best ignored. All the working pride in the world would never change that. It was one of those moments in which a piece of the world magically clicks into place and I realized that all the anger and bitterness that had begun to infect my work days as I toiled for others suddenly made sense. I returned to the hospital, vowing to start a novel I'd been putting off. A week later I finished my last carpentry gig, hung my tool belt in the basement, and began writing. It became my job. I woke early and stumbled out of bed, working ten, sometimes twelve hours a day, pouring all of my stored-up job rage into the writing. It was time to put up or shut up. So I put up, because I knew that if I quit or faltered that I would have to snap on the tool belt and start looking for work. What scared me was that it was an easy thing to imagine.

Six months later, about the same time my daughter was learning to crawl, I finished the novel and sent it off. It sold and just like that I ceased being a carpenter. I was a writer—a guy who went into a room in the morning and returned several hours later, looking none the worse for wear and with nothing to show for his labors except for a few pitiful pages of rough prose.

My dream had come true, but something was missing: hard physical work. When we moved to a farm in upstate New York I found a balance. I busied myself with projects—refinishing old furniture, tapping maple trees, planting massive vegetable gardens, hauling, chopping, mowing. The days had rhythm and shape. Mornings spent writing were followed with long, brain-dead afternoons of physical labor. I went to bed tired and full, ready for the next day.

But it didn't last. Seeking better schools, we moved to an apartment in Brooklyn. The careful equilibrium I'd managed to attain began to dissolve. There was no yard to take care of or wood to haul or trees to prune. I was just a writer, a guy who sat in a chair all day shoving words around. All the work muscle I'd built maintaining the old farm quickly went to flab. My hands softened and I began to dread my daily descent into the basement to write. My brain was working, but my body seemed confused and bored. I grew restless, unable to sit still for the necessary hours the writing life required. My work began to suffer. It took me longer to produce the pages and ideas came seldom and hard.

Then I looked in the mirror. I was soft and dangerously close to becoming a full-blown pussy. But unless I wanted to sweep streets there wasn't much work begging to be done in Brooklyn. That left gym work. And as much as I hated to even contemplate it, the sallow-eyed thing smirking back at me in the mirror left me no other choice. So I joined a gym and began working out for the first time in years. My body resisted at first, but then quickly fell into a routine. It wasn't work, but it was the next best thing—the thing I'd tried to leave behind all those years ago when I'd turned my back on football. I needed the sweat and strain and didn't care if I looked like just another chubby, soon-to-be-middle-aged dude trying to stave off time and gravity. An hour or two of mindless repetition and I stumbled home spent and body-proud. In return I had the mornings to toss words around without guilt.

I'm a writer who doesn't wear black or smoke unfiltered cigarettes in coffee shops. I avoid universities and refuse to dissect my writing in high-falutin' language. It's just brain work—good work, but not physical. And I've learned that the only way I can keep this hopped-up working-class kid from Cleveland happy is to get my hands dirty or lift and run until all of me is sore, hands and muscles burning just like they did all those years ago on the football fields and wrestling mats. It's who I am. My heroes haven't changed. I still look at my father's dirty, work-stained hands with pride and envy. And now not a day goes by where I don't pine for a massive field to mow or a pile of wood to stack. Work is the one thing I know how to do, the most important thing.

Listening

For me it was law school, my father's profession. For Bruce Main it was stock brokerage and business, the career choice of his elders. I thought of lawyering as my default career, a safe, respectable path to follow if nothing else worked out—in other words, if I couldn't figure out what I really wanted to do. Even now, though, that's not a completely honest statement. Law was my default career if I didn't have the guts to do what I knew I should do.

Like a lot of young men just out of college, Bruce Main agonized over what to do with his life. He felt a compelling need to do good work, but also felt competitive pressure from his peers, who were jumping into highly paid jobs, and from his parents, who wanted to see him independent, financially secure, and capable of supporting the family they knew he wanted. His decision: he cofounded UrbanPromise, a ministry that serves children and teens in Camden, New Jersey, one of America's poorest cities. It's not an easy thing to find your calling, as Bruce testifies. For it takes real courage just to listen for the call in the first place.

Finding Your Calling

Bruce Main

What are you willing to give up to ensure your own unfolding and the unfolding of what is holy in your life?

GREGG LEVOY

I rushed through my rounds—locking windows, shutting off lights, and bolting auxiliary exits. It was late, 11:30 P.M. I longed for a few oblivious hours of sleep before the chaos and excitement started all over again—another day leading the high-energy activities for 150 inner-city kids.

I stepped out onto the cement stoop in the balmy July night and tripped over something soft. I flicked on the porch light and was startled by what I saw. There, cuddled like a house cat, lay the body of a little boy sound asleep—an angelic five-year-old kid, arms tucked up inside a dirty Chicago Bulls T-Shirt. It was Peanut, a neighborhood kid who had been attending our day camp for the past few days. I scooped him up and loaded him in our van. His mom must be terrified, beside herself, I thought, her five-year-old baby wandering dangerous streets in the middle of the night!

At a little past midnight I waited at his housing-project apartment for someone to answer the door, cradling my sleepy friend against my shoulder. He had hardly stirred since I picked him up. I could hear a television blaring inside. I began banging the door with my fist, hoping not to awaken everyone in the complex. Finally, Peanut's four-year-old sister opened the door.

"Is your mom home?" I asked.

"No."

"Your grandma?" She just shook her head.

I peered into the apartment. No furniture. No pictures. Just a little black-and-white TV with a coat hanger antenna. A few Chinese food containers and potato chip bags littered the corner of the room.

Peanut's brother, who didn't bother to look up, was lying on the stained carpet, his eyes glued to the television. He was seven. "When is your mom going to be home?" I asked him. I was near the edge of rage. The kids shrugged. The numbed indifference, the complete lack of concern for their mother's whereabouts, was shattering.

I was a college junior, raised amid the comforts of a protective, upper-middle-class, suburban, two-parent family, encountering for the first time a separate reality. What mother would leave three children under eight alone in an apartment with no phone, no beds, and no food? How could a five-year-old boy wander the streets at midnight and be missed by *nobody*? I was shaken. When I think of critical events and epiphanies that shaped my career—my calling—this is the most formative one.

Like many men entering their early adult years, I was at a cross-roads. Family and friends were beginning to ask me, predictably, "What are you going to do with your life?" After high school I had spent a year as a stock trader on the floor of a small exchange in the Pacific Northwest. At night, I studied for a brokerage license. As I witnessed my coworkers spending their days flipping stocks and making thousands of dollars, my interest only intensified. Colleagues my own age were driving Porsches and BMWs. I decided this was my calling.

Then the market went south.

College sounded like a good idea and I began to save. Then I got a hot tip and invested my tuition money in a small mining company that was about to release its latest exploration reports. Since the market had already slumped, and since the soil samples were "rich in valuable minerals," I was guaranteed to make enough to cover a few years of college. Two weeks later my stock crashed. It was delisted and never returned to the board. I ended up earning my tuition by spending the summer on a garbage truck slinging trash.

Every ninety-plus-degree, fourteen-hour day was an exhausting reminder that my talents were not best rewarded in the securities field. Hoping to secure a useful degree that would provide well for a future family, I entered college as a business major. With an accountant for a father and two entrepreneurial grandfathers, I felt a business career made sense. But I soon fell under the influence of a charismatic English professor whose passion and love for books and great stories enthralled me. I decided that if I was going to heave garbage cans to pay for classes, I would study with the most highly regarded professors on campus—the men and women whom the students talked about in the cafeteria and snack bar. These people would help me find my calling and provide the direction I was seeking. They would become my mentors.

I found my home in the English and theology departments. From old Dr. Sawtell I learned that our best mentors and lifetime guides could be found in the characters of a novel and that human nature was revealed more clearly by a Shakespearean drama than by a Myers-Briggs personality profile. From theology professors Dr. Baloian and Dr. Hartley I was introduced to the great themes of Christian faith and some of the saints of the church. Dorothy Day and the Catholic Worker movement, Oscar Romero and his fight for the poor in Central America, Dietrich Bonhoeffer and his resistance to the Nazi regime, and Mother Teresa of Calcutta became my heroes and sources of inspiration.

My adopted mentors challenged me to put faith into action. A summer of volunteer service sounded like a good place to start. This is how I found myself at midnight, on the doorstep of an apartment in a housing project in east Camden, trying to figure out what to do with Peanut.

As the volunteer director of a neighborhood-based day camp program, I came to realize that the obstacles faced by Peanut inside his home were only a few of the challenges he would encounter in his community of Camden, New Jersey—one of America's poorest. This postindustrial town, once known for its thriving economy, good schools, and healthy neighborhoods, was now a grim reminder of corporate irresponsibility, political corruption, and crushing tax ratios. And the children were paying the price. In the second most dangerous city in America, Peanut would have to protect himself from continual community violence. With public schools graduating only 40 percent of their students, sending less than 5 percent to college, the odds were against Peanut getting an education that would prepare him for adult life and gainful employment. With about 50 percent of Camden's population under the age of twenty-one, adult role models were scarce. With few organized sports, boys' clubs, and youth programs Peanut would most likely spend his spare time just hanging out and getting into trouble. And with little industry and few jobs left in the city for teens, the probability of Peanut resorting to the lucrative drug trade would be very high.

The jarring reality of this five-year-old's existence challenged me. Could I just walk away at the end of the summer with my idealism intact—my insights about urban crises enriched—and add the experience to my résumé? Sure, my volunteer efforts would look good on grad school applications. Could I continue to take advantage of all my privileges and just ignore the sense of responsibility I was beginning to feel for kids like Peanut? I was beginning not to think so.

A significant spiritual awakening only intensified the questions I was asking. Reading the Gospel narratives for the first time as a young adult, I was struck by the social implications of Jesus' teaching and his mission. While growing up in a Christian home I had always thought that my faith was about avoiding the seven deadly sins, holding correct doctrines, and getting into heaven—not living a life of service and fighting for justice. But after a closer look at the biblical witness, I saw that there was little mention of heaven in the Old and New Testaments but a lot of discussion about the kind of world we are told to create. Whether reading the prophets Jeremiah, Amos, and Micah, or reading the words of Jesus, it became clear to me that God is concerned about the worldly condition of people— especially the oppressed, the poor, and those who have no voice. I could no longer read the Gospels without feeling challenged by a Jesus who committed himself to those whom society had forgotten or found of little value. I needed to decide: Was I going to curse the darkness or light a candle?

I also had to decide what I was going to tell my family. My parents were supportive of a brief stint as a volunteer. But when I returned to Camden as a volunteer during the summer before my senior year of college and again after my first year of graduate school, the family began to get a little nervous.

I was not "outgrowing" my idealism. Three summers in a row stretched their patience. When I mentioned the possibility of dropping out of grad school to start a full-time program in Camden, they got *very* nervous. I remember my grandfather's reaction. A hardworking survivor of the Great Depression, he sat me down one day and said, "I really thought you were going to make something out of your life." He always believed that social problems were somebody else's responsibility. Gramps could not understand me. I knew he loved me deeply. But his words stung.

Friends, too, who were beginning to scale the ladders of personal success, would roll their eyes and ask, "Are you ever going to get a real job?" or "Are you ever gonna work for a summer?" whenever I would call and ask for financial support. As they were interviewing for better jobs with better stock options, I was begging for their donations so I could pay for food and gas and take the kids to the Jersey Shore on the humid dog days of August. In their eyes, volunteering a summer to play midnight basketball with angry teens or coordinate afternoon softball games was something an idealistic young man might do once in his life—not three summers in a row!

Who, and what, would determine my calling? Would it be conventional expectations of what a man is supposed to do with his life? Would it be the subtle pressure of my peers? The desires of my family who wanted me to find security and a stable job? Or would it be my spiritual convictions and growing sense of personal responsibility?

In the end it was my involvement with kids like Peanut that convinced me to dig in, establish some roots, and try to implement some of the programs I believed would help young people in the community.

First, though, I had to convince the young woman I had been dating in California to marry me and move to the East Coast. The prospect of continuing a cross-country courtship did not appeal to me. This seemed like the perfect time to add one more commitment to my life. She agreed! Since I had no place for us to live, I had to convince a local church to let me use its abandoned manse for housing and its basement for program space. The parishioners liked the idea of having a young couple take care of their property. Things were beginning to happen.

My new bride and I honeymooned across the country in a U-Haul van driven toward our new work. Saying good-bye to the sun and fun of Los Angeles and moving to the heart of an impoverished East Coast city was no small feat for Pamela. We were somewhere in New Mexico, I believe, when she struck the first deal of the marriage. For the first five years I could pick where we lived; the next five would be her choice.

For five years we lived next to the church where the programs of UrbanPromise were started. It was a critical time for building trust in the community and being able to provide something many kids do not enjoy—the stability of a home. For the children who came from chaotic households in which there was little routine and few traditions, our home became a very special place. Neighborhood kids regularly joined our family to celebrate their birthdays and holidays, or just to have a special meal. Pam always pulled out the best linen and the best cutlery for the kids. Even a meal of boxed macaroni and cheese would seem like a five-star meal for some of these children. Simple events, like a Sunday afternoon meal, became an occasion that kids would talk about for years.

On New Year's Eve of our sixth year, a Vietnamese man was executed, gangland style, across the street from our home. Pam reminded me of our deal. She had put up with the drug dealer next door, vandalism of the vehicles, and crack addicts who would pound on the door at 11 P.M. looking for work. She'd had it. With three of our own kids now, all under the age of six, it was time to get a little distance from ministry. We moved to another community in Camden.

Those first six years provided an important foundation for the ministry. The word on the streets was that the program was here to stay. The number of kids served had mushroomed from a handful to hundreds. The staff grew from Pam and myself to over a hundred workers during our peak seasons. The outreach expanded from one neighborhood to many throughout the city. The variety of programs offered evolved from summer day camps and after-school clubs to job training, small business development, performing arts programs, college readiness workshops, and alternative schools. Our teen programs started graduating 95 percent of the young men and women and began to send them to colleges and universities such as Cornell, Howard, LaSalle, and Rutgers. Young people who never dreamed of college now considered careers as teachers, doctors, child psychologists, and youth pastors. Now, as UrbanPromise programs have expanded beyond Camden into other inner-city communities such as Wilmington, Toronto, and Vancouver, my responsibilities require more time raising money and managing staff. Yet even as my duties shift, my sense of calling still finds its root in the incredible potential for both greatness and tragedy that can be found in the life of a single young boy.

My little friend Peanut, whom I had lost track of for a few years, continues to inspire my commitment. By the time he was eight his mother had moved fifteen times. I tried to keep him connected but he moved far away from our center and had no phone or real address. But every now and then Peanut would reappear. As we talked and tried to catch up, I discovered that he was becoming farther and farther behind in his schoolwork. Uncontrollable emotional outbursts were becoming more frequent.

Then I didn't see Peanut again.

One day while reading the paper, I came across a story about a fourteen-year-old who had gotten in a skirmish behind a housing project on the east side of town with a homeless man. The story graphically reported that the man had stolen a toy car from the teen. In a fit of rage the teen shot the man, fled to New York, then was apprehended and eventually tried in court. He was given a sentence of twenty years. He was that sleepy little kid I'd found on my porch almost ten years before, Peanut.

After eighteen months of trying to sift through prison bureaucracy, a staff worker finally tracked Peanut down and wrote to him. In a few weeks Peanut responded.

Today they read the names for mail, he wrote. *When they called my name I thought it was an angel. You see, I've been in here close to two years and nobody has written or visited me.*

I wrote Peanut back. I asked him if he ever thought about the great times he had at summer camp and if he remembered anything about the program. A few weeks later, a response.

Sometimes when I lie here in my cell, the only thing that helps me through these long days are the memories of summer camp—the trips to the shore, the fun, the games, the Bible stories, the counselors. Sometimes I dream about those times all day long.

Sadly, Peanut will spend the best years of his life in prison. In a recent letter he told me how he had "busted up a guy real bad." He said that he had to do it, otherwise he would have been perceived as weak and somebody would have killed him. He was moved to a new prison and put in the hole for four hundred days. He assured me that he was trying to do his best, but "this prison is a tough place to do right."

The night I picked this little boy off the church steps fifteen years ago is a continual reminder of why I do this work. As I enjoy the excitement of travel, the advantages of education, the love of a family, I think of my young friend who spends night after night in the hole. And the ifs begin to haunt me.

If I had had more staff, could someone have kept in better touch with Peanut?

If our job program had been running at the time, could Peanut have developed the job skills he needed to believe he had a future?

If our alternative school had been started, could he have made up lost grades and dealt with his anger in positive ways?

If I had had a male mentor on the staff who would have committed to find Peanut when he disappeared, would things have worked out differently for him?

I believe they would have. For this reason I continue to commit each day to gathering the resources and people needed to create opportunities for children and teens—kids from our most desperate urban communities—to become all that God has created them to be.

This is my calling.

✦

There is a significant difference between a job, a career, and a calling. Jobs are what we do to keep bodies, souls, and families together. They can be temporary or they can last until retirement, but a job ends at quitting time. Punch out and you resume your life where it left off in the morning.

A career can be a calling, but not necessarily. Usually a career occurs when we stick to an occupational path— accounting, advertising, law, publishing—because we do what we do quite well and get paid well enough for doing it. So we stick around. Sometimes careers resemble long-standing domestic arrangements, marriages in which passion is exchanged for comfort, security, and predictability in an uncertain world. Of course, there is nothing wrong with this choice; for many people it is exactly the right one—though some may wonder what psychic price is being exacted for playing it safe. It is certainly true that every day we don't strive to live authentically we do pay a price, with compound interest.

Many of us eventually move from jobs to careers, but often we hesitate to answer an authentic calling, especially in midlife, because we're torn—between the financial realities of raising children and caring for aging parents, between a proven track record and the unknown, between a regular paycheck and uncertainty, between circumstance and creative choice. But it's a mistake to accept as our reality the illusion that many are called to fulfillment, such as Bruce Main, but few are chosen. What Spirit has done for other men and women can be done for you—when you're ready. The truth is, we're all chosen; most of us just forget to RSVP.

"In saying yes to our calls, we bring flesh to word and form to faith. We bring substance to dreams, to passions, and to the ancient urgencies," Gregg Levoy *writes in* Callings: Finding and Following an Authentic Life. *"We ground ourselves in life and bring ourselves into being as alchemists and magicians in their finest hours."*

—SBB

CHANCE

How do you define authentic success? By your paycheck? Your title? Your peace of mind? The quality of your family life?

At a crucial point in his life—at the peak of his earning years, in fact—Millard Fuller decided to redefine what success meant to him. His health was bad, he was focused exclusively on career, and he felt hollow inside. Most troubling, his marriage was failing.

Fuller went on to found Habitat for Humanity International, which in the past twenty-five years has built 85,000 homes for nearly half a million indigent people. He has received numerous awards for his humanitarian efforts, including the Medal of Freedom. And he has raised four kids.

To find authentic success, Fuller had to undergo a personal crisis, fall, and start over. He had to take a hit.

And then he had to see that the hit was actually a gift.

A Planned Life Can Only Be Endured

Millard Fuller

When your ship, long moored in harbour, gives you the illusion of being a house . . . put out to seas! Save your boat's journeying soul, and your own pilgrim soul, cost what it may be.

ARCHBISHOP HELDER CAMARA

When I think about the philosophical issues that have engaged me for much of my life, it seems they all boil down to simplicity versus complexity and scarcity versus abundance. I was a

273

wealthy man, materially, in the same days that I was close to spiritual bankruptcy. I have been comparatively poor, yet at the same time felt richer than at any other period in my life. In order to learn what I know about a woman's love, I had to nearly lose the woman I cherished the most. And in order to learn what I know about a man's true responsibility to God and his fellow man, I've had to turn my back on financial wealth and apply my talents to providing simple, decent homes for people in need. I have come to measure my own worth by God's measuring rod, as revealed in the Bible, however foolish that may appear to the world.

I grew up in a small Southern town, where a person's worth was measured by the size of his bank account, the length of his automobile, and the extent of his land holdings. I got involved in the world of commerce when I was six years old, when my dad, who ran a small grocery store on the edge of an Alabama cotton-mill town, bought me a pig. My instructions were to fatten him up, sell him, and make myself some money. That I did. More pigs followed, then chickens and rabbits, and a small enterprise in firecrackers. When I was about twelve years old, my father bought a farm. I decided to sell my assets and invest in cattle. Until my senior year in high school I remained in the cattle business, and that income helped pay my way through college at nearby Auburn University.

Later, as a law student at the University of Alabama, I launched a series of business ventures with a fellow student, Morris Dees. Our enterprises included student apartment-house rentals, fancy birthday cakes, student telephone directories and desk blotters, and a mail-order business offering products such as holly wreaths, doormats, and trash cans to youth groups throughout the country for fund-raising. By commencement day we were making $50,000 a year.

After graduation, Morris and I opened our law practice and continued to launch new business ventures, which eventually included a dozen subsidiary corporations. We expanded our mail-order business, offering more products to more youth groups and other organizations. Selling tractor cushions to Future Farmers of America brought us a $70,000 profit in one three-month period. We gave away Ford tractors as prizes to the groups that sold the most cushions.

Next, we published a cookbook and offered it to Future Home-makers of America chapters for fund-raising. Soon we were the largest publisher of cookbooks in the country. Then came tooth-brushes and candy, and other publishing ventures.

Eight years after our first business deal at the university, we owned a modern office building in Montgomery, Alabama, with our names emblazoned across the top of it. We employed 150 people and our sales totaled more than $3 million a year. As president of the company, my annual salary was $100,000.

One day in 1964, I was sitting in my office when the treasurer of our companies came bounding in and tossed a stack of papers on my desk.

"Congratulations," she exclaimed. "You are a millionaire!"

"A millionaire? Let me see those papers!"

It was true. I looked up at the treasurer.

"Congratulations, Millard." She said it again as she stood there beaming at me from the other side of the desk. "What is your next goal?"

"My next goal? Why, ten million! Why not?"

"Okay," she replied. "Why not?"

"Good. Since we agree, get back out there and go to work on it. Time's a-wastin'!"

She hurried out of the office. I spent a few minutes thinking over the past. In a very short time, I had amassed a fortune, with all the trimmings.

But my life was a thunderstorm about to burst. I was under thirty, but I could not breathe properly. The pressures were so great that several times a day I would grasp the arms of my chair, push myself up, and gasp desperately for breath. A big sore had developed on my left ankle and would not heal. Doctors told me it was stress-related. The close and loving relationship I enjoyed with my wife, Linda, had cooled. We had everything—a successful business, two beautiful children, cattle ranch, cabin on the lake, speedboats, expensive clothes, Lincoln Continental, big house, and plans to build a mansion. But deep in the recesses of my mind I was beginning to wonder: Is more and more of this to be the sum total of my life?

I had been raised in a Christian family and had been taught from earliest childhood the precepts of the Christian faith. I had embraced it. Accepted it. Was baptized. "Seek ye first the Kingdom of God, and all else shall be added." I had believed that, and tried to live by it.

In high school and college and in recent years, I had been active in our church. As business demanded more and more of my time, however, my interest in the church declined. One day in 1964, I received a letter from the national stewardship council of my church denomination. They wanted me to visit African missions, study them from a layman's point of view, then return to the States to interpret the work for congregations and conferences.

My first impulse was to accept. But the business was growing rapidly. My whole mind was wrapped up in it. I took out a pad and pencil and did a bit of quick figuring on the cost of such a junket. Not the cost of airplane tickets, food, lodging—that was insignificant. I figured the cost of being away from the business, the loss of potential income and profits. That expense, I calculated, was too high. I said no.

All that can come later, I reasoned, after I've secured my fortune. Now is the time to make it, and store it up. Later, I'll have more time and money to give and then I'll put the Kingdom first. I pushed questions of conscience back into the deepest, darkest corners of my mind.

In November of 1965, Linda brought the whole matter to the crisis point when she suddenly and firmly announced one evening that she had decided to go to New York to think about the future of our marriage. She left me with our two young children, Chris and Kim. I was in agony.

I began to examine my life. An image came into my mind of the day I would stand before God to explain what I had done with it. I could hear myself bragging pathetically, "Lord, I sold a hell of a lot of cookbooks." In the presence of God, that sounded so ridiculous I could only cringe.

After a week of misery I could sit still no longer. I asked a pilot in our company to arrange for an airplane to go on a trip.

"Where to?" he inquired.

"I think I'll go to Niagara Falls," I replied.

"But why?"

"Because I've never been there!"

"Okay. It's your money!"

That evening in my hotel room, I caught the beginning of a movie on TV that featured a young woman missionary in China. She fell in love with a young military officer. He wanted to marry her, but it would mean the end of his military career. He went to an old village leader—a mandarin—for advice. The old man thought for a moment, and then replied, "A planned life can only be endured."

Those words penetrated my innermost being.

A planned life can only be endured.

With those words ringing in my ears, I phoned Linda and persuaded her to let me come to New York City to talk to her. She had been counseling with a pastor we knew, but had not arrived at a decision about our marriage.

That evening we decided to go to Radio City Music Hall. The show was entitled *Never Too Late,* a prophetic title.

After the movie, Linda suddenly broke down and cried. I couldn't get her to stop. Finally, in exasperation, I grabbed our coats and we stumbled out into the cold November night.

We walked around for a while just holding each other. We sat down on the front steps of St. Patrick's Cathedral and talked. Then we walked some more, eventually ending up in the doorway of a shop just off Fifth Avenue. Linda faced me and bared her soul. She confessed the ways in which she had betrayed our relationship. I poured out my own agony and regret for ways I had betrayed her. The wall was broken down, and love rushed in. We grabbed each other and held on. After a long while we took a taxi and returned to our hotel. We stayed up all night talking, singing, and praying.

We both felt a strong sense of God's presence, calling us out of this situation to a new life, a new way of living. To prepare for this new thing—whatever it was—we felt it necessary to leave the business, sell our interest in it, and give away all the proceeds.

The following morning we left our room and went downstairs. I hailed a taxi, and we climbed in. But the driver didn't drive off. Instead, he turned around to us with a big smile on his face.

"Congratulations!"

"Congratulations? For what?" I asked.

"This is a brand-new taxi. You are my first passengers!"

I turned to Linda. Another favorable sign. She was already crying.

"Driver," I said, "take us on a drive through Central Park. I've got a story to tell you."

FAILURE

For a lot of men, "failure" is not a part of their vocabulary. There's "stumbling block," "bump in the road," "a little setback," but "failure" connotes a face plant of such humiliating degree as to be banished from the realm of professional possibility.

So what could a very successful man, the founder of five companies now publicly traded on the NASDAQ exchange, possibly know about what it means to fail? A lot. For instance: until you do, until you reach that milestone, you'll never truly know much about success.

To Err Greatly

Stephens Millard

We are all failures—at least all the best of us are.

JAMES M. BARRIE

Let's face it, it's better not to fail. I've known men who have lost their jobs or had their businesses go under just fall apart. Their marriages break up, they retreat from friends and family, curtail their aspirations, and settle for a job way beneath their talent and potential. Some men, as we all know, have killed themselves. A lot of a man's self-esteem is tied up in his job. Women may have many of the same opportunities men have today, but they're still attracted to those who are successful and men are deeply aware of that. There is nothing the culture, no matter how much it's changed or will continue to change, can do to alter that fact. There are some ancient dynamics at work that spur men on to achievement and success and cause them a lot of humiliation and suffering when they don't attain them.

Still, I think most men take a professional setback a lot better than many women do. Women define their world more in terms of relationships, so they tend to experience failure more personally. Men have evolved to be able to tolerate defeat better. Men see the business world as one in which there is limited loyalty; it's dog-eat-dog, and people have selective memories about what you can and can't do. All successful men know that at some point they will fail, but that they won't necessarily lose the respect of their colleagues and peers if they do. The willingness to fail is admired because it suggests the courage to try—and try again. For almost all successful men, failure is a necessary rite of passage; like a Prussian dueling scar it bespeaks fortitude, character, and resilience.

In Silicon Valley, you don't hear much about failure these days. But it's more rampant than ever, because for every company that makes it there are dozens that don't. That interplay between success and failure is what drives the world forward. George Bernard Shaw said, "The reasonable man adapts to the world. The unreasonable man tries to adapt the world to himself. Therefore, all progress depends on the unreasonable man." Today, you can just substitute the word *entrepreneur* for "unreasonable man." It's the risk-seeking entrepreneur who's willing to risk success and failure upon whom progress depends.

That's not to say there's great glory in failure. I learned this mid-career, when I left the cozy corporate world for the risky start-up world. I was working for a Fortune 500 company in the Midwest, where I found myself reduced to going to bowling alleys at night, seeking any kind of stimulation. I'd had a partnership for a couple of years with a software engineer—he did the software, I did people, we used to say (we still say it, in fact)—and I was using my Christmas-card list to raise money for this guy. One day we got lucky, we got our first funding, a total of twenty-seven million bucks over several years from a big oil company. I quit a job as a divisional vice president—a job that offered a lot of opportunity and promise of going forward—and headed west. Manifest destiny. It was scary, damn scary.

My decision didn't go down well with my wife. She came from a well-known family in the Midwest and thought I was an idiot to leave a good job, a good salary, throw over a promising career for this. She stayed in Ohio and I went back and forth for two years. Finally, I convinced her to come west. The next thing you know, oil prices dipped, our backer pulled out and kept us from raising money from others, and we went under.

Not surprisingly, the marriage didn't survive the bankruptcy. I consider that as big a failure as the loss of the company. But when you're working eighty-hour weeks and your whole life is wrapped around keeping your company alive, there's no time for the homefront. One reason you're obsessed with keeping the thing afloat is because of the people—the employees and investors—you've brought on. I could have cared less about making out at the end as long as my employees could have kept their jobs and friends who invested in the company were made whole. You take care of your friends and those who trust you. And sometimes those concerns simply overwhelm the one personal relationship that means the most to you.

So there I was with a failed company, a failed marriage, a big mortgage, and a smirking corporate America ready for me to slink home with my tail between my legs. But I said, The hell with it, I'll stay. I'm absolutely convinced there's no substitute for persistence, pressing on, never giving up. At any point I could have said, What am I doing here? I could be running a major division of a Fortune 500 company where the biggest decision every day is where to have lunch or whether I should get on the company jet and go to the hunting camps. I was well thought of, I could have gone back. But I concluded that, on my deathbed, I didn't want to have to regret the fact that I had a chance and didn't take it. Why live a bland life?

I was also still naive enough to believe that I could pull off something else. A personal flaw of mine is that I tend to look only for the good and I've been deceived, taken advantage of, more than once in life because of that. But I also tend to forget when bad things happen. I guess if you're not an optimist you shouldn't be an entrepreneur, because every day you get up and there's a new problem that could represent the end of your dream.

So out of the ashes, after a reorganization, came a true phoenix—a business that was later sold to a major Silicon Valley company for $4 billion. After all the dilution we didn't fare as well as we had hoped, but we did all right. We started another company that went public a few years after its founding. Over the next dozen years my partner and I started seven companies, five of which went public and two of which went under. Not a bad record. We made out all right.

After that first flame-out, it was simply a matter of picking myself up off the carpet and making it happen. They don't teach you at Wharton or Kellogg Business School what you're supposed to do after you've been stabbed in the guts. You just do it. Or you don't. You either choose to take the hit as a gift, examine the positive utility of failure, or you crawl off to a corner, wring your hands for the rest of your life, and dream of what could have been. You can learn a lot more from failing than you can from succeeding. You analyze the decisions you made, look at whom you relied on too much or too little, what you didn't pursue that you should have. And you get back to work. If you don't fail you never have any reliable measure of what it means to succeed.

I'm biased. I've always believed that the business world runs on relationships. I have the ability to pick up the phone and say to a guy, Here's an opportunity, and because he knows I've treated him right in the past, he'll listen. I place a lot of stock in my Rolodexes—I've got maybe a couple thousand names of people I can call. That's why when my company went under, the venture capitalists took us back in their good graces. I had nurtured those relationships and now, even though we'd failed, it didn't matter. We could still muster the support of people who trusted and believed in us.

Of course, part of that is because men have respect for other men who try hard but stumble. It wasn't like Joe Frazier "failed" when he lost the Thrilla in Manila to Muhammad Ali. A fighter who loses is almost always given the opportunity to fight again. But that attitude about failure is peculiarly American. If you go bankrupt in England, you'd have trouble getting a job driving a taxi cab. In Germany there's a powerful stigma attached to failure. America doesn't have the stratification you find in England and to a lesser degree in France and other Western European countries. We're still the Wild West, a nation of ladder-climbing immigrants. Almost everybody is related to someone who once fled something—persecution, poverty, injustice—and arrived here dissatisfied, disenfranchised, and lacking the social connections to get a prestigious job. We should also remember that dukes did not emigrate. So a lot of these boot-strappers start their own companies—they don't have any alternative.

Failure is foreign to the vocabulary of these men. They think of themselves as being on a desert island with their boats just burned and nowhere else to go. Either they make it or they starve. They look at every setback as temporary—an opportunity they can turn to their advantage. They know that people who think they're going to fail always do.

In the back of their mind, of course, they know that somewhere down the line they will stumble, too. What they don't know is that it may be the best thing for them. Failure humbles you. There's a saying that fame is a vapor, popularity an accident, that riches take wing and only character endures. Theodore Roosevelt, who knew something about character, had great respect for the man who is "actually in the arena, whose face is marred by dust and sweat and blood, who strives valiantly, who errs and comes short again and again, who knows great enthusiasm, great devotion, and spends himself in a worthy cause, and if he fails, at least fails while daring greatly so he'll never be with those cold and timid souls who know neither victory nor defeat."

Neither victory nor defeat. Neither success nor failure. Now that would truly be a curse.

✦

Webster's *dictionary defines success as "the attaining of a desired end," as well as "the attainment of wealth, favor, or eminence." When we succeed we "prosper, thrive, flourish." When we don't, we want to sink to the center of the earth until the shame subsides. Success and failure are a black-and-white issue. They're never good or bad, a lucky break or tough luck. Actually, they're none of these things. Failure and success are the two forces in the universe over which we have absolutely no control. We keep forgetting that all we can control is our* response *to failure and success.*

I'm a big fan of failure—in retrospect, that is. You wouldn't have wanted to be around me when I was actually recovering from being hit by destiny's two-by-four. Still, every great success in my life, personal and professional, was born out of failure and depression. But try telling this to your child who's just gotten a low SAT score or a friend whose business is on the verge of bankruptcy. You can't. Why? They won't believe you. Not until later, not until they've learned like you to recast failure into an exciting chapter of their amazing saga. What you can tell them is: You can only fail if you didn't do your best. You only stay a failure if you don't try again. *It's bumper sticker wisdom, but they're not listening anyway.*

However, I know that I started to recast the idea of failure after I heard what the Irish playwright Samuel Beckett had to say about achieving success. "Ever tried? Ever failed? No matter. Try again. Fail again. Fail better." This I could do. I might not succeed, but I could learn to fail better. Fail with infinite grace, class, and style. And you know what? That's when I started to succeed.

—SBB

REWARDS

Retirement. *The word is sobering, a little sad, a little ominous. After all, what comes after it? There is no other stage, no other Eriksonian developmental task to complete, no fifth season. A lot of us can't wait to get there, but then what? Idleness is not kind to men. Epidemiologists tell us that those who quit working are more likely to die than men who keep their job—or some facsimile of it.*

A certain kind of man, though, learned early in life to make his avocation his vocation. Thus, only when he gets tired of doing that thing he has always loved to do will he quit working. And, given his passion, by the time that happens, he'll be on the other side of retirement. The writer Reynolds Price is one such man. He'll be writing in Heaven.

A Lucky Choice

Reynolds Price

> *People think that if a man has undergone any hardship, he should have a reward; but, for my part, if I have done the hardest possible day's work, and then come to sit down in a corner and eat my supper comfortably—why, then I don't think I deserve any reward for my hard day's work—for am I not now at peace? Is not my supper good?*
>
> HERMAN MELVILLE

While children are often asked what they plan to be when grown, few of them have any real sense of the meaning of the phrase "a life's work." It would be interesting to know how the answers of American children have differed through, say, the past century. For one thing, it's sadly clear that few contemporary ambitions can include a life in agriculture or in the countryside. Born in 1933, a child of the deepest Depression years and the son of a housewife and an electrical appliance salesman, I do know that from the age of six or seven onward, I'd invariably say that I meant to be "an artist." For me, an artist was someone who drew and painted every day.

There was no professional painter in the known history of either parental family. My father's eldest sister had taken lessons with a local woman and produced a small array of creditable landscapes, but she abandoned the skill early. I don't recall my mother's ever drawing so much as a smiley face; but from the age of three, I know that my father would sit at the kitchen table with me and help me draw my favorite creature—the elephant. Reared entirely at home, I had no experience of nursery school or kindergarten with their opportunities for slathering paint on hapless surfaces. It must have been my father's welcome company then—and a rapidly growing fascination with the look of the world and a longing to reproduce that look on paper—that launched me on a passion of my own.

An only child till I was eight, I had hundreds of hours of solitary time on my hands. Fiercely devoted as she was, my mother shared the assumption of her time that children were best left to their own devices for entertainment; so I filled a great many indoor days with my drawing and painting and the invention of whole cities from a big set of highly aesthetic building blocks—a gift from our only rich relation, a cousin in Chicago. And with no formal instruction or other encouragement beyond the mild praise of my family, I continued the work—above all, the painting—right through elementary school. Since I remained something of a lone-eagle boy, it brought me a very substantial part of the pleasure I experienced in childhood.

Surviving examples of the long effort show that I wasn't an entirely hopeless aspirant. I had from the start a certain talent for transporting natural objects—especially human beings—onto paper and canvas. But by the time I was midway through high school and had begun to write verse and prose with the encouragement of a superb teacher, I was also coming to see that most of my pictures had a fatal lifelessness. Luckily, it was a realization that I came to on my own. Thus I had no necessity to buck or deny the unwelcome observations of a critic. Recognizable as my portrayals instantly were, they lacked any form of radiant intensity to distinguish them from a million other dutiful copies of the face of reality. They were, in short, not close relations of the work of Vermeer, Chardin, Cézanne, or the great American landscape painters of the nineteenth century, all of whom had been among my respected elders.

My relatively new interest in writing quickly expanded to cover the disappointment, and soon I was learning how closely the two pursuits resembled each other. They were each means of closely observing the physical world; and most congenially, they were each forms of solitary work, performed in deep silence. Despite the usual apprentice years of fumbling and waiting, writing has proven a rewarding choice in all senses. But at virtually the same time as my writing began in earnest, I conceived a parallel intention.

From the start of my years in public school, I'd had an almost unbroken line of superb teachers. Since I was better at school than at all the other skills expected of a child, I quickly became the kind of boy who almost invariably fell in love with my teacher. With only one sadistic exception, those generally unmarried and childless women became benign creatures for me, far larger than life; and I labored mightily for their approval. By the time I was a junior in high school then and encountered opportunities for "career guidance" counseling, I heard myself saying that I'd made those choices already. I was going to be a writer and a teacher.

My parents, inexperienced as they were with any such precedents, showed no reluctance to approve my choices. I proceeded through college and graduate school with both goals in sight and have lived my life in both brands of harness. More than forty years into those careers, I can reflect on them with considerable distance. I've mentioned the rewards of my writing. The returns from teaching are more difficult to assess. Indeed, few professions can offer their adherents a more mysterious stream of returns than teaching (the priesthood may be a rival).

Students seldom thank or blame us. In four decades of steady work at Duke University, I've taught more than three thousand undergraduates. I haven't kept count but I'd be astonished to learn that I'd received as many as fifty favorable letters from old students. Not that a serious practitioner teaches for praise; any innocent who nurses that hope will soon be selling ice cream cones. In my own case, as the years have mounted, I don't believe I'm deluding myself when I continue to claim that the main reasons I teach are few but strong.

—I relish the chance to stand before mostly interested groups of students and investigate with them some text which I've come to love or am at least intrigued by. A good part of that relish is similar to the pleasure an actor or other public performer takes in the presence and interaction of an audience. For better or worse, good teaching is a histrionic skill. Again, however, the performance seldom triggers applause and may well be suspect if it does.

—As a childless man, I've profited by years of annual contact with young men and women at the near edge of maturity. Occasional students can be as maddeningly indifferent or inexplicably contrary as my friends' adolescent blood descendants, but (without quite claiming martyrdom) I've tried to take them on with level-headed patience as at least a civic responsibility.

—And the final reason: my faculty colleagues, while not often my most intimate companions, have constantly provided me with the kind of decent and affable workplace and the trustworthy friendships that I don't always hear of from my friends in business, the law, publishing, the theater, or elsewhere. To be sure, I've witnessed regrettable outbursts of ego—I've launched a few myself—

and, at a distance, I've known of a few personal tragedies. But the overwhelming balance for my years has been welcoming and often invigorating, and I've often wondered at the specific sources of my good fortune.

I'm an unusually slow learner, so it was only as I rode home from the annual Christmas faculty dinner this past December that I suddenly thought I could explain it. The friend who was with me commented on the good feeling of the evening—among other pleasures, for the second year in a row I'd indulged in a bout of frenzied wheelchair jitterbugging—and he wondered aloud how Duke had managed to assemble such broadly miscellaneous but generally civil, and in many cases better, band of colleagues.

At first, I cautioned him against rose-colored vision and offered him a couple of hair-raising bad memories; but then I knew that his sense of the drift in the crowded ballroom was broadly just. As human lots went, we assembled teachers—ranging in age from our mid-twenties to our late seventies—were a good lot. I gladly conceded as much, and my friend wondered why. The answer came fast but I think it came truly. I said "Because no one ever chose to be a teacher in the hope of real money."

All university teachers know that a few members of certain departments make dramatically more than others—physicians and lawyers are famously well rewarded among us—but despite the jokes about them, and occasional glares in their direction, even they can seldom have entered the profession with their prime sights on lucre. If so, in this age of teenage cyber fortunes, they were sadly misguided.

I've reflected, since that night, on the range of my academic friends and on the degree of satisfaction they seem to have taken from their work (and not altogether incidentally I might add that an older colleague once said to me "Name three good reasons for teaching—June, July, and August"). Only a few years ago I attended a high school class reunion at which most of my contemporaries rose and, to my considerable surprise, spoke of longing for their imminent retirements—they dreamed of much travel and long visits to their scattered grandchildren.

I'm wary of claiming unearned virtue for me and my teaching fellows; but I've yet to hear a handful of us say any such thing—nor any significant number of my fellow writers, craftsmen, artists, and artisans. A great many of us seem entirely prepared to tumble into eventual graves while working at the projects that have fueled our lives. Harmless drudges though we may have been, and dim guides for our young charges, we often prove as nearly inextinguishable as humans get to be. A self-applauding cheer then—and for far more than me—to the men and women in classrooms and cabinet-making shops, on stages, in gardens, and wherever else, who've thrown in their lot early in life with the less-than-money-bound. We may not last significantly longer than our dollar-bound siblings nor amass more virtue in the eyes of Heaven, but aren't the lights in our aging eyes a little less flinty? Aren't our houses likely to contain fewer mirrors? Would *mellow* be the word?

FREEDOM

Like a lot of men, I have recurring dreams about flying, always under my own power. Flight, of course, is a grand metaphor for freedom—from the dull pull of gravity, earthly chores and duties, even, were we to travel fast enough, time. When I was a kid, my flying dreams were especially vivid and magical. After all, what could be more enchanting than the ability instantly to flee ornery parents, picky teachers, the boredom of Sunday school, the wrath of the neighborhood punk? Now, my nocturnal hallucinations are more impressionistic; I awaken knowing only that I've been aloft, airborn for some indeterminate time, unable to recall the precise details. The dream sage Freud says these flying fantasies are about sex. This is an idea I've never been able to grasp.

Until recently, when I met Bruce "Buck" Rodger. Buck flies 747s for United Airlines, transport planes for the air force, and an F-5 "Freedom Fighter" for two wealthy Seattle businessmen. The Vietnam-era F-5 is still used as a frontline fighter for many countries, capable of carrying air-to-air ordnance, air-to-ground ordnance, bombs, missiles, and sidewinders. The businessmen, one of whom is learning to fly the plane, bought it from Norway for $6 million. They were going to buy a MIG, but visited a MIG manufacturing plant in Russia and were instantly dissuaded. Buck tells me on the phone that he may be able to illuminate this connection between flight and freedom, but that I'll understand it better if I meet him in Seattle and fly with him in the F-5.

On the morning of my flight—that is to say, on the morning of the second most exciting day of my life—Buck picks me up at the hotel and we drive to Boeing Air Field. There are some instructions he has to run by me—nothing serious, I don't have to take notes or anything because I'll remember them, just a few protocols to follow if it looks like we're going to crash. As Buck races his rented car through heavy traffic, one finger on the steering wheel, hardly ever looking at the road, I feel a squirt of acid attack my stomach wall. Crash? *I'll be in the rear cockpit seat, Buck tells me, and like him I'll be sitting on about fifty pounds of explosives—a hot seat leased from the navy—that will blast me through the canopy and out of the plane when I deploy it, which he hopes won't happen.* (Hopes? *Another squirt of stomach acid.*) *Before I eject, it's essential that I get in good body position. I'm to make myself as small as possible, pull my knees together with my head up and back straight. Like a battering ram, my head will be helping shatter the cockpit Plexiglas. With the handgrips raised, I squeeze the trigger. We can't eject each other, so if he says, "Bail out," Buck tells me, I'm to bail out. He won't be kidding. It's a good idea if I go first, he says, because his rocket blast goes into the rear pocket and could fry me up pretty good.*

Now, there are four kinds of ejection—controlled with and without the intercom and uncontrolled with and without intercom. If we're in trouble and lose the intercom and he holds up a flight book, that means prepare for ejection. When he turns his head to face me—that's called a face curtain—that means go. If we still have intercom and are gliding after the engines flame out, I should try to bail out at above two thousand feet. Whenever ground impact is imminent, he says, bail out. If we take a bird in the plane—shattering his cockpit, for instance—and he gives me a thumbs up, it means don't bail out.

As traffic races by, I suddenly feel the need to write everything down. What if I confuse the signals and bail out unnecessarily? My breakfast feels hot and liquid in my intestines. Buck continues. Once I've been blown out of the plane, everything should be automatic. The seat should kick me out, but if it doesn't, I should find the seat belt and release it. If that doesn't work, there's a handle at my right thigh. If that doesn't work . . . well, I'm kinda screwed. But it will. The parachute has a device that tells it what altitude it's at, so if I'm above fifteen thousand feet and I have no canopy I shouldn't panic and open it manually. If I do I'll suffocate before I freeze to death, or freeze to death before I suffocate. Once the canopy opens, I can steer with the red rails. When I get close to the ground I should try to land into the wind. If I'm

293

going through trees, I should protect my neck with my hands to prevent decapitation or severing a jugular; if slipping through power lines I should make myself as thin as possible. I'll be carrying an emergency locator device whose signal can be picked up by airplanes, but if I want to talk on the radio I first have to turn off the device in the parachute harness.

That's it, Buck says cavalierly, as we drive up to the airplane hangar. Any questions? Now suffering from severe gastrointestinal distress, I ask him to point me toward the nearest men's room.

But once in the plane, fully outfitted in helmet, mask, gloves, combat boots, and antigravity suit, tightly strapped in atop my private cache of dynamite, I'm ecstatic. The F-5B has a tiny, paper-thin Courier wing, a precursor to the better-known Delta wing, which means the plane has to take off and land at an outrageous speed— almost two hundred miles an hour—otherwise it will fall out of the sky. We scream down the runway and in no time are out over the Pacific, where Buck demonstrates an aileron roll. He brings the nose of the plane up, flips the plane upside down, then completes the roll. He checks on my condition. Far from nauseated, I'm giggly with excitement. He does a split-S turn—takes the plane straight up like a rocket, turns upside down to counter the negative G forces, which would bust the vessels in our eyeballs, as he pulls out and then heads straight down. Seven seconds and two miles later he pulls out again and now we take five and a half G's; the drag on my body is equal to five and a half times my normal weight. I do the insane breathing Buck has taught me— sucking in a breath, holding it, and squeezing my lower body as though trying to void my bowel, which is now clean as a whistle, raising my blood pressure and forcing oxygen to my brain. Buck lights the afterburners and, although we're already going six hundred miles an hour, the plane delivers a head-snapping kick of acceleration. He takes the plane straight up again, tells me to look at the tip of the left wing as he pirouettes the plane and the wingtip traces a full 360 degrees of gorgeous, ethereal horizon. How am I doing? he wants to know. My civil-

ian inner ear and stomach were born to fly. I want more thrills and Buck, unexpectedly, delivers the big one. "Take the stick," he says. The front and rear cockpits have identical instrument panels and controls. "Go wherever you like." The local air controllers have given us three miles of vertical airspace to play in and I use it all. I do aileron rolls, several in a row, corkscrewing through the air. I drop down to chase clouds. I bank around great smoky pillars, dip and climb and twist and dive, in the embrace of tremendous speed and power.

It's glorious. Better than a dream. And Freud was right: very sexy.

The Wild Blue Yonder

Bruce Rodger

Freedom's just another word for nothin' left to lose.
KRIS KRISTOFFERSON

I don't know whether you've ever experienced a moment when it feels like a curtain is lifted on the future and you can see perfectly clearly how you want your life to turn out. But that's what happened to me when I was five years old and flying on a Western Airlines DC-10 by myself from Santa Monica to Vancouver to visit my grandmother. After I walked onto the plane I instinctively turned left into the cockpit (which I now do routinely), where a friendly pilot sat me down on his lap and let me play with the controls. I can remember it like it was yesterday—the pilots in their freshly pressed shirts with gold wings and epaulets, the view through the big windshield out onto the tarmac. I felt this tremendous sense of excitement and I could see at that moment, with the curtain fully raised, that one day I would be a pilot. I was only five, but I could see that flying was my path to freedom and joy.

I suppose I had a typical pilot's childhood, if there is such a thing. I was a daredevil skateboarder and did some pretty insane things on my bike. I used to love to see how long I could hold my breath under water, often scaring my parents sick. I was the kid who never got invited back to a friend's house because I'd taken apart his dad's stereo and left it in a hundred pieces on the living room floor—covering up the *Playboy* magazines I'd brought over and left behind. When I was eleven I distinguished myself by driving the family car onto the freeway at two in the morning and receiving a police escort home. I was an only child, good at entertaining myself (particularly in my parents' car), and always looking for a new kick. Later, my mom and dad told me I was the reason they didn't have another kid. I was out of control.

But I always kept my eye on flying. Up in the air, I wouldn't have to worry about police escorts. As soon as I was old enough to work I began saving money for flying lessons. I scooped ice cream, sold clothes, delivered cheesecakes, washed airplanes. Everyone always told me I was lucky because I was so focused and knew so clearly what I was going to do. It was true. My schoolmates would ditch school to smoke pot and I'd ditch school to fly airplanes. I lied about my age to start flying lessons and got my pilot's license at eighteen. I immediately got interested in aerobatics—flying upside down, screaming toward the ground while being in complete control—a total high. Flying was all I could think about. I knew right away I had a very special talent. My thought processes, my brain, my hands, my vision, my hearing—when I was in the air, they all connected and I had this feeling of oneness with the plane. I have it every time I'm in the cockpit. God gave me a gift to pilot airplanes. I was born to fly.

After high school, I set my sights on flying the most exotic and challenging airplanes in the world—the ones owned by the United States Air Force. My dream was to become a fighter pilot, then a test pilot, and close out my military career with NASA as an astronaut.

I advised my parents of my plan and said that they may not have had to take me seriously when I was five and on my way to Grandma's, but now they had to. My dad laughed and said I didn't have the right stuff. Four years later, I received my officer's commission into the air force with a pilot-training slot at one university and an aerospace-engineering degree from another. I had to wait eight months before the air force pilot-training class started, so I got a job at McDonnell Douglas as an aerospace engineer monitoring the manufacturing of the DC-10—the same plane on which I had my vision when I was five. My father was very proud, and stopped laughing.

All the people who graduate from the air force pilot-training class are good pilots, but the best are what's called fighter-qualified (as opposed to bomber-qualified). When you've got high-performance airplanes carrying heavy ordnance, you want the best guys in them. After getting fighter qualification, I went home at Christmas and found out my mom had terminal cancer. The news rocked my world more than anything had before, and more than anything since. I told the air force I wanted to be near her and they stationed me in San Bernardino, fifty miles away from my parents' home in Santa Monica, where I flew the transport C-141. That gave me a year with my mom before she passed away, a year I'll never forget. But it effectively aborted my career as a fighter pilot. After she died, I was devastated, but set a goal to get back on my original track.

Because I was fighter-qualified, the air force allowed me to instruct in the T-38, a two-seat supersonic trainer used to get future fighter pilots ready for the real thing. This got me to Edwards Air Force Base, where all the action was. A few years later, Edwards had a position open as a research pilot, which I turned into an instructor's job at the USAF Test Pilot School. The job also involved finding a variety of airplanes to instruct students in. So I got to fly all the air force fighters, navy fighters, everything from F-15s, F-16s, and F-111s to P-51 Mustangs, T-6 Texans, B-17 bombers, B-26 bombers, even a blimp—about thirty planes in all.

It was the best experience of my life. I've flown about every modern military plane that's ever been made.

A big part of the appeal of flying is intellectual, which I couldn't foresee when I was five. We've taken metal and engineered it into an airfoil and been able to accelerate it fast enough to where it creates lift and vaults 500,000 pounds of machinery into the sky. How cool is that? It's amazing what we're doing with air, how we're able to manipulate and compress this invisible stuff we breathe. Beyond the physics and engineering, you have to know about different mechanical systems—hydraulics, generators, engines, and avionics. Add to that meteorology, aerodynamics, the rules of flying, the rules of engagement, dogfighting, instruction—all of it engages the mind at a very high level.

The greatest appeal is harder to describe, but this I did glimpse when I was five. If you could fly with me in a fighter and do split-S turns, aileron rolls, scream across the sky upside down, you'd get it. If you could fly a hundred feet above the desert at six-hundred-plus miles per hour—at a speed and altitude only a split second from disaster—you'd get it. If you could experience the thrill of solving geometry that's always changing and find yourself locked on to an opponent with your fangs bared, ready for the kill, you'd get it. And if you could experience just once the joy of cloud chasing, you'd really understand.

Imagine a column of cloud that rises to fifty thousand feet and you fly slow aileron rolls around it, kissing its edge with the tips of your plane, seducing it, gently touching it. It's there only for you to play with. It's very serene. When you drop into the clouds you experience this tremendous rush of speed, like they've suddenly given you life. You're skimming along this ephemeral barrier between heaven and earth and you're overwhelmed by this total sense of freedom and joy, like you belong to both worlds at the same time but are beholden to neither. Like heaven on earth. Totally free. It's the only way I can describe it.

Once you experience that kind of freedom, it becomes a lifestyle. If I know I'm flying that day, I wake up with an incredible sense of excitement and anticipation. And if I'm not flying that day, I wake up just as excited because I know I'll be trying to go after that rush I get when I'm in the air. I've traveled all over the world—surfed in Hawaii, Costa Rica, South America, trekked in Antarctica, hiked the Italian Alps, motorcycled across Thailand. My home sees very little of me.

The cost of this freedom is women and relationships. It's hard to fit romance into the mix. Not that I haven't tried. I got married when I was in the air force, just after my mother passed away, and my wife couldn't wait for me to get out. After eight years, when my commitment was up, I had to make a decision: either I signed on for another four years, in which case I planned to apply to NASA, or I left. My wife thought it crucial to the survival of our marriage that I leave the military, so we moved to Seattle, where I found a job flying a corporate Lear jet. Thrillwise, I expected this to be a significant demotion, but the job turned out to have a fabulous upside. The businessmen I was working for had bought an F-5B, a two-seat supersonic fighter still used as a frontline fighter by many countries. This was the closest I could get to Edwards-style flying in the civilian sector.

Unfortunately, after giving up my chance to join NASA I found that it wasn't the air force my wife didn't like but being married to a pilot. I was always on my way to some exotic place, or at the exotic place, or coming back from it. But never home. She left because my first love wasn't her. It was flying.

I love to be with women, maybe even more so now than when I was younger. I want to settle down, have a child, a monogamous relationship, but I so love what I do. My passion for flying has nothing to do with money or power, which is why a lot of guys love their jobs. It has to do with freedom. I don't know why every man wouldn't want to be a pilot. I fly two weeks a month and am free to chase thrills around the globe the other two. I'd love to be with a woman who could live that life right next to me, but I haven't found her yet.

But honestly, flying is also a transcendent experience, and I've never had that with another human being, who is far more complex and unpredictable than an airplane. Flying and sex are both arousing, but when it comes to intimate human experience, I'm not in control and that's probably why I find it uncomfortable. I want the unknown, I like not being in control a little bit, but I like being in control a whole lot more. I've had powerful experiences in airplanes, been very close to death. I was in the Gulf War from the beginning to the end. I got pumped on adrenaline every day. A woman can't take me to that spot, she can't give me the ultimate, at least every time. I know I should be able to get to that place with her, but I haven't figured out how yet.

Even so, I couldn't ask for a better life. I feel like there's somebody watching after me. I don't know if it's my mom, my dad, my grandmother—I'm not sure who or what it is. I've felt its presence in the airplane—once, critically, when I was instructing a fighter over Edwards AFB. We were flying heavy, with extra fuel in a center-line gas tank under the belly of the jet. At around eight thousand feet the student asked to do an aileron roll. I said okay, we had enough altitude for a quick roll, and bent over in the cockpit to change radio frequencies. When I looked up, we were headed straight down. He had failed to roll the aircraft fast enough so that when we were inverted, the nose dropped and the airplane headed straight to the ground. I looked at the altimeter and saw we were seriously lacking the altitude needed to pull out. You normally need ten thousand feet to pull out of a dive like that. We had six thousand feet. I thought, This isn't good, and started to prepare for ejection.

In a crisis, and I've been in a few, I experience temporal distortion—time slows way, way down for me. I pushed the throttle to afterburner—it was counterintuitive to accelerate as we were heading to the ground, but I decided we needed speed to pull out. As we were gaining air speed I was taking a little bit out of the vertical, trying to pull the jet out of this terminal dive. The altimeter was spinning down, I kept pulling on my stick, then relaxing as the airplane started to buffet and shake. Meanwhile, the student was grabbing his ejection handles waiting for the final signal from me to bail out. I couldn't let go of the stick to grab my own ejection handles and continue to take little bites out of the vertical. Finally the airplane settled down in the horizontal. I swear there was an angel working there with us, giving us a little push from the ground. We pulled out at five hundred feet while going six thousand feet per minute. We were a split second—well, five, anyway—from a crash.

I felt the same thing once, a little push, when I was surfing a ten-foot wave in Costa Rica, wiped out, and was surely on my way to drowning. Again I felt this little boost—it could have all been in my mind—a little push to the surface, and the next thing I knew, I was breathing air. I felt it again on a test mission when I was the photo chase following an F-16. On that flight, things went terribly wrong, we took a lot of negative G's—the F-16 pushed too far. My aircraft couldn't take it—our bodies couldn't take it—and my copilot passed out. My tail just barely cleared the belly of the F-16 as its exhaust scorched my canopy. We avoided impact by inches but at the cost of overstressing the wing of our plane. But again, I felt just a little nudge out of harm's way that I had nothing to do with. We landed uneventfully, even though we had a bent wing.

Pilots are very superstitious. I carry a Saint Christopher's medal and other medals my mother gave me in my flight suit. I see what's known as pilot's halos all the time. A pilot's halo is caused by the reflection of sunlight off the plane, which creates a little rainbow-colored corona on the clouds below. In the center of this halo is the shadowed outline of the plane. It's a beautiful thing, very cosmic, it follows you as you fly along, and pilots feel blessed and protected when they see it. I see it all the time.

I don't know why I keep getting saved. I don't know why I've been just so incredibly lucky—allowed to live this unfettered but magnificently scripted life I envisioned when I was five. I don't know what my purpose is. But I have to think it's to keep flying airplanes. Maybe it's because there's going to be a situation in which I'll be required to save a life. Maybe I've already done it. I don't know.

I do know I was born to fly.

Thoughts for the Road

Ten Questions a Man Should Know the Answers To

Jake Morrissey

1. Do I love you the way I should?
2. Why do I go to work every day?
3. Who made me the man I am?
4. Have I thanked him/her/them?
5. Are my heroes truly worth looking up to?
6. What makes me so angry?
7. What makes me laugh out loud?
8. What makes me cry?
9. How bad are my bad habits?
10. How much of an effort do I make, really?

PART FIVE

DIVERSIONS AND DETOURS

*If I had no duties, and no reference to futu-
rity, I would spend my life driving briskly in a
post-chaise with a pretty woman.*

SAMUEL JOHNSON

HUMOR

What do women really want? They want to be entertained. They want to laugh and smile. That's why they almost universally look for a man with a good sense of humor when scanning the mating universe. A man who can make them laugh puts them at ease socially. Shared laughter also brings them closer to attaining the common feminine raison d'être: connection.

By those standards, Garry Marshall, the creator of some of television's most popular sitcoms and director of such blockbuster movies as Pretty Woman *and* Runaway Bride, *would have to be a major ladies' man. And he is. One lady's man, that is.*

Accustomed to Her Laughter

Garry Marshall

We cannot really love anybody with whom we never laugh.

AGNES REPPLIER

I have been married for thirty-seven years to the same woman and I'd have to say that at least once every day we have laughed. Sometimes we laugh at the same thing. Other times we laugh at different things. Often, I laugh because of something she's said. The other day we were watching a hot, steamy love scene in a movie and my wife said, "You know, sex feels a lot better than it looks." Laughter is the single shared element we value the most because it helped shape the course of our marriage and my career.

When I was growing up in the Bronx during the 1950s I wasn't the best athlete. I wasn't the best-looking boy. And I certainly couldn't throw the hardest punch. I had to figure out another way to set myself apart, so I told jokes. I relied on humor to entertain old friends and make new ones. My specialty was insult jokes: "Eddie is so fat he wore a yellow T-shirt and on the way to school three people tried to hail him as a cab." I made the guys laugh.

However, when I told the guidance counselor at my high school that I wanted to be a comedy writer, he was not amused. He said if I had to pursue a career in writing, it should be in journalism because then I could possibly make a dollar to live on. My parents agreed with him and sent me off to study journalism at Northwestern University.

At college I wrote jokes into all of my articles, even when they were about fires and murders—perhaps especially when they were about fires and murders. Straight news was so depressing and I thought people should laugh instead. During my years at Northwestern the school had several losing sports teams, so I even made sports funny: "Northwestern's football team is so bad that by the time 'The Star-Spangled Banner' is over they're behind by seven points." My professors failed to see the humor in my writing, but my friends didn't. I made the guys laugh.

After college I served in the army and worked at a radio station in Korea. Again, I was able to make the guys laugh (which is not so easy when the audience members are holding guns). So, when I came home from Korea I decided I was finally going to get my chance to write my own material as a stand-up comedian.

As it turned out, my material was better than my delivery. Other comics would come up after my act and ask to buy my jokes. I could make a better living selling them than telling them. I wrote routines for Jack Paar, Joey Bishop, Danny Thomas, and others. One day Joey said, "Do you want to go to Hollywood with me and write for my new TV show?" And I said sure. I'll make the guys laugh and they'll pay me for it.

In my personal life, I had always used humor to win women over. I once dated a woman who wanted to become a teacher and I said to her, "Did you hear the one about the cross-eyed teacher who couldn't control her pupils?" Silly as it was, my approach led to my marriage to my wife, Barbara Sue Wells. I was a hypochondriac and she was a nurse so we hit it off immediately. What clinched our relationship was the night she mentioned a joke she had heard on Jack Paar's *Tonight Show*. He had said, "Traffic was so heavy today that I drove five miles in neutral." I wrote that joke for Jack. She was impressed I wrote it and I was impressed she laughed. We've been together ever since.

In those early days, working as a television comedy writer was a dream career for me until I got a staff position on *The Dick Van Dyke Show* and had to write for Mary Tyler Moore. Suddenly I got stuck. Aside from writing a nightclub act for a transvestite comedian named Christine Jorgensen, I'd never tailored material for a woman before, especially not a woman like Mary. She was so elegant. How could I make her funny?

My wife, like Mary Tyler Moore, was elegant but she could also make me laugh. So I decided that in order to write better jokes for Mary, I had to study my wife. One night I was supposed to drive to Las Vegas for a comedy writing job, but instead I decided to come home and go the next day. When I came through the front door of my house, I bumped smack into a pyramid of Campbell soup cans and knocked them down. My wife came running out of the bedroom.

When I asked her what was going on, she explained, "Whenever you go away I put the cans up so I can hear if a burglar comes in and knocks them down." The soup barricade was her very own homemade alarm system that she used to protect herself and our newborn baby. The next morning I marched into work and gave the entire soup can bit to Mary Tyler Moore. The other writers loved it and so did Mary. She laughed.

A few weeks later when my wife saw her alarm system on *The Dick Van Dyke Show* she said, "How could you? You stole from my life." I tried to explain to her that it wasn't exactly stealing. If I ever did it again, she said, I'd owe her money. So every time she noticed something I wrote about her in a series, I had to pay her $25. Over the next four decades, my wife made quite a bundle. As my price went up, so did hers.

From the time I wrote for Mary, it sparked something inside of me as a writer. Creating comedy for women was more challenging, but also more rewarding than doing it only for men. Until the 1950s the philosophy was that the pretty girl was elegant and the ugly girl was funny. But I started to think that it could be different. Why couldn't the elegant girl be funny? Not many comedy writers in the sixties and seventies cared about writing for women, so I made it my specialty.

I examined the differences between men's and women's humor and decided, *Vive la différence!* After Mary I spent three years writing for Lucille Ball, and then in the 1970s I created *Laverne and Shirley* for my sister Penny Marshall and Cindy Williams. Later I directed comedy films starring Julia Roberts, Goldie Hawn, Bette Midler, Diane Keaton, and others. With each new series or movie, I tried to make the women involved look beautiful and act funny, whether in *Beaches* and *Overboard* or *Pretty Woman* and *Runaway Bride*.

The more I wrote for women, the more I figured out what worked and what didn't. For example, women hate the humor of the Three Stooges and most sexy jokes about bosoms. (Women don't like the Three Stooges because they behave like they are drunk, which is not especially appealing to women. And boob jokes are degrading.) Women like campier humor about daily living and friendship. (Most men only permit friendship jokes during times of war.) I noticed that Lucy was the bridge between men and women. She fell down like the Three Stooges, but she did jokes about her hair and makeup that appealed to women. When I created *Laverne and*

Shirley, I patterned it after Lucy's style of humor and the show was a big hit with both sexes. I now made couples laugh.

Throughout my career as a television writer and movie director, my wife has continued to help me understand the essence of what makes men and women laugh. She demonstrates most often by example—unconscious example—using her special brand of Gracie Allen humor that in our family we have nicknamed "Zeligs," after an incident that happened near the Plaza Hotel.

One day my wife and I were walking by the hotel and I said, "There's *Zelig*." The Woody Allen movie was playing at a theater next door to the hotel and we wanted to see it. Later in the day I overheard my wife tell a friend that we had seen the actor Tom Selleck standing in front of the Plaza. I was startled and said, "Barbara, when did we see Selleck?" She said, "Well, I didn't see him exactly. You did. Remember, you said, 'There's Selleck.'"

Another time, my wife confidentially told a table of people that Rebecca DeMornay was one of her favorite authors. I had to correct her and say, "No. That's Daphne du Maurier. Rebecca starred with Tom Cruise in *Risky Business*. She was a hooker, not an author." That's why we get along: I always know what my wife is talking about.

I can't spend an evening with Barbara unless I have a pad and pencil in my hand. Comic material sails from her mouth and I simply catch it. If I didn't marry her when I did, I might be trapped right now writing jokes for some terminally unknown guy in a smoky New York nightclub. She showed me that women value humor in both sexes because it can make a dull person interesting and mend a fight faster than chocolate or flowers.

My wife taught me how to be funny with women and I've now built an entire career on that knowledge. I still make both men and women laugh, but my specialty is that I help beautiful women be funny. Much to my high school guidance counselor's surprise, I even make a living at it.

✦

Can a woman ever forget the first man who made her laugh and laugh—truly, madly, deeply? Laugh uproariously, in short peals, squeals, and spasms of delight, until aching sides and shortness of breath made you scream, "Stop, no more!" though you hoped he never would.

What a rush of pleasure laughter brings to any relationship, passionate or platonic. Laughter can turn a complete stranger into a companion, a friend into a lover, or, as Garry Marshall points out, a wife into a mistress.

"Laughter is the lightning rod of play, the eroticism of conversation," the writer Eva Hoffman confided, probably because the more a man makes a woman laugh, the quicker the seduction begins.

—SBB

BEAUTY

The question of what men and women look for in each other has enlivened a good many dinner-party conversations. Kindness, generosity, and the ability to be a good parent top both men's and women's wish lists. But beyond that, real differences emerge. Despite women's financial independence, they still highly value a man's status, or at least his potential to achieve it. Men, on the other hand, weigh far more heavily a woman's physical attractiveness than they do her earning power. These preferences have resisted enormous social and cultural change, and seem almost encoded in our genes, regardless of how unpolitically correct they are.

But what, in a man's eyes, constitutes beauty? Scientists have come up with some objective standards. Anatomical and facial symmetry are major determinants of what most people deem attractive. But that leaves a lot of room for personal interpretation, not to mention psychological history. Who we find attractive may be some composite of our mother, first girlfriend, and Madonna. Or, depending on how those relationships turned out, she may be the opposite of our mother, first girlfriend, and Madonna. Novelist Benjamin Cheever decided to explore how he would define female beauty, and was surprised with what he came up with.

Eye of the Beholder

Benjamin Cheever

Barukh attah adonai eloheinu melekh ha olam
shekakhah lo ba olamo.
Praise to You God, our Lord, Ruler of the world,
that such do You have in Your world.

Hebrew prayer to be said at sighting a beautiful woman

The first truly beautiful woman I ever saw was entirely naked. She stepped out of bed, walked into the kitchen of her Manhattan apartment, and ground coffee on a hand mill. While she worked the crank, she kicked her right foot up in the air behind her, as if preparing to score a field goal. I could smell the coffee beans. I could hear the traffic on the street below. Light streamed through the windows.

I was thirty-one years old at the time. And no, this wasn't the first naked woman I'd ever seen. Not even if you exclude my mother. It was simply the first time I'd ever slept with a woman and not felt afterward that I was in her debt.

That same day I saw my second truly beautiful woman. This, too, was in the city of New York. I still don't know her name. A flash of silver caught my eye. She was on the north side of Seventy-ninth Street, heading slowly down the sidewalk toward Riverside Drive. It was spring. Spring in the city.

I grew up in the country. We have spring in the country, too. We have snowdrops and then daffodils, the lawns go emerald. This takes your breath away. In Manhattan we have women in the spring. They knock the wind out of you.

The second truly beautiful woman I ever saw had a fresh face, which she had tilted upward toward the sun. She had a great figure. She also had dreadful taste. She was wearing a tunic of leopard spots, stiletto heels, a skirt so tight it made it difficult for her to walk. The flash of silver caught my eye.

It wasn't silver, actually, but an aluminum walker, which reflected the morning sun. The second beautiful woman I ever saw was helping a much older woman down the street. The young woman was beaming. That's important. Her face was wreathed in smiles. Obligation seemed to having nothing to do with it. What passed between those two was freely given. The woman who might have been nineteen looked handsome. As did the woman who might have been 105. I could hear laughter.

That day I'd stumbled on a secret. It is possible—however difficult this is to imagine—for a gorgeous, sexy woman to also be kind. But you have to be looking. Or willing to look.

This I never would have guessed. Not in a thousand years.

Mothers are women, of course, and we all know that mothers are selfless, nurturing creatures, plump and aproned, dusted with flour. The mother gods stand right at both thresholds of consciousness. Rule out male obstetricians, and female is the first person anybody meets. *Mother* is often the last word we call out before dying. "Oh, mama!" GIs used to shout when they'd received a mortal hurt.

For most of my life this sort of woman was not the type I was interested in. A home-cooked meal is a glorious event, but by the time I was ten I could feed myself.

The women I was interested in weren't known to cook. Or engage in any other even mildly altruistic activity. Many of the women I was interested in were both delicate and mean. They didn't like to get wet. They didn't like to get dirty. They didn't want their hair mussed. Especially, they didn't want to be touched.

Up until the morning of the coffee mill, I had divided the world into two camps: the men, who were trustworthy. The women, who were not trustworthy.

Once I began to use deodorant, my contacts with single members of the opposite sex could have been completely understood in terms of an undeclared game of capture the flag.

Not that we ever mentioned the contest. The woman and I would speak about colleagues, literature, even the weather. The more beautiful the woman, the more ridiculous the conversation. This is not just because many beautiful women are not talented conversationalists either. In order to think clearly, I need blood in my head. When I was talking with a beautiful woman, most of my blood was elsewhere. The whole time we talked, I was trying to figure out how I could get at her flag, and she was trying to figure out how to put me in prison.

Looking back now I can see that women probably weren't all as treacherous as I took them to be. You get what you look for. My dislike of the opposite sex had a good deal to do with the intensity of my longing. The men I knew didn't have anything I craved. And if they did have something I wanted—take, for instance, a chain saw—they'd often lend it out. Whereas most women had something I wanted desperately. And most women wouldn't share.

Plus, they were tricky about it. They said yes, when they meant no. They said no when they meant yes. They were always looking around for a better deal. There were fickle men, of course. There were men who wouldn't lend you their chain saw. But once I'd figured this out about a man, I'd avoid him.

One of the first serious girlfriends I had stood me up at the high school prom. She got a better offer. She spent that weekend out with a college man. Now, if she had been a man, I never would have spoken with him again. This girl, I married.

When it came to men, I looked for sterling character or, barring that, at least an interesting story. When it came to women, it was beauty I wanted. And my idea of beauty was a very limited one.

I think the camera had something to do with this. Many of the women I saw were in pictures. When I read the newspapers, I saw them in lingerie ads. In magazines they wore tight sweaters or else poured out of bathing suits.

I'm talking mainstream magazines here. Not *Playboy,* which I read for the short stories.

It was with the creatures from still photographs that I peopled my imagination. Out in the world, I looked for the flesh-and-blood women who reminded me of the imaginary ones.

Fortunately, I was gross enough in my appetites so that when I did actually convince a woman to get undressed, I was still delighted. Other men I knew became so attached to their imaginary lovers that they didn't have a lot of sympathy for the real ones. I had a friend once who told me how shocked he was the first time he'd seen a breast that wasn't in *Playboy.* No airbrush. "You could see veins in it," he told me with real dismay.

I wasn't that foolish, but foolish enough to think that the single most important feature of any woman was how she looked. Not how she acted, but how she looked.

I persisted in this folly, even while the evidence piled up. I got older and so did the women I knew. When you get older, your face isn't an accident anymore. Often it's an accomplishment. You look quickly at the face of a thirty-year-old and you can tell if she's generous or not. You can tell if she reads books.

If she's been disappointed in life from the get-go, you can see it around the mouth. Also, there are lights in the eyes. In some people those lights go out. In others, they burn brighter with time.

Of course there's no scientific proof that you can read a human face. There's also no scientific proof that if somebody looks at the back of your neck for long enough, you know to turn around.

Certainly, you can be mistaken, even fooled by a countenance. You can also be mistaken about the balance in your checking account. The information is there. You have to collect it and then process it correctly.

In order to really judge a face, you need to see it in motion. Here's where the camera comes in again. The camera always shows a face in repose. Models look beautiful in repose. Actresses often do. You see cheekbones, the shape of the nose, the proportions.

What you see on these faces isn't beauty, it's orthodontia, and a lucky role of the genetic die.

What does she look like when she's cut her finger? Horrified is not the correct answer. What does she look like when you've cut your finger? If she's bored, that's not good.

Watch her eyes when the dog pees on the rug. Watch her face after the baby has vomited on the shoulder of her favorite dress. What does that pretty face do when the tire goes flat? When she learns that you've forgotten to fix the spare?

Does she laugh easily? Is there actual mirth in the noise she makes? How much does the income of the joke teller have to do with the quality of her laughter?

It sounds as if I were a Sunday school teacher prodding you to do the right thing, not to be wicked or ever have any fun. But then it's not actually a lot of fun to spend your life pursuing women with wooden heads.

There may not be anything morally wrong with treating females as if they were objects, but unless you're a moron yourself, you're going to be spectacularly bored.

I've been married for nearly twenty years now to the woman who made the coffee. She's my second wife, and who says we don't learn from our mistakes?

I know, I know, there's nothing less compelling than a man who loves his own wife. "The amount of women in London who flirt with their own husbands is perfectly scandalous," says Algernon in Oscar Wilde's *The Importance of Being Earnest.* "It looks so bad. It is simply washing one's clean linen in public."

But here's the good news. I have reason to believe she's not the only one out there. Since I met her, I've met a lot of other women like her. I never would have seen them if I hadn't seen her first. Because of her, I know that there are beautiful women who are also kind. There are women who like their hair mussed. They look great in the rain. There are women who like to be naked.

✦

I believe that, given a choice, a woman would prefer to be told by a man that she's beautiful before he says he loves her. (For my male readers, this secret should help if you're phobic about the L-word.) For in a woman's mind, if she's beautiful, she's assured love. This is, of course, a mass hallucination, for some of the world's great beauties are the loneliest women on the planet.

But to be born a daughter of Eve is to be born blind to the knowledge of your own radiance. The Irish poet W. B. Yeats described this insidious birth defect insightfully, but then for thirty years he adored a woman celebrated for her beauty, and many of his poems read like dispatches from behind the front lines, documenting the destruction of them both because of it.

> To be born a woman is to know—
> Although they do not talk of it in school—
> That we must labour to be beautiful.

It's interesting to note that when Yeats finally married for the first time, after fifty, it was to a woman whose plainness shocked his friends.

Ben Cheever's charming description of what makes a woman truly beautiful in a man's eyes reminds us how powerful love at second sight can be. Artifice has its place on a woman's dressing table, but the truth is that a woman is more beautiful when she doesn't labor, but lusts, laughs, lets her hair down, and lavishes love extravagantly.

319

However, just as a tip, should a woman ask a man, "How do I look?" do not for one moment think that she's soliciting an honest critique of her comeliness. This is a trick question periodically posed by Venus, the goddess of Love, to evaluate a man's appreciation of just how good he has it. In which case, the appropriate reply is "Rarely have you looked more lovely, my darling."

Because, after all, isn't her beauty in the eye of her beholder?

—SBB

THE WEDDING

Someday, I will have to marry my wife again. Why? I didn't do it right the first time. And it's not like all that much was expected of me. Two of our best friends, our witnesses, met us at City Hall, where we all gathered in a faux wedding chapel/chambers before a rent-a-judge who stood before us and fed us our vows. I guess I was a little nervous, for as the rent-a-judge asked me whether I was in it for thick and thin and told me to repeat after him, et cetera, I stared straight into his eyes in the hope of convincing him of my sincerity and good intentions. (Was I protesting too much? Let's not go there.) I was taught you look a person in the eye when you're spoken to. I didn't know that the wedding ceremony is a significant exception to this rule. While I gazed into his eyes, my not-quite-yet wife gazed into my left ear. The marriage has survived, but it comes up.

Weddings aren't designed for men, as Roy Blount, Jr., who has messed up a few himself, attests. They are completely for the benefit of women. If it were otherwise, we'd have to marry the same woman three, four, six times before getting it right. And we'd still probably never hear the end of it.

Still, most of us must take that hike. So here's a proposal: maybe women should just go ahead and have the wedding without us, and we'll show up later at the reception.

The Great Groomal Expo

Roy Blount, Jr.

In olden times sacrifices were made at the altar—a custom which is still continued.

HELEN ROWLAND

I attended a wedding in Washington recently where I had a couple—appropriately enough—matrimonial insights, which in the end canceled each other out.

Wedding and reception were lively and pleasant. Champagne flowed, dancing was rampant, and my researches turned up someone whose role in the drama of matrimonial preparation was one I had not heard of before: "I am the neighbor," she told me with quiet pride, "whose house the bride has been going to, to cry about her dress."

"I thought it was a *nice* dress," I said, and immediately I felt like someone who has just said "I thought it was a *nice* play" to someone who has held Shakespeare's hand through the long, harrowing process of writing and preparing, for this opening night of all nights, *King Lear.*

I did not hear any great new wedding stories, but that's okay. The important thing was that no disasters occurred that would go down in great-wedding-story annals.

No groomsman's failure to pace himself during prenuptial fetes caused him, just after he extended his arm to the bride's grandmother, to topple over backward in the aisle, taking Grandma with him.

No bridesmaid became so caught up in the ceremony, and no groomsman became so inattentive to his role in it, as to join full-voicedly in the first "I will."

322

No stray dog wandered onto the flower-bedecked outdoor altar just before the "I now pronounce you" part and started heaving and making horrible *gakkkk* noises in a protracted effort to throw up parts of the maiden of honor's missing slipper.

The groom when bade to rise did not remain kneeling for several minutes despite strenuous efforts to bring him to.

The reception got nowhere near so dramatically out of hand as one I heard about some years ago, at which the groom's friends, in attempting to kidnap the bride, set off an earnest melee that ranged over most of the bride's parents' home, involved the police about halfway through, and remained unsettled until at length the groom's friends stood up bloodily one by one and recited formal apologies, and then kidnapped the bride anyway.

No brother-in-law of the groom attempted—as I am afraid I did once at the Colonial Country Club in Fort Worth, Texas—to limbo while his sister-in-law was riding on his shoulders. I still regret this incident, but I want to take this occasion to deny, for the record, the allegation that I had forgotten that my sister-in-law was there. *I thought I could do it.* I thought we could do it. And, although she denied it in the emergency room (just a precaution— I tried to tell everyone there was no concussion as soon as she was able, on her second guess, to tell the caterer how many fingers he was holding up), *so did she at the time.*

The groom did not cry.

The only development that was at all untoward, I believe, was that during the reception a great many fine Honduran cigars were distributed. It is probably not a good idea for several dozen people to boogie while waving eight-inch cigars. No one's pretty party outfit burst into outright flames, but it is a good thing for several dresses and jackets that they were black to begin with. And the hall became so dense with smoke that my own lovely dance partner observed, while giving my own *robusto* a wide berth, "This is what happens when *anything* is organized around the groom."

It was that observation that sparked Insight Number One: *Wouldn't it be interesting if an entire wedding were organized around the groom?*

As we know, the traditional duty of the groom at a well-conducted wedding is just to stand there, smile, and bear in mind that this is not about him. If he puts his own interests forward in any way, he is likely to be remembered forever as the one who ruined what should have been the most beautiful day of a woman's life.

That role, if the groom can manage to contain himself long enough, will eventually be filled by someone's uncle. Or, in some cases, brother-in-law.

If the groom is prudent and fortunate enough to stay out of focus for the entire proceedings, he will be spared what happened to a groom on Fifth Avenue in Manhattan many years ago when I happened to be driving down that avenue with my formidable Texas then-grandmother-in-law, whom we shall call Gammy, in the car.

We stopped at an intersection just as an elegantly got-up wedding party was emerging from a church on the corner. They all looked snappily cosmopolitan until Gammy thrust her leonine head through the car window, gave out a loud *Humph,* and then remarked, quite audibly to all in the epithalamic cluster, *"Well, look at the groom!"*

Everyone did look at him. As if for the first time. He even attempted, in pained bemusement, to look at himself. In the rearview mirror, as I drove hurriedly away, I could see a general deflation spreading ineluctably outward from the suddenly, regrettably, centric young man.

"Weak chin," Gammy explained.

Everyone wants everything to be just so for the bride, which puts her under the pressure of a pitcher with a perfect game going in the World Series, but consider the poor groom, the catcher, who will be remembered only if he drops a third strike.

So let us imagine a wedding organized around the groom.

Now we're talking something more along the lines of slow-pitch softball. Get a keg, and invite some friends in, and if we do get hitched sometime during the festivities, and we still remember it the next morning, well, fine; it was meant to be.

Hey, aren't the lines between genders blurring? Today there are probably male strippers at bridal showers, and I wouldn't be surprised to hear that 6.8 percent, say, of contemporary brides have at least one tattoo. So why do weddings have to be so backbreakingly feminine?

It might be objected that groom-centered weddings would eliminate a considerable chunk of the Gross Domestic Product. When I picked up a copy of *Modern Bride* magazine the other day, I thought for a moment I had thrown out my back. Nine hundred and forty-four pages, virtually all of them advertising or uncritical advisories. An article entitled "105 Great Wedding Ideas" ("Moroccan brides are pelted with figs, raisins, and dates," "Float flowers in Pfaltzgraff's Galaxy Collection 'Pillar' candles for drama," "For your Easter wedding, have baby chick soaps in the restrooms, and a marzipan bunny on your cake!") filled five pages that took me twenty minutes to track down amid all the ads for gowns (a line called Nah Nah, which sounds awfully negative, is "available in missy and petite sizes," which surely excludes a lot of gals), Victorian wedding certificates ("Record History as it was meant to be"), and the Kenny Kingston Psychic Hotline ("THE MOST IMPORTANT PHONE CALL YOU WILL EVER MAKE").

Another vital element of the American economy today, I gather from a recent article in *The Washington Post,* is something called the Great Bridal Expo, a traveling show that features booths at which people acquaint prospective couples with attractive new options in not only honeymoons, flatware, goblets, and wedding-planning software, but also plastic surgery. At one booth in Crystal City, Maryland, recently, a 10 percent discount on liposuction for the wedding party was being offered, and at another, according to the *Post* story, "Free computer imaging can instantly show prospective patients how they might look with bag-free eyes or whittled wattles. 'Hi,' a young nurse greets a passing bride. 'What are you interested in? New breasts?' "

Whereas there is no *Modern Groom* magazine. There is no Great Groomal Expo. There is no such word, in fact, as *groomal.*

If weddings *were* organized around grooms, however, appropriate magazines and expos would surely emerge. "Days You Definitely Don't Want to Get Married" might be a useful service piece for the magazine—listing all crucial televised weekend sporting events for the coming year, particularly in June. Groomal expos could be held in conjunction with boat shows. If *groomal* is too dorky to catch on, how about, I don't know, *seminal* or something.

How would a groom's ideal wedding end? Not, I think, with the tossing about of bouquets and rice. On the plane back from D.C., I read an article in the *Washington Times* about an incident in the Civil War. It seems that a troop of federal cavalry were haplessly pursuing Mosby's Rangers, the dashing Confederate horsemen led by John Singleton Mosby, the "Gray Ghost," when word reached the Yanks that one of Mosby's men was to be married that afternoon. Perhaps the Gray Ghost could be nabbed at the wedding! Here, according to the *Times* article, was the denouement.

"At 2 A.M., the federal contingent staggered back into camp, minus four men. Sheepishly, the lieutenant reported that the Union force had arrived half an hour late for the wedding, surprising the noisy Confederates just as they were making their way out the front door of the hotel. In a street skirmish, one federal trooper was killed and three were wounded before Mosby's men disappeared into the night."

Wouldn't that be a groom's ideal wedding finale? You walk out of the church with your bride on your arm, surrounded by your boys, and right off the bat you kick butt in a noisy skirmish!

It was that realization that sparked Insight Number Two:

There is a good reason why weddings are organized entirely around the bride.

COMPANIONS

Different stages of life call for different companions. In extreme youth, you need a guy to head down to the river with you. Not much fun to fish alone. Usually, this pal will move away or go to a different school. When you're a little older, in early high school, your first real best buddy is somebody with whom you play sports and have your first discussions about girls. A few years on, the friendships of late adolescence and early adulthood are intense, intimate, often unpredictable, just like the life you're living. Those that survive the inevitable graduations and marriages and geographical separations often endure for a lifetime. Friendships formed in middle age are a blessing, but rare; there's not enough time to develop a history. And of course there's the buddyhood of marriage.

Occupying a special place in this pantheon of relationships are a series of companions who are ever loyal, always eager to play, and will never move to California or divorce you. They have four feet and a tail, which they tend to wag a lot.

Heartbeat of the Running Dog

Rick Bass

Dogs' lives are too short. Their only fault, really.
A. S. TURNBULL

A month after Ann, my beagle-mix hound, died, I am still paralyzed, unable to read or write, numb to the beauty of autumn. But I also feel an obligation to Colter, my young German shorthaired pointer, to his youthful heart and burning eyes. I want him to see a sage grouse, which I've read about but never hunted—I've heard they seem as large as turkeys when they get up out of the sage. Plus, my old truck isn't going to make it through the winter. So early one afternoon, Colter and I drive down to Missoula, Montana, where I trade the old truck for one that's even older but in better condition. Then we head farther south and east, toward Dillon, where I've heard there's a huge ranch where the public is allowed to hunt for sage grouse.

We arrive in Dillon well after midnight. There's a rodeo in town the next day, so all the hotels are full. I spread my sleeping bag in the back of the truck. It's a cold night, and I try to show Colter how to get in the sleeping bag with me. But this is a thing that is definitely not in his blood, so he spends the night draped across my knees, shivering but never whining, getting up and pacing, teeth chattering, waiting for morning, until settling his bony frame back down across my knees again, where he shivers so hard that the truck rocks. A Texan and a shorthaired pointer. What are we doing this far north?

The sun's slant still has enough bite to burn the frost off quickly the next day. We drive out into the country, find the vast ranch, park on the side of the road, and I wait for a few minutes, savoring the blue sky, my freedom, the health and vigor of my dog, and the scent of sage. A distant line of willows snakes through the prairie, beyond which are foothills. Colter's raring to go, but I want to sit a moment longer, soaking in the autumn and this new place and new pursuit.

I make sure I have everything in my vest: shells, pocketknife, water, lunch. I close the truck and unload Colter, and we set off. I have complete confidence in his nose and know that if there is a sage grouse within our range—roughly twenty miles today, with him covering easily five times that distance—we will find it, and I will shoot at it: There's a one-in-five chance I might hit it.

Some days—probably only a few in my lifetime—I'll go three-for-three, or three-for-four, or four-for-six, but there are longer stretches where I'm oh-for-twelve, or one-for-twenty-five. It averages out to about one in ten, and Colter, bless his wild heart, knows it, and does not back off a bit for knowing it. If anything, he pushes on harder than ever, and I think that it must be a kind of bravery for him to do this, to continue to hunt so hard for such a lousy shot.

There is a kind of joy in bird hunting that is like passing through long stretches of shadowy forest toward patches of sunlight—brief shafts and columns of it through the forest. A huge part of the joy is that the artifice and ego, the veneer, of almost everything else in the world, except for one's family, is revealed nakedly, under only the eye of God and the sky. Pushing hard into a north wind with a big running dog in big country, there is only the moment, only the one bird, or the one cover, somewhere out there in the shadows. There are so many shadows and so little light that when you pass into it, you know it, and the dog knows it.

It's a good thing, I think (though it can't be articulated too well), that dogs can't speak our language. That we have to leave the shadows and step onto some new ground, into a new place, where we learn their language: the language of muscle and desire and the vision of scent; and that they, too, learn this middle ground that exists between dog and man.

We push out onto the prairie: my first steps of any consequence, of doing anything, since Ann died. All of the old clichés of rebirth, or healing, are so time-tested and maddeningly true. On that bright morning after traveling far through the night in a new old truck and stepping out into a new place with my pal, my hunting partner, I feel a return of the senses after a long numbness and confusion. The edges of things seem to have a sharpness they did not possess the day before.

We launch ourselves into the wind, into the vastness of the

country before us, making our way through hard-grazed stubble toward the winding green corridor of a creek and the foothills beyond. The young dog is happy simply to run, casting perfectly, casting hugely, and it relaxes a thing in my heart to watch the grace and ease of his long legs and to see his continuous joy, uninterrupted by even the shadow of a fleeting negative thought.

Newborn, but older, I follow him, ever conscious of my responsibility to participate in his joy. He needs me.

It's hot. We strike the willows and he crosses the creek in a herculean bound—easily fifteen feet—and I wade it to join him. We travel upstream through tall grass and willows. He catches scent and moves in tight to a clump of willows and goes on point, though it is a tentative point, with a bit of a hunched back.

I've seen him staunch on birds a thousand times, and he has never, ever been wrong. Not once, even as a puppy, has his body betrayed him. When his stub tail stops twitching—when it locks— the bird is there; not the scent of where the bird was just a moment ago, but the bird itself, now.

He's not staunch now—not on full point. But such is my grogginess from the month of grief that I want to force things—to force my dog to learn some restraint, even as I, at the age of forty, have been unable to learn it.

"Whoa," I tell him. He whoas, and I kick at the brush, wondering what will emerge. Nothing. "All right," I tell Colter, "get that bird up."

He creeps in, just as he's supposed to—I'm so proud I could burst—and I urge him on.

He catches sight of his unfamiliar quarry and lunges. A porcupine! And I mean to tell you—a big one. Colter yelps, backs away, and then, furious, attacks it again and again—two, three more savage bites. Colter is still attacking as I wade in and pull him off the beast, blood everywhere. An ivory pin cushion obscures the face of my dog. He yelps with pain as he tries to spit out the quills lodged in the roof of his mouth. Every time he barks or pants or yelps, he stabs himself again and again with the mouthful of daggers. No quills in the eyes, thank God, but all around them, so that he looks as if he's wearing a clown's mask.

Like a rookie, an amateur, I am not carrying hemostats. I didn't even bring any on the trip with me. Perhaps I do not deserve this dog. I do have some scissors in the truck, so we head straight back to it. You can't just pull porcupine quills; you've got to snip the ends off to deflate them, then snatch them out. Otherwise, it's like trying to pull fishhooks. It's a Sunday, of course, and we're damn near a hundred miles from a vet.

I ask Colter to heel so I can pet him and soothe him as he trots alongside, but he won't have any of it. As ever, he races out ahead of me, still hunting hard, casting.

I think that's when the next phase of my renewal kicks in: the return of joy.

We spend only two and a half hours pulling quills, though it seems like days. I stop counting near two hundred. Bits and pieces of clipped quills are scattered all over the road, all over the tail-gate/operating table. Quite understandably, Colter doesn't want me tugging on those quills, snipping and then gripping each one, saliva-slippery, with the needle-nose pliers, and jerking as he squalls and yelps like a pack of coyotes—lunges and twists and writhes. He's far too strong for me to restrain and pluck at the same time, so I've got him trussed and haltered and bound, stanchioned every which way. But still he twists and rolls like a pretzel, winding himself (and me with him) into a corkscrew, and then back out again, so that the scene out there under the big sky and the lone prairie, unobserved by the eye of another, is like that of an anaconda wrestling with a hapless deer.

I don't know how it ever ends, but it finally does. I offer Colter some water, but he doesn't want it. I try to entice him to kennel up, but it's no dice: He skitters away, dances out into the field, anxious to go hunting.

To feel the world again, to taste it, to see it, drinking it in like gulps of air. We jump a lot of deer out of the willows, but Colter's learned not to chase them. I'm worried he'll go after another porcupine, demanding a rematch—his heart is larger than his considerable brain—but I know that we have to get back out there and try.

We make it over to the foothills unscathed, and we break even: we find nothing, but nothing finds us. There is one tense moment when, moving hard through the sage, zigging and zagging, Colter springs right over the top of a snarling badger. I'm right behind Colter, and as the badger charges out of his burrow, all I can see are teeth. But I veer hard left, to the north, while the badger's rush carries him south. For a long time afterward, the image of the badger's teeth and rank musculature sticks in my mind, and I begin to wonder if there is some hellish gauntlet, some series of challenges, through which all dogs and hunters must pass to reach the land of sage grouse.

We push on up a dry wash, and the sage makes a rich smell as Colter smashes through it and I crush it with my boots. I want to know what the meat of a bird that feeds on sage tastes like.

We pound those hot hills for an hour, finding no birds, but there are beautiful flecks of turquoise underfoot, some of which I pocket to take back home. I stop often and pour water into my cupped hand for Colter to drink, but as usual, he's too jazzed to drink. He'll drink all the water in his bowl in the motel room tonight, and then, at four A.M., as I'm trying to sleep, he'll get up and lap all the water out of the toilet bowl—but today he doesn't have time for water.

After a long while, we give up on the hills and turn back down toward the flats. There are some abandoned outbuildings a mile or two distant, shimmery in the haze, and I point Colter toward them without a word. He reaches the creek, dives in, swims in circles, and the autumn light ignites his eyes like gold candles. He grins like a kid as he swims in the deep hole. Then he hauls himself out, ribs tight against the slick skin, shakes once in his goofy, rattling, disjointed hound way—the back half shaking totally independent of the front half—and then he is off again, galloping, fluidity and grace, and for a moment I catch a whiff, an inkling, of how it must feel to be running cool and damp through all that hot, dry air and to be that young and strong.

He makes game near the old homestead—snuffles about, darting this way and that—seeming crazed and frantic, a million pieces of data igniting in his brain. There are grouse scat and downy feathers everywhere; he makes his read and dashes off toward the creek, and I follow. But after hours of walking, I am not ready, I am not alert—I am just out walking rather than hunting. When he goes on point and I move toward him, the birds, too many of them—big as Dallas—flush out ahead of me, and I take too much time choosing one, and I fire twice at a distant, going-away bird, missing both times.

Colter holds staunch. The flock sets down not far away, and we move in. He stops after a few steps, points again—a single is still hidden—and when this one gets up, no excuses, no one could ask for more, I miss by a mile, shooting so far behind the bird that to a casual observer it might seem that I was *trying* to miss. And at the sound of my shots, the rest of the flock gets up again, and this time they fly a long, long way south until we can't see them.

We travel for a long time toward the horizon over which they disappeared, but we do not find them again.

We flee north, to look for sharp-tails, and to draw closer to home and family—as if I have overextended, getting so far from home, not yet having regained my heart's stamina. We stop at a motel in the state capital. It's raining like hell, sleeting, with thunder and lightning, too. We walk down the hallway like tired businessmen—it's after midnight—and I set the alarm for dawn.

As the sun is rising on a clear day, we are up and driving north along the Rocky Mountain Front; the towering reef of mountains rising above us, as if beneath a frozen wave of stone, with us tucked right in there against the base, the only things moving, the only signs of life on that sea.

A distinctive mesa rises out of the prairie all by itself. There is a brightly painted farmhouse at the foot of the mesa, shrouded by a dense oasis of fruit trees. I turn and drive slowly down the gravel lane toward the house. Fierce rooster pheasants run cackling down the drive before darting beneath the fruit trees. Red and golden apples litter the green grass.

A woman appears at the door. She is dressed nicely, as if on her way to some important meeting.

"You must be a bird hunter," she says. "You can probably find some birds over by that silo," she says, pointing across the road. "There are about three hundred acres over there."

I thank her and drive off toward the silo. We launch ourselves into the grass, quartering the wind. We will patrol the perimeters like a combine, then clean up in the middle. Colter will eat the half-section like a giant threshing machine.

He goes straight to the first covey, but he bumps them; or rather, they get up wild. I shoot anyway, so excited am I to hear them chuckling and to see the white undersides of their wings flapping like banners against that blue sky. They are flying high and fast and away and I shoot twice, missing, and Colter runs after them, barking, and bumps more. I shoot at those, even farther out, and miss them, too. Colter becomes unglued—I shot when he did not make a staunch point; I changed the rules on him—and he accelerates, running after those birds and howling.

For a moment, I feel like sitting down and weeping. Instead, I shout, whistle, and wait. Colter comes slinking back, knowing he's done wrong. He also does his trick of pretending to scent game right in my vicinity—snuffling for a moment, feinting, darting—so that for a moment, I can't help but wonder if there's a bird hid-

334

den right under my feet. Only once in maybe a thousand such times has there actually been a bird, but I fall for Colter's trick every time, and my anger fades.

We settle in to the real hunt. Colter casts big, runs big for about ten minutes before making game again, this time moving forward with a strange combination of recklessness and caution that is beautiful to see, especially in a dog so desirous of running with the throttle wide open.

He gets as close as he possibly can—creeps, points—and then the birds must skitter away beneath some tunnel of grass, because he pussyfoots forward again, being careful not to run up over them in his enthusiasm. With my heart beating about two hundred times a minute, I step in to flank him. The birds go up, and I shoot one and it tumbles. Like a pro, Colter still holds until I release him. He bounds over to the bird, mouths its sharp-tail blood, his first ever—the best-eating bird there is, I'm told—and though he does not bring it all the way to me, he comes halfway. I reach down and take it from him and spend a long time letting him know that he is just the most amazing damn animal on Earth.

We repeat the process twice more, so that we have three of the beautiful birds in hand. They seem to bleed more than other grouse, and there are drops of bright red blood stark against their snowy chests. We sit on the roadside and draw the birds; I won't pluck them, but instead will take them back to the valley where I live, to show my family, as if returning with rare and interesting specimens from the deepest Congo.

Though I love to hunt with friends, these moments of grace have come only when Colter and I have been alone in the field, in big country. The visual palate is gold wheat and brown dog, or brown bush and gold dog. The dog is ranging big and steadying into the wind, head up, charging, in perfect casts uninstructed by any trainer and dependent upon the terrain. And the hunter, also strong, is moving steadily forward into that wind, walking briskly. The dog has adjusted his casts to fit the hunter's steady progress.

There is nothing ahead of them but more country—no borders. Everything is behind them: everything. There are two lines of movement—the north-south stride of the hunter and the east-west stitching of the dog—both of them wanting only one thing, a bird, and wanting it so effortlessly and purely that they come the closest they will ever come to shared language. For several minutes they travel across the prairie like that, indistinguishable from each other in heart and desire until finally the scent cone is encountered, and the dog must leave that place-in-time, that striding harmony, and accelerate, supercharged, into his own greater, vaster capability to desire that bird. The hunter feels a supercharge of excitement as well, but much of it comes from the dog. The hunter hurries forward to the completion of things, with the dog dashing and darting now, chasing the bird, running it, trying to capture it as a tornado perhaps tries (in flinging up trees and houses) to capture the soil.

These are the moments you remember after the season is over—not whether you got the bird or not, but the approach—the process, the shadow of the thing, more than the thing itself. It's very strange, very beautiful.

Nothing but prairie, sky, wind. Nothing. You're walking along, keeping up with the heartworks of the dog, and he with yours. Sometimes you laugh out loud at how conjoined the two of you are.

I think that in these moments—these perfect moments—when we are crossing the big fields like that, an observer looking down from a mile or two above—a bird's-eye view—would not believe that we were earthbound. I feel certain that the observer would see the two animals, man and dog, moving steadily across that prairie—one casting and weaving, the other continuing straight ahead—and would believe that they were two birds traveling in some graceful drift to some point, some location, known surely to their hearts.

CARS

Which happy event occurred first in your life—girlfriend or car?
Most of us remember their arriving simultaneously, but, truth to tell,
the car always came first. Given a choice between the ignominy of being
chaperoned by your mother or having no date at all, Saturday night in
front of the television with your kid brother was always preferable.

Perhaps it's because a car represented liberation, status, a new level
of cool, and a guaranteed makeout venue that it continues to occupy
such a lofty position in the hierarchy of our favorite objects for the rest
of our lives. Scratch a guy's new "vehicle" and it's like a fingernail to his
heart. Not by accident or default do men affectionately use the femi-
nine pronoun to refer to the buff and perfectly tuned bundle of horse-
power in the garage. She's runnin' real good now.

Twenty-five years ago, I sold Bill Morris, who went on to write
Motor City *and other novels, a car that was then twenty-five years old.*
He still has it, and it looks better than ever. Recently I observed that
Bill has had a longer relationship with his car—our car—than he's
had with any woman.

Well, yeah, he admitted, he's a bachelor. But he wouldn't exactly
refer to himself as unmarried.

Hers Is a Lush Situation

Bill Morris

*It is a curious fact that the all-male religions have produced
no religious imagery. . . . The great religious art of the world is
deeply involved with the feminine principle.*

KENNETH CLARK

It was love at first sight—not because she was perfect, but because
she was so lush with possibility. The object of a man's love is like
that, always possessing highly specific virtues while emitting a
sense of what she has a chance to become.

In this case she possessed curves that were ample, sometimes
breathtaking, but never vulgar. She sparkled. She turned heads.
She looked like she was in motion even when she was standing still;
and when she moved, she flew. Her skin was bad in spots, a terrible
dark color. But as I say, she was not about perfection, she was about
possibility.

And the price was right. I picked her up for $250.

Even then, during Nixon's second term, that was a steal for a
1954 Buick Century in good running condition. Yes, the uphol-
stery was frayed, the starter sometimes balky, and there were rust
spots sprouting on her atrocious midnight-green paint job. Yet her
charms were undeniable. Her bulging contours, lavish slabs of
chrome, and three fender notches left no doubt that she was from
an earlier era—a time, as John Cheever put it, when New York City
was still filled with a river light and almost everybody wore a hat. It
was different from the time when I bought the car, 1974, when
Americans were getting used to oil embargoes and disco and the
notion that their president was a crook and Detroit was sinking

into its deepest stylistic Sargasso. I think of the seventies and I think of Ricardo Montalban purring about the "rich Corinthian leather" inside that bloodless box, the Chrysler Cordoba.

While I still believe that much of American pop culture from the fifties—music, fashion, architecture, and, especially, cars—was superior to what was to be found twenty, thirty, forty years later, I have come to understand that the Buick's appeal was built on more than mere nostalgia.

I was born in 1952, when my Buick was just a series of sketches and clay models in General Motors' futuristic Tech Center, and I grew up not far from there, in northwest Detroit, where my father had migrated shortly after my birth because Ford Motor Company offered to double what he was making as a journeyman reporter at *The Washington Post.* I don't suppose you had to grow up in Detroit in the fifties and sixties to become so obsessed by a car. But I'm sure it helped. So much of our life was lived in cars back then. Our family's summer vacations were epic voyages in overloaded station wagons, frequently on back roads because interstate highways were not yet universal. A driver's license was the Holy Grail, entry into a world of hamburger stands, lovers' lanes, and drag racing on Woodward Avenue. There were drive-in movies, drive-in banks, even drive-in churches. And why not? Cars were freedom, cars were escape, and they seemed to fall out of the sky. One summer during high school a price war drove gasoline down to nineteen cents a gallon.

So when I saw that midnight-green '54 Buick for the first time in 1974, I saw a chance to say something about who I was, about the time and the place I came from, its peculiarly American exuberance, its swagger, its shameless love of excess. As it turned out, the car did all that. But then it did something altogether unexpected, which is what cars do and why men love them.

That Buick became my muse.

*   *   *

Before she could become my muse, however, she had to become herself. The paint job came first. I chose "Tahiti coral" for the midriff, black for the roof and the side panels below the swooping chrome spear. Other factory colors were tempting—"Condor yellow," "Cherokee red," "Malibu blue"—but I decided nothing was more fifties than pink and black. Next came pleated red vinyl on the tops of the seats and black fabric shot through with silver threads the rest of the way. Then full-moon hubcaps, black carpeting, and a red steering wheel.

This attention to appearance was coupled with a virtual indifference to the car's mechanical workings. Oh, I changed the oil religiously and tuned the engine and performed minor repairs, but I never fancied myself a mechanic. I know nothing about gear ratios and I never learned to love grease the way some men do. This is important because I have known men who are indifferent to cars and men who harbor a deep loathing of cars, but every man I have known who loved a car always loved a specific car for specific reasons, much as he might love a woman for the sound of her laughter or her mind or the way her hair catches the light or the music she makes when she makes love.

A man might love a car for its gonad-tingling power, which he strives tirelessly to maximize. Or it might be its shape, which he strives tirelessly to customize. Or it might be the way the car tells the world he's rich, daring, eccentric, a pimp, a Mexican, or a Republican. In my case, this particular Buick told about the particular world that made us.

Once she'd been returned to her original state I started studying the windshield—and everything changed. It's a wraparound windshield—a "panoramic" windshield in the advertising lingo of the day—and in 1954 it was a radical innovation. As I admired the graceful S curves the doorposts made to accommodate the sweep of the glass, I remembered that my father used to joke that everyone in the car business after 1954 was gripped by an obsession he called "wraparound windshield-itis." Nowhere was the malady more severe than at Ford, which was getting pummeled by General Motors' popular innovations, first the panoramic windshield and then, most spectacularly, the tail fin.

My curiosity about the windshield led me to an issue of *Industrial Design* magazine from the fifties. It stated: "The impact of the panoramic windshield was tremendous, and the whole appearance of the upper structure changed. Whether or not the panoramic windshield improved vision as much as it would appear does not alter the fact that it was a major achievement for automotive stylists and glass manufacturers; and it did more than any other single development to make last year's models out of date overnight."

This was a revelation. This was the first time the Buick taught me something I would be able to put to use. There, in one short paragraph about the windshield, was a whole web of implications about the way America worked in 1954. If the wraparound windshield was a "major achievement for automotive stylists and glass manufacturers," then it was also proof that form was now more important than function. Appearance was all. Whether the windshield improved vision as much as it would appear, *Industrial Design* conceded, was beside the point. (I knew for a fact that it didn't improve the driver's vision at all; it improved the car's appearance, and that was the point.) I kept digging and soon learned that GM's stylists, operating under design czar Harley Earl's edict that cars must be made to look longer and lower, had come up with the wraparound as one way of achieving this goal for the redesigned 1954 models. But the technology for curving glass did not yet exist. So it was made to exist by the Libbey-Owens-Ford glassworks operating under brutal deadline pressures. And as soon as it existed it neatly achieved another of Earl's stated goals: to make cars seem hopelessly out of date as soon as the next year's models rolled into the showroom.

*   *   *

My Buick had begun to reveal its true purpose. It was giving me a way to write about the world that made us. I already knew that America in 1954 was flush with victory, eager for the seductive flash of consumer goods, poised for blastoff. The more I learned about that pivotal year, though, the less it had to do with the stereotype of bland Eisenhower conformity. Rather, I came to see it as a year of bubbling ferment—artistic, political, social, sexual, racial. It was a year that had room not only for the wraparound windshield and the H-bomb, but for everything in between—the first recordings of Elvis Presley, the final defeat of the French in Vietnam, the beginning of the end of school segregation, the censure of Joe McCarthy, the marriage and divorce of Joe DiMaggio and Marilyn Monroe, and the appearance of color television and McDonald's golden arches. Nabokov was finishing *Lolita* and Kerouac was finishing *On the Road*. This rich frenzy formed the backdrop for what would become my first novel, the story of how General Motors managed to conceive, produce, and sell more than half a million Buicks in 1954, including the one I drive to this day. That car managed to insinuate itself into the two novels I've written since, and into the one I'm writing now. It won't leave me alone.

Deborah Allan, writing in *Industrial Design* in the mid-fifties, got my Buick exactly right: "It was not designed to sit on the ground or even roll on the ground; it is perpetually floating on currents that are conveniently built into the design. . . . The heavy bumper helps pull the weight forward; the dip in the body and the chrome spear express how the thrust of the front wheels is dissipated in turbulence toward the rear. . . . [The roof] trails off like a banner in the air. The driver sits in the dead calm at the center of all this motion; hers is a lush situation."

In other words, the car is more than car. It's a five-thousand-pound emblem of impulses that were at work throughout society at the moment it was made—the tireless quest for the new, the triumph of styling over engineering, the dovetailing of fantasy and mass production. As the architectural critic Reyner Banham put it, the car brilliantly captured "the kinship between technology and sex."

So a man's love for a woman and a man's love for a car turn out to have at least one thing in common: when they're genuine, both types of love are always specific, never general. For this reason, I scorn men who collect cars almost as much as I scorn men who collect women. The womanizer does not love women; he loves the narcissistic notion that he is irresistible to them, and when they fail to resist his charms, as often as not, he despises them for it. Similarly, a man who collects a warehouse full of gaudy cars does not do so because he loves them all equally and well. He is most likely indifferent to them *as cars,* much as the womanizer is indifferent to, even contemptuous of, women *as women.*

I had great respect for Jerry Brown when he was governor of California and drove a frumpy Plymouth sedan, while I never felt the slightest tingle of awe or envy for Reggie Jackson when he tooled around in a Ferrari or a Deusenberg or a Corvette. That Plymouth said something worth knowing about Jerry Brown, while all those Deusenbergs and Corvettes told us the one thing we didn't need to be told about Reggie Jackson: that the world was just a mirror where he could gaze upon his own celebrity with boundless self-loathing masquerading as joy.

A harem can be full of female flesh or it can be full of flashy sheet metal, but it's still a harem, a monument to an incomplete male ego. So keep your warehouse full of exotic cars. Give me a garage, or a car port, or even a shade tree where I can park my '54 Buick out of harm's way and dream of new ways to pamper my muse and make her even more beautiful than she already is. Hers is, indeed, a lush situation.

✦

Cars are to men what shoes are to women. For the wings of imagination that begin to soar when a man is behind the steering wheel are not unlike the flights of fantasy a woman enjoys when her foot sensuously slips into a sole-mate. Remember that and you won't ever have to hide another shoe box in the trunk until he's not looking.

Bill Morris may think that he's written a simple ode to his best babe in this sassy and evocative essay, but for me, he's penned a feminine emancipation proclamation that frees us from our self-imposed tyranny of perfection. Could there be anything more glorious than recognizing that, like Bill Morris's Buick, we are "lush with possibility"?

Read those three words again. Lush. With. Possibility. *Say it slowly aloud, as if the phrase were a foreign language, for it probably is.*

Yours is a lush situation. Now say it in the first-person singular.

I am lush with possibility. *And, baby, you can drive my car.*

—SBB

FANS

Sports are a great training ground for life, we are often told. On the fields and courts and in the gym, a boy learns about discipline, fairness, courage—character. As his interest in a particular game grows, he emulates the sport's icons, particularly the stars of his hometown franchise, and memorizes their "stats." Now living and breathing his game, the boy, all of ten years old, decides he, too, will be a pro. Somewhere in his teens, though, no later than early adulthood, he gives up the dream, his skills having fallen far short of the professional level. Oddly, his allegiance to the local pro team remains resolute, and no matter what else is happening in his life he finds that his spirits and personal pride rise and fall with the successes and failures of the Yankees or Dodgers, the Knicks or Celtics, the Cowboys or Packers. They, and he, are alternately glorious warriors and lazy bums. But he's not even playing. What happened? He morphed, as novelist Jim Shepard did, into a sports fan. But as Shepard himself discovered, fandom, too, can be a great training ground for life.

They Killed Our Fathers and Grand- fathers and Now the Sonsabitches Are Coming for Us

Jim Shepard

I carry from my mother's womb a fanatic's heart.

W. B. Yeats

I have next to my desk a color photograph from an old issue of *Pro Football Weekly*. At the time the photograph was taken, *Pro Football Weekly* was not what one would call a high-quality magazine. None of its images was really suitable for framing. The photo in question is raggedly mounted, and in any event not the sort that would make the cover of *Sports Illustrated*. It shows Frank Pitts, Kansas City Chief wide receiver, and Paul Krause, Minnesota Viking free safety, after a tackle. They're both on their rear ends, starting to get up. They're leaning into each other a little, for leverage. They look like two boys who aren't really friends together in a sandbox. The image is from 1970. I write this some three decades later.

The photograph is as eloquent about me then as it is about me now. I framed it soon after I first saw it, to commemorate, apparently, one of the bitterest and most sorrowful moments of my life up to that point. And I still have it by my desk, some thirty years later. Over those three decades, there have been, however rare, God knows, positive events, even highlights in the Minnesota Vikings history. Yet that's the image that I framed, and that's the image to which, during my working day, my eyes continue to return.

On January 11, 1970, late in the first half of Super Bowl IV, the underdog Kansas City Chiefs, who'd been chipping away at my mental health for about an hour and a half with a steady stream of field goals, finally broke the game open with a sucker play—a trap, designed to take advantage of the other team's growing desperation and defensive aggressiveness—and scored a touchdown, thereby escalating the score from a deeply worrisome 9–0 to an absolutely catastrophic 16–0.

The first half ended. The halftime show began. I left the television in a mental state that only Thomas Hardy or Malcolm Lowry could describe. I wandered the house. I was beside myself. I was thirteen years old.

I'd been following the Minnesota Vikings for a year. I'd watched them lose to the Baltimore Colts the season before, upset but only dimly aware of what I was letting myself in for over the next thirty years. Leading up to the Super Bowl, the following season had been a joyride. Crushing victories. Lopsided scores. Stirring playoff wins. (In the first round they stormed back from a 17–7 halftime deficit against the other colossus of the league, the Los Angeles Rams, and then hung on to win when their All-Pro defensive end, Carl Eller, sacked the Rams' quarterback for a safety, and their All-Pro defensive tackle, Alan Page, intercepted a last-second pass.)

I'd had all sorts of uneasy premonitions before the game. All of them seemed confirmed during the player introductions with the visual shock of seeing the Vikings stream onto the field in their white "away" uniforms. Up until that point, because of their infrequent appearances on television, I'd never seen them play in their road uniforms. Their home purple, for me the nearly visceral symbol of their dominance, was gone.

The second half began. Outside my bedroom, on the second-floor landing, I could hear the announcers gearing up for the kickoff. Time was slipping away, along with the Vikings season, and I was going to have to witness it all. I had to do something.

I threw myself down the stairs.

My father and brother left the television and rushed into the hallway to see what had happened. Such was the state of my commitment to the Minnesota Vikings that they didn't have to ask whether the fall had been an accident.

My feet were in the air. My shoulder was on the bottom riser and my head was between the riser and the leg of a rolltop desk. I stood up with my knee bleeding, both elbows skinned, and a piercing pain in my lower back.

Exasperated and frightened, my father, after some ineffectual scolding, followed me back to the television. He suggested turning it off. That idea didn't fly. While I sat there dazed, arching my spine against the pain, the Vikings started running the ball with some success. They made a first down. They made a string of first downs. They marched the length of the field, for the first time, and scored. It was now 16–7.

There was, I now saw, a direct linkage: if I threw myself down the stairs, they would score. I got up, playing with pain for the sake of the team, and left the room. My father and brother assumed I was getting something from the kitchen, since there didn't seem particular cause to worry after a Vikings score. I threw myself down the stairs again.

As far as my family was concerned, this was going too far. I was allowed back into the television room but prevented from returning to the stairs. My second tumble, meanwhile, had apparently had no effect on the Vikings' intensity. One of their cornerbacks pinched a nerve covering a simple out pattern, and the rest of the second half was like a slow-motion execution. The game ended with me lying on the floor in front of the television and the score 23–7.

The colors of the photograph, taken late in the game, are muted. The gloom captures the mood I remember viscerally, thirty years later, from the second half of that greased slide of a loss. It was late in the third quarter. The Vikings, who that year won largely by dominating defensively, were confused and tentative. Their expressions were bewildered but game: the expressions of professionals who'd expected another outcome but saw where this was headed. Paul Krause wears that expression in the photograph. He's just tackled Pitts after yet another end-around has produced yet another demoralizing first down, and what's going on behind his eyes is a formulation that Sartre would have recognized: *Okay. So. That's the way its going to be, then.*

In other words, he's carrying himself well, in a difficult situation. The Vikings often did. I almost never did, watching them. They lost one playoff game on Christmas Day. They lost another on a Hail Mary miracle pass on the game's last play. In the latter case, their quarterback's father, watching at home, had a heart attack and died. They've played wonderful first halves and been annihilated in the second; they've played miserable first halves and mounted heroic but insufficient comebacks. They've lost countless playoff games, three NFC championships, and four Super Bowls. The one thing that's been consistent over the last thirty years is that their seasons have ended with a loss.

The Vikings over the last thirty years have been an encyclopedic workshop on losing—the cosmos taking me by the hand and murmuring, Here are all the ways of getting beat. And here are all the ways of getting through it. Learning about losing, after all, is not a bad way to begin learning about loss. And as many before me have pointed out, loss is a seminar in which, sooner or later, we're all going to be enrolled.

That's the high-minded explanation for my undying devotion. But of course, the lunacy of being such a fan is not simply a matter of gaining instruction on the subject of losing. There's also something more dysfunctional, and pitiable, however necessary, going on. Being a rabid fan, as we're joltingly reminded whenever we catch a glimpse of face-painted, bare-chested yahoos brawling in the bleachers, is not all about leading oneself toward maturity.

Being miserable about the Vikings over the years helped me avoid spending time on—and perhaps coming to terms with—more serious issues. It was also a way, almost certainly, of focusing or venting more inchoate and possibly dangerous if articulated dissatisfactions. It was also then, probably, a way of punishing myself for the sins of omission outlined above. (I was, after all, raised a Catholic.) Even the most rabid adult fan knows on some level that his behavior is silly. And even the most self-conscious and rational fan knows that what he's doing, in a deeply pleasurable and shameful way, is refusing to sort through and prioritize impulses toward maturity and impulses toward childishness.

At the heart of the irrationality here is the simple fact that while both the pain and the pleasure are intense, there's always more pain, and it's always more intense. I don't enjoy the pain—I never have—and yet I put myself through it. Which suggests that in some way I think I deserve it.

Even at the top of the stairs that first Super Bowl Sunday, I knew that if I was playing with pain for the sake of the team, a kind of inverse was also true: my family was playing with pain for the sake of me. They worried about my obsession, and it made their lives miserable every Sunday, but they gamely soldiered on, respecting my need to watch. Was this only about football? they asked themselves. How could it be only about football?

I'm not still thirteen years old, but I am, by profession, a fiction writer. I wander around in made-up worlds. I muck around trying to imagine, and retrieve, moments of pain and loss and reconciliation. That self-mortification is both high-minded and foolish. Right next to my desk, then, is a little touchstone of agony—immature agony, but agony nonetheless—to give me, should I need it, that shove in the right direction. Or at least in the direction my favorite team has always gone.

My loved ones have continued to consider my condition an

affliction, and treat it like a drinking problem that recurs once a week for four months a year. They hold out the hope that I'll outgrow it—unlikely at this point—or that perhaps the team will transform itself so dramatically (the Albuquerque Vikings?) that even I will register the arbitrariness of my loyalty and drift away. But over the past few years there are ominous signs to the contrary. In a recent season, the Vikings became an offensive juggernaut and went 15–1 over the campaign, raising the hopes of even the most determinedly pessimistic of their fans. But if history teaches us anything, it's that one cannot be as creatively pessimistic as the situation warrants when it comes to the Vikings. Their season ended ignominiously when their kicker, who two weeks earlier had become the first kicker in NFL history to go through the entire season without missing a field goal or extra point, missed a chip shot that would have won the game. They became the first team to go 15–1 and not win the Super Bowl. The following year, they lost in the first round of the playoffs.

I've often been asked: In the event of a Super Bowl win—a season that actually ended with a victory—would I feel a euphoria to match the devastation I feel after a loss? It's a question that doesn't require an answer. As a Vikings fan, I'll probably never find out.

My eight-year-old son, when asked what he wanted for Christmas last year, led off his list with a request for a Vikings helmet. He got one, of course, a children's version. Every so often I look at it and think, What could be a more diabolic product for children?

At such times I flash on an anecdote related by Peter Gammons in his coverage of the 1986 World Series between the Boston Red Sox and the New York Mets. Gammons recounted watching the Red Sox's staggering collapse in Game Six (remember Bill Buckner?) with a group of lifelong fanatics, one of whom, streaming tears, cried out, "They killed our grandfathers and our fathers and now the sonsabitches are coming for us."

Well, yes. But even worse: we keep inviting them in.

HUNTING

Unless you stalk prey for a living, as Tony Dyer has done for much of his life, it may be difficult to understand the atavistic attraction of the hunt. In fact, though, men still hunt every day—if only for their weekly bonus. The tracking and survival skills we learned eons ago on the savannah may not be so clearly relevant to our safe and bountiful suburban lives, but the primal instincts that underlie them are ever with us, and ever will be.

Tony, who was born into a pioneer farming family in Kenya close to what was then, in 1926, primeval forest, grasps this deeply. He went on his first "short-foot" safari with his father when he was four, accompanied in classic style by three porters. In 1949, he began hunting professionally with the American Museum of Natural History expeditions and later founded Hunters Africa, Ltd. One of the most highly regarded professional hunters in the world, he served as the last president of the East African Professional Hunters' Association. He now lives in the center of a ranching and wildlife area on the northern slopes of Mount Kenya, where he's involved with the aerial and radio monitoring of lion and elephants ranging over about six thousand square miles. An avid conservationist, Dyer still thrills to the hunt—as do all men, albeit in their own modern ways.

Basic Instinct

Anthony Dyer

There is a passion for hunting something deeply implanted in the human breast.

CHARLES DICKENS

You can take the boy out of the country but you cannot take the country out of the boy. That saying very succinctly explains man's love of hunting. For from the beginning we have been countrymen and hunters, every one of us. Over the eons we have evolved into the greatest predators on earth. No creature on land or sea or even in the air is safe from us.

You may polish and refine a man, condition and discipline him, soften and civilize him, blunt or sharpen him, even move him from country to city—but he will still remain subject to the primeval instincts and urges of the hunter.

You may not believe that you still hunt, but give me half a chance to dig around for a while and I will find some remnants of your atavism—somewhere.

We should first investigate the meaning of the word. *Hunt* means to seek, to search, to follow tracks and signs and scent until you find your quarry. More hunts end in failure than those that are rewarded by success.

Although man has many advantages over wild animals both in armament and superior reasoning capacity, wild animals still make fools of men more often than not. The senses of animals are much more acute than ours and they possess a form, or forms, of extrasensory perception, which warns them of danger. There are old, old rules for hunters that advise us never to look directly at, nor to concentrate our thoughts upon, our quarry. For he will know.

Hunting has no direct connection with killing. Antihunters generally think only in terms of the act of killing and are unaware of the long human history and culture of hunting. They seek to deny or denigrate this second basic urge, which is inextricably tied up with man's more urgent one—to procreate. When we were still real countrymen, our ladies sensibly chose the best stalkers among us. They knew that the most successful would keep the larders full.

In olden days all over the world young men were subjected to initiation rituals and "braves tests." Very few ever failed these tests because the penalties were severe. Risks were great and rewards were high. Among the Masai, those who spear a lion single-handedly or meet its charge or hold its tail while their fellows spear it are entitled to wear the lion's mane as a headdress. When they come to a tribal meeting wearing these badges of honor, the ululating maidens rush to them.

Who are the modern hunters? Certainly those striving for a trout in clear water with a tiny fly, or for salmon in a raging river with a larger and more ornate fly—a remarkable form of masochism. Why do they do it? Because it is hunting in its purest form. The wildfowler freezing in the marshes at dawn is as happy and content for as long as his protesting body allows. The hunter who follows elk tracks all over the Rocky Mountains is doing more than tracking—he is obeying his natural instincts. He can visualize the great antlers on the wall of his den, there is special space in his freezer for all that venison, and he is anticipating the feasts ahead. A lot of the pleasure of hunting and fishing is in anticipation, and much of this anticipation is gastronomic.

Detectives are hunters. They use all their old tracking skills together with intuition, observation, patience, and persistence. The fact that they are hunting criminals adds the requisite danger to the hunt.

Fighter pilots are hunters of their fellow men and are held in the thrall of the chase. The fact that they are risking their lives is accepted with pride. It would not really be hunting otherwise.

Investment bankers and market traders are hunters. Their daily hunt begins in the Tokyo stock market and ends with the closing of the New York Stock Exchange. It is a long day and they are on the trail all the time. They are hunting anyone who is less alert or slower off the mark. They move in for the financial kill with the ruthlessness of a stalking cat. Then in the evening they go back to their dens and brag about their coups to their mates.

Even modern conservationists are hunters. In the area where I live there are about forty wild animals carrying radio collars on strong belts around their necks. Elephant, lion, leopard, and even hyena are monitored by us so that we can learn more about their movements. Tranquilizing these animals with a dart fired from a pneumatic gun is hunting of the highest order. We have to find them at regular intervals, usually from an airplane with a special scanning receiver that's tuned to each animal's specific frequency. We are searching over an area of up to six thousand square miles. When you first hear the *pip, pip, pip* of their signals, you instantly savor the thrill of the hunt.

After the hunt there are the memories. Ernest Hemingway made much of the "moment of truth" in his descriptions of being face-to-face with large and dangerous animals. Such memories remain vivid and warm in later years.

Come and join me in a hunt for a lone bull buffalo that has been acting cantankerous toward the herdsmen on our ranch to the north of Mount Kenya. This is always a worry for us: five men have been killed by buffalo or elephant around here in the last few years.

We will not tell you of the three days of fruitless hunting that have been, if nothing else, an excellent preparation for today. You are fitter than when you arrived here and we have had ample time to talk about many things.

The cape buffalo of Africa is the finest sportsman's quarry on earth. He makes full use of his keen senses of sight, hearing, and smell. He is brave and cunning and determined. If you wound him and follow him into thick bush, he will ambush you and charge you and quite possibly kill you. I have lost several friends this way and have escaped myself—after being well gored—only by miraculous providence. He threw me so far that he lost me for a moment. Just where I fell there was a tall termite mound that enabled me to climb a tree, to which I clung, bleeding, until I was rescued by my men. They had to kill the old bull, who was trying to get up the tree. Had we been alone he would have waited at the foot of the tree until he died or I fell. It is only in recent years that I have shed the arrogance of youth and come to realize that I owe my life to the termites that built that colossus in that exact place.

You, I, and George, my Turkana tracker, start our hunt before dawn. The buffalo usually drinks in the evening. Then he climbs back up five hundred feet of steep hillside and over the top into the next valley, where there are many thickets of bush, and sleeps for the day. We hope to pick up his tracks over the brow of the hill, where there should be some dew on the grass that will make the tracks visible. Sunrise is beautiful and soon the snow on Mount Kenya is pink for a rare moment. Such sights are the rewards of the early morning hunter. There are other rewards, too, for we see four mountain reedbuck, which I have not seen for a long time.

Finally we find the tracks we are looking for. The line they take poses a problem, for I know that the wind will soon change and the buffalo will be downwind of us. We must walk a long semicircle around the back of the area where we hope to find the bull asleep in one of his several known "hotels." These hotels are carefully chosen shady arbors where he sleeps through the heat of the day.

By the time we are in position to start exploring the buffalo hotel chain, we have been walking for over two hours. We approach each patch of bush as quietly as possible and with the wind in our faces. The first three thickets have hidden no buffalo, although in one we have found evidence that he had slept there the day before. This gave us a little charge of adrenaline. Adrenaline is an excellent but addictive drug. I can get a jolt of it by merely scenting fresh elephant droppings. This charge is not limited to big and dangerous animals. I get just as much excitement stalking a guinea fowl for the pot.

Such is the magic of hunting.

The most promising thicket is still ahead. When we get close to it George hears the *tsick, tsick, tsick* of the red-billed ox peckers, or tick birds. In the old days, when rhinos were everywhere, these birds gave you advance warning of the presence of a couple of tons of possibly aggressive animal. This warning gave you a moment to find a tree to climb or hide behind when the great animal came charging downwind at you—for he had also been warned by his friendly bird sentries.

I am sure that the birds are with our buffalo. Now the real stalking begins. We cannot afford to make the slightest sound. Any wind shift will betray our presence. The tick birds themselves may go on "tsicking" until their friend gets the message. Even if he does not run off he will stand up and all his senses will be fully alert. We creep along and time seems to stand still. Fatigue is banished by adrenaline.

The old bull must be very close now—not more than thirty yards away, and we can't afford to get much closer or he will in one way or other sense that we are there. I am convinced that an extrasensory perception plays its part.

We have to stoop as low as our backs allow and I decide that it will be easier for us to crawl. So crawl we do.

Ah! Now we can see him lying with his head up and facing slightly away from us. He senses the presence of danger and is on his feet with surprising speed and looking, head held high, straight at us. From our prone position he looks huge and menacing. I am sure he can hear our beating hearts. The benefit of our being so low on the ground is that we do not look like humans, and while we remain still he does not fear us. This is the great difference between man and beast. A human would instantly recognize us as armed humans lying prone on the ground in a place where they had no business. The buffalo just sees low objects.

We cannot move while he looks at us. Then something distracts him and he looks away, giving you a quick chance to aim your rifle. Then he swings around and looks ever more menacing. He takes a step closer.

You line up and I can see you quivering with excitement—so much so that I know you will jerk the trigger and ruin the shot. I touch you on the elbow and you look around and I give you a sign with my fingers to count to ten. You are puzzled for a moment and I mouth the numbers: one, two, three, and on to ten. Finally, you *squeeeeeze* the trigger. The bull rushes off. For a second or two we hear his hooves and then all is quiet.

We discuss the shot in whispers and you are anxious to go forward. My long and painful experience rules otherwise. We must wait until we either hear his death bellow or his fall to the ground. Patience and caution are now essential. To follow straight after a wounded buffalo is rash. His charge is difficult to stop in thick cover.

This is the time for doubts. Was the shot good enough? Was the bullet deflected? How much easier it would be if we could send in a pack of brave dogs. I am thinking with a cold heart of the many times that the buffalo has nearly got me.

Twenty minutes have passed. There has been no sound from our old bull. Now we are coming to our moment of truth—the acid test of our resolution.

There is a good blood trail to follow and his heavy running hooves have left deep tracks. We go forward, you and I, side by side, so neither of us is in the other's line of fire. We are standing upright with our rifles held high and ready. George is close behind and looking everywhere and even sniffing. He is unarmed and has to trust us to shoot well if the buffalo charges.

An hour has passed and it could have been five minutes.

We must be close to him now. I have had too much of this over the years. I won't confess that my nerve is gone but I will concede that there is a kind of stubborn, irrational obstinacy dominating me. If I had any sense I would not even have started this crazy business, let alone invited you to join me as my guest!

George suddenly touches my shoulder and points down and to our right. There, ten yards away, half hidden by branches, we can see the dark form of the buffalo. Which way is it facing? Is it alive or dead?

If there is any doubt, always, always get in another safety shot. You don't need any prompting from me and shoot right in the middle of where it looks biggest. The buff does not move. His days of chasing our herdsmen are over.

As always: I am now sad for the death of any animal, great or small.

What a magnificent old gentleman he is! The tips of his horns are blunt with age and his boss is deep and heavy. I am afraid you cannot have the horn, for there is no sport hunting allowed in Kenya. His horns will join others on the side of the old garage at the ranch headquarters. But his tongue will be on our luncheon table tomorrow and George and his friends will feast on tripe. None of the meat will be wasted and the hide will be cut into a long strip and made into a rope.

There is a heavy feeling of anticlimax and the walk home seems much longer than the walk out.

From now on the three of us are bonded together in a camaraderie that will endure. We have hunted together and our lives have been changed.

ICONS

*As a journalist/raconteur, Harold Evans has had quite a high time.
Forget, for a moment, his recent incarnation as highly civilized writer*
(The American Century) *and editor (publisher of Random House for
much of the nineties). Ignore the fact that he has headed, or even
started, some of the most successful magazines around. The man's true
cowboy spirit is revealed in his bronco-busting newspaper career, which
he began at sixteen in rural England, interrupted for a stint in the
Royal Air Force and a bit of education, then resumed at* The Times *of
London, where he eventually held the top job. For investigative series
on cervical cancer detection and Thalidomide, among others, he
earned a variety of honors, including Campaigning Journalist of the
Year and Editor of the Year.*

*Cowboy—the tough, independent, and honorable manly icon
almost universally admired by men and women—is an appropriate
description of the legendary Evans. Enamored of the American West
since he was a schoolboy, Evans would be thrilled to be considered one.
As a young man, he was awarded a fellowship for travel in the United
States and spent time at the University of Chicago and Stanford—
gateway to the West and the West, respectively. The cowboy journalist,
at last, had found his way home. Let the cowboy ride.*

Some Real Good Men

Harold Evans

Heroing is one of the shortest-lived professions there is.
WILL ROGERS

If those folks Upstairs had not got into some tangle with their computers, I would have been born on a ranch on the high plains of Wyoming instead of a red-bricked terraced house in sooty Manchester, England. My father was convinced he had been destined to be a cowboy. Instead, thanks to that system glitch, he spent his working life on the hot, clanging footplate of an Iron Horse: he was for forty years the driver of a steam locomotive on the London, Midland, and Scotland railways—an engine driver in the precise English nomenclature, an engineer in the inflated American. So instead of big sky and cottonwoods, and box canyons where rustlers or renegade Cheyenne hid out, we had to fashion our dreams against a landscape of cotton mills and the railway tracks we could see from our backyard, ascending bleakly to Oldham through a forest of tall chimneys.

We tried. My nostalgic ear catches now the refrain of "Home on the Range," which Dad puff-cheeked out of his jolly little mouth organ, sitting round our kitchen fireplace just as he would have played it by the prairie campfire under the stars before rolling up in his horse blanket, the saddle for a pillow. Sometimes he sang it sweetly to us and the words lay a trail we could follow through the mesquite and chaparral:

> "Oh, give me a home where the buffalo roam,
> where the deer and the antelope play,

where seldom is heard a discouraging word,
and the skies are not cloudy all day."

Why should the cowboy have so excited the imagination of an
English working stiff? Maybe, trapped in the hierarchy of an English, class-bound society, he responded to the equality and openness
of Western life in the Zane Grey yarns he read. The fraternity of
Riders of the Purple Sage counted more than the go-it-alone style
of Hopalong Cassidy. Then, again, why was Grey published—and
read—in Russia, Spain, and France? Why did so many novelists,
movie directors, historians, artists, and ballad makers transmute a
bowlegged man eating dust on horseback into the American cava-
lier? And why does the legend of America's most popular folk hero
continue to transcend nationality, race, and social culture? It's not
that they all got turned on by the testosterone. The cowboy had
plenty, but he wasn't Rambo on horseback. His high levels of the
manly stuff were filtered by the circumstances of the West. There's
one hint in the lines of "Home on the Range," whose most relevant
words are not zoological but ethical. "Seldom was heard a discouraging word" speaks to bonding and fraternity. My father took it to
heart; I'm glad, because I grew up when boys were not infrequently
beaten by their fathers.

The commonplace to explain the cowboy's popularity is to picture him as a loner who epitomizes the spirit of rugged independence
that made the West, but that is too simple and unhistoric. Certainly,
the pulse beats a little faster at the image of one man and his horse
venturing into an infinity of beauty and danger. Certainly, even in
these speedy days, there is hardly anything to touch the exhilarating
sense of freedom of cantering across the Arizona desert. I am just back
from my annual Walter Mitty fix at a dude ranch, which was as
replenishing as ever—though it also always reinforces the conviction
that I would not have long survived as a cowboy. Trying for seven or
eight minutes to follow one yelling wrangler's chase of a loose steer

was more unnerving than a black-diamond ski run in a whiteout on an iced-up mountain.

The West could not have been settled by the timorous, but it also required a powerful impulse to community. The covered-wagon pioneers did not go it alone; when the Sioux paid a call, the homesteaders survived by circling the wagons. The long cattle drive, where the legend of the cowboy was born, was a communal effort. The cowboy had three critical relationships—with his beloved horse, with the landscape, and with his companions, who all acknowledged, as he did, the unwritten moral precepts known as "the code of the West." It was unambiguous. There were good guys and there were bad guys. Good guys never drew on an unarmed man and used the six-gun only in self-defense. Bad guys shot you in the back. All ranch women were to be treated like mothers. Only bad guys branded cattle they did not know for absolute sure were theirs. A rancher who did not offer the best of everything to a stranger riding through was an outcast. The stranger must leave his gun and belt hanging on the saddle horn before entering the house. Hats could be left on at the dining table unless ladies were present. And nobody asked damn fool questions. A man was what he was, not what he or his family had been. "We take a man here and ask no questions," said an 1880 trail boss. "We know when he throws a saddle on a horse whether he understands his business or not."

Without losing one iota of their individuality, and never missing a chance for a practical joke, cowboys worked good-naturedly together in a hostile environment, bound by the ties of comradeship and more by the code than the written law. Larry McMurtry's *Lonesome Dove* has it right, but let the veteran 1880s Texas rancher Charlie Goodnight speak for the breed: "I wish I could find words to express the trueness, the bravery, the hardihood, the sense of honor, the loyalty to their trust and to each other of the old trail hands. They kept their places around a herd under all circumstances, and if they had to fight they were always ready. I wish I could convey in language the feeling of companionship we had for one another. Despite all that has been said of him, the old-time cowboy is the most misunderstood man on earth. May the flower prosper on his grave and ever bloom, for I can only salute him—in silence."

It makes sense. Small groups of contentious or fearful men could never have succeeded in working together for ninety days to drive 250,000 head of fierce Texas longhorns across the Red River into Indian territory and all the way to Kansas and Missouri. That was how it all began in 1866, when beeves that were $4.50 a head in Texas fetched $40 at a railhead in Kansas and $56 if you forked left for San Francisco.

Spur forward now and catch them before they vanish over the horizon and head into the vast unknown. They are slim young men in their early twenties, superb horsemen with two mounts apiece. There are two riders for every three hundred steers, point men at the front of maybe three miles of cattle, swing men on the peripheries, and drag men in the dust at the back. They'll be in the saddle from dawn until sundown for ninety days, driving an average of one thousand longhorns ten miles a day, hoping that the cook up ahead with his chuck wagon has found a bedding ground with plenty of water and maybe killed a deer to vary the diet of cornmeal, sorghum molasses, and mast-fed bacon. Just when they're daydreaming about having a good time in Abilene, there's a treacherous swollen river to cross with the herd in frenzy. Of one Red River crossing, Andy Adams's *Log of a Cowboy* records that the river was merciless: "for though this crossing had been in use only a year to when we forded, yet five graves, one that was less than ten days made, attested to her disregard for human life." Or there's a thunderstorm that spooks a stampede and they're gone forty miles before they can be turned back, always presuming the cowboy is not unhorsed and trampled to death. Or one night, worst of all, there's a passel of predatory Kiowa in among the horses. There was only one thing a cowboy feared as much as a decent woman, observed

E.C. (Teddy Blue), a cowpuncher in the 1870s and '80s, and that one thing was being set afoot. The man on horseback was a superior being; the cowboy on foot was a lost soul, and the code of the West sanctioned the utmost violence against the horse thief.

It was an egalitarian culture, but with a debonair style. Owen Wister introduces us to the hero in *The Virginian,* a slim young man lounging at ease against a wall: "His broad soft hat was pushed back, a loose-knotted, dull-scarlet handkerchief sagged from his throat, and one casual thumb was hooked in the cartridge belt that slanted across his hips. He had plainly come many miles from somewhere across the vast horizon, as the dust upon him showed." In short, he looked like one of those glamorous Ralph Lauren ads, but there was purpose to the accoutrements. High-heeled boots give a good grip on the stirrups; if you are thrown, the pointed toes mean there is less risk of having a foot caught while the runaway brushes the desert with your spine. The kerchief is a dust filter and neck mask against the sun. The broad Stetson, as my Arizona wrangler put it, is "my umbrella against sun and shade." The leather chaps deflect against cactus thornbrush; the gloves are vital for the flesh-burning roping maneuvers, and the spurs for lightning movement of horse and man. And then there's the "equalizer," the six-gun Colt .45.

The combativeness of the cowboy has been misunderstood. There is hardly a movie that does not feature a saloon slugfest, but the testimony of old-timers is that cowboys did not fight with their fists. Miners, railroad gangs, buffalo hunters did, but the cowboy considered fistfighting on foot demeaning for a white man. Cowpunchers were common men without education, but they set themselves above the riffraff. As Pier La Grange put it, "If God Almighty wanted me to fight like a dog he'd have given me long teeth and claws." As for the six-gun, it was indispensable on the range, against the rattler, the redskin "varmints," the runaway herd, the lamed calf, the horse thief, and it was a neat firecracker on a spree in town. But, as the historians Joe B. Frantz and Julian Ernest Choate,

Jr., testify, the average cowboy was not a gunman, nor did he have a notch in his Colt, and, after the metallic cartridge came in, only strapped two of them. Forty thousand cowboys were spread over the Great Plains in the trail-driving years. "Isolated a good part of the year from outside companionship and convivialities," conclude Frantz and Choate, "he produced his share of one shot and habitual hell-hounds. But as a class he does not deserve the lawless tag." Robert W. Wright, the mayor of Dodge City in part of its heyday, thought cowboys delighted in appearing rougher than they were. "There are less cutthroats and murderers graduated from the cowboy," he wrote, "than from the better class who come from the east for venture of gain."

Of course, there were deadly killers in the West, men like Jesse James, Doc Holliday, Wyatt Earp, "Wild Bill" Hickock, William H. Bonney (Billy the Kid); but save for the Kid (a fourth-rate cowboy who became a first-rate killer), the Boot Hill dispatchers were not cowboys.

The image I prefer to keep intact in my mind is the flashpoint scene my father liked of Owen Wister's Virginian. Abused by the bad guy, Trampas, he replies with laconic lethality: "When you call me that, SMILE."

LIFESTYLE

Boys, on the whole, chase risks and thrills much more than girls do. Occasionally, a boy feels an affinity with a thrill-copping activity at a time when some serious neurological wiring is being laid down. He's imprinted by the experience, and the pleasure center in his brain is coded to seek that thrill again and again. Chasing the high becomes a lifestyle.

That's what happened to Corky Carroll, a five-time U.S. national surfing champion. One day in his extreme youth he found himself in the tube, in the hollow core of a great breaking wave, and knew that he never wanted to leave. He found transcendence. He has lived it ever since.

In the Tube

Corky Carroll

Live all you can; it's a mistake not to. It doesn't much matter what you do in particular, so much as you live *while you are doing it.*

HENRY JAMES

So I'm sitting here, having just passed my half-century mark, filling out tax returns. I have to smile when I come to the box that asks for my occupation. I'm sure even the IRS computer does a double take when it reads that this fifty-year-old geek claims he's a professional surfer. *Does not compute. The guy must be delusional.* I can't really argue against that. Surfing is and has always been my life. I never got over it, never outgrew it, never learned to think of it in a way mature men are supposed to think of their youthful recreational obsessions—as history, in other words. The thrill of being "in the tube" pulses through my veins like an oceanic life force. Some dudes grew up and got real jobs. I couldn't. Miller Lite even got wind of my extreme reluctance to join the adult world and made a commercial with me. In the ad I was supposed to threaten to get a real job, but then after thinking about it for about three seconds let out a resounding "Naaaaaah." Not much creative thinking in that script. It was the fact.

I gotta surf. Being an older, more full-figured, and slower dude than I once was, I can't compete on the pro tour anymore. No problem. I run a surfing school, design boards and surfwear, write about the sport, even sing about it. Surfing is the only life I know, the only one I want.

The best thing that ever happened to me was when my parents decided to move to the beach south of Los Angeles when I was a little kid. My dad was an electrician and my mom was a singer. Neither of them ever learned to swim. But they wisely decided that the beach was a better place to raise a kid than the land-bound Los Angeles suburb. Our house was right on the sand in a shabby little beach colony appropriately named Surfside. Walking, talking, and learning to surf all came at about the same time for me. If I never thanked them for the lifestyle choice they made, I'm doing it now.

I grew up in the ocean, and the ocean became part of me. I could tell what the surf was like each morning by the sound coming in my bedroom window, never even had to open my eyes. I could feel it vibrating my bed and my bones. I knew how big it was, what the tide was doing and the wind. I became an addict, I just had to have it, and as much as I could get. Before school, after school, at night, all day every day when school wasn't in session. I plastered posters and surf photos all over the walls and ceiling in my room. Everything else in my life was secondary, even girls. Surfing came first, period, although my priorities never exactly hurt my chances with the babes.

By the time I was in my early teens I had firmly decided that I would be a professional surfer. I got sponsored when I was thirteen, got free surfboards, wetsuits, clothes, accessories from companies. When I was fourteen, I worked for Hobie Alter, of Hobie Surfboards, but after a couple months he figured out it was better to have me out surfing on one of his boards than being in the factory. So he put me on salary to surf every day. What a job! Then Jantzen sportswear signed me to wear their gear. I was a surfing billboard, a showcase every time I dropped a toe in the water. Getting paid to just go surfing was unheard of back then. But I pulled it off. I opened the doors for endorsements and pro contracts for surfers, and today's top guys make several million dollars a year. But do they ever thank me? Of course not.

It's not like my passion is unique, though. There are zillions of surf addicts out there. We all have our different levels of commitment, but we are all users. It's not just something to do—that something being the most joy-producing activity I know—but a way of life to many people around the world. It's a living art form, really. You find the same sort of thing with skiers—the fabled "ski bum." But that isn't really the right description because very few are really bums. They find a way to spend their lives doing this thing they love, this thing they *have* to do, and supporting themselves at the same time. Some artists and musicians are in the same club. They feel a compulsion that cannot be denied. Anti-nine-to-fivers for sure. Surfers have it the worst.

For us, the charm has to do with the combination of this relaxed lifestyle and, conversely, the extreme thrill factor of the ride. The relaxed lifestyle—no real job—speaks for itself. The intensity of the thrill factor directly correlates with your desire to get "tubed." It's like sex. No matter how many times you get it you still want more. The craving is as deep as bone marrow. Oh, it can be calmed for a time, like right after an all-day screaming-hot session in perfect waves. But the next morning it's right there again. *Boing!* Surf erection! Want more. Need more. Need more now. Get more now. Gimme more.

Getting tubed is the art of riding inside of a breaking wave, deep in the hollow part behind the curtain of water that descends as the wave breaks. In places of the world that have waves that peel off in one direction or the other you will find surfers. This can be anywhere from some sandbar off Long Island to a dangerous reef near a remote South Pacific atoll. The more perfectly the waves form and peel off, the more desirable the wave is. It has been said that surfers are always searching out the perfect wave. They will go to the farthest ends of the earth to find it, too. Zillion-hour plane rides followed by days on a bus and fifteen-hour hikes through tiger- and snake-infested jungles just to get to the one dude who has the boat that will take you there and drop you off. You just don't get that kind of commitment from bowlers.

Most surfers will tell you, though, that the ultimate tube ride would be found on the north shore of Oahu, at a spot they call the Banzai Pipeline. The Pipeline is one of the world's most dangerous waves. It has an extremely shallow lava rock and coral bottom. Huge swells generated by storms in the North Pacific come marching out of very deep water and suddenly hit the shallow reef, pitching out into fantastically dramatic and hollow tubes. Waves five and six times a person's height will sometimes break in as little as three to five feet of water. All this takes place remarkably close to shore, making Pipeline one of the best to watch and most photographed surfing spots anywhere. You can actually hear dudes screaming as they are gettin' the ax. It's gnarly. A fall almost certainly means hard contact with the bottom. You're lucky if you get away with some nasty scratches and coral cuts. Broken bones, and broken surfboards, are normal, daily fare. Head-first can mean a broken neck. The extreme danger is part of the vibe of riding the place. The terror part. Death is always hovering somewhere nearby.

The object is somehow to make it down the face of the wave as it is beginning to throw out. This alone is an extreme challenge as the wave is very steep and fast. Once you're at the bottom, the ideal thing is to time it so that you turn down the wall of the wave and pull inside the tube just as it throws over and peels off down the reef. As you climb into the slot it seems that everything goes into a sort of slow-motion mode. The sound is mesmerizing, like being behind an enormous waterfall that's inside a tunnel. Sort of a massive roar with some echo and delay added to the mix. And you're straining with every fiber in your body to surf through this thing and come out the other end. It would be similar to the feeling that you would have if you were in a car and racing a screaming train to the crossing and it was pretty much a dead heat. It is both terrifying and thrilling at the same time. If you are really good, and have the nerve and experience, your concentration and focus will win out over the fear and you might make it out the end. And when you do, it is a real adrenaline rush. Talk about being alive. You are. And some of those who let the fear take over aren't. Pipeline can and will kill ya. Just like that big ol' train coming down the tracks.

Of course, not everybody goes for the really big tubes. It is still a thrill getting inside even a little tube at a spot with a sand bottom, particularly for this old dude. And that thrill keeps us comin' back. Makes us not want to have real jobs. Hang out on tropical islands with exotic native babes to keep us busy while we are in between surf sessions. Like I said, it is lifestyle art. I imagine that's why dudes in Cleveland want to wear Hawaiian shirts and dream about being surfers and leading the life. Some just surf for recreation and do other stuff. To really lead the life takes something of a sacrifice—regular income, for instance—although most who do will tell you that it really isn't a sacrifice at all.

I heard the call before I even knew what it was. Some hear it later in life. I just taught a dude sixty-eight years old how to surf. Last I saw of him he was in his camper headed out to Mexico to ride a mile-long wave that is down there. He hoped to meet a couple of tasty señoritas along the way. Told the IRS to drop his refund south of the border.

Thoughts for the Road

Ten Things I Want My Lover/Partner/Wife to Know

Greg Bestick

1. Emotionally, we have to take turns being on top.

2. I can't form words around my feelings as fast as you can.

3. I love you.

4. Don't confuse preoccupation with indifference.

5. Even though I'm paranoid, I really do know you're not out to get me.

6. There are really times when silence is better than talking about it.

7. I know I can go farther with you than without you.

8. I think you are beautiful, no matter what you look like on any given day.

9. Of course, on any given day, you look great.

10. When we get lost in each other, I find myself.

PART SIX

TRUE NORTH

*A man travels the world over in search of
what he needs and returns home to find it.*

GEORGE MOORE

SOULMATE

Who among us cannot remember his first kiss? I had to be coaxed into mine. I was "slow," by the standards of my eighth-grade peers. But as is true with foreplay, it was well worth the wait. I fell hard, real hard. In my rough-and-tumble adolescent world, it was a shock to learn that this innocent bit of intimacy could be so enjoyable. Of course, it was just the beginning, but the imprint from that first romance influenced every subsequent one.

For Terrence Deacon, a distinguished neuroscientist and author of The Symbolic Species, *his first serious high school girlfriend was also just the beginning—of a lifelong love affair. Only in their case, thirty years, a couple of marriages, and several kids interrupted the bond. But now it resumes.*

Boys and men fall hard. And they never forget.

First Love, Again

Terrence Deacon

To see coming toward you the face that will mean an end of oneness is—far more than birth itself—the beginning of life.

HOLLY ROTH

The dark road becomes slick, forcing me to slow down, pay it more heed. It's lined with irregular walls of snow thrown up by the plows, now shaped like a shadowy throng of children lining a road at a parade. As I round the last, quiet corner, my house comes into view, a sentry at the edge of a perfectly flat snow-covered lake.

One light has been left on since morning, a single ember of warmth beckoning the house's lone occupant.

A little more than an hour ago, I had been rocking uncomfortably, half awake, in a too-familiar aluminum cylinder suspended miles above the Atlantic shoreline. My day had centered around presenting a scientific lecture in Washington, D.C., but I was not now thinking of the web of ideas I had spun or the insistent conversations that followed. Instead I was trying to imagine the caricature that those rapt listeners might have unconsciously sketched of me as they followed the path laid down by my words. And I mused at the dissonance that reality hid.

If these hundred attentive faces could only now see this man they'd come from distant cities to hear, could see him shuffle up his snow-covered walk, force open his sticking front door, and enter a partially finished room in this not quite quaint, and for him scarcely affordable, fishing cabin of a home, what would they think? If these same scientists, eager to shake his hand or ask him their long-prepared questions or have him sign their copy of his book, could see his arrival to an empty house, to no word of greeting, to no eyes turned toward the door, what would they say? If they could hear with his ears the awful pause, like that moment at the end of a presentation when the audience isn't sure whether to applaud—if they could *feel* that terrible silence as he hears it, pouring out the open door and filling the night, would they be surprised, confused, or just a little more satisfied with their own quiet lives?

More than halfway through my life, I am now spoken of in intellectual conversations in a dozen nations and have realized some part of the daydream I had formed at eight years of age while memorizing the names of scientists and learning about their discoveries in encyclopedias and textbooks. But perhaps too true to that childhood cartoon vision, this one enviable fragment of my life now stands almost like a cardboard prop on an otherwise empty stage awaiting a new play to take shape and lend it some illusion of solidity.

A couple of years ago I would have opened the front door to a more animate scene—a TV flickering in the corner next to the dark fireplace, faces lit by the glow looking up from across the room and greeting me with questions about my trip. A child might have taken my bag, offered me leftovers, or cleared a space to sit on the couch next to her. Even though my partner in this marriage of more than two decades would offer no welcoming kiss as I entered, no move to make up for time without touch, no sigh that signaled that my arrival was a relief for loneliness—even without these gestures of intimacy, I had no doubt that this was home.

Oasis or mirage? A strangling thirst for companionship compelled me to leave it, and where its dry fountain once stood there are now only scrambling lawyers sifting through the debris—like scavengers recycling the marital corpse. I chose to risk losing all, to risk wounding my loved ones with my sudden excision, to stop acting my part in this play, to gamble on there being something more real, not feigned. To reach for it I had to sacrifice the dream of family that I had nurtured and protected against reality for so long. The death of the dream haunts me continually, particularly at moments like these, when I enter my empty new house. But now a blinking light on the phone catches my attention. Without setting down my bags or removing my coat, I cross the room toward that electronic wishing star and push the button.

"Hi, honey!" comes her velvet greeting, the tone slightly depressed, expressing her disappointment at finding only a recording at the other end. "I've been thinking of you all day today. I am just a little worried. How are you feeling? How did it go? Call me when you get in. Please. I love you, sweetie." I fall back onto the couch with my coat still on, bag on my lap, and I am smiling.

Why did I fly all the way across the country to attend my thirty-year high school reunion? I had avoided all others, and now three decades later, I had inexplicably given in to this curiosity. With adolescence now as remote as the events of a biographical novel, I had no particular reason to reintroduce myself to these long-forgotten minor characters in the story of my life, but somehow I suspected that there was unfinished business waiting from my past. Embarrassed and feeling foolish, I walked anonymously into the rented bar chosen as the meeting place. Around me, I saw only the faces of strangers— unrecognizable after years of subtle change and the decay of memory. After a few greetings and handshakes, I told myself, I would just quietly slip out and spend the remaining hours with my parents, who still lived in the area.

But something intervened to change my mind—and my life. As I reached for a name tag, a distantly familiar voice called my name in a quizzical and hopeful tone. I turned and looked directly into the light of her soft blue eyes—eyes that had seen me once, as no other eyes had seen me, and, I now knew in an instant, like none others had seen me since. It was as though we had parted just yesterday, and the feelings were unchanged, beautiful, timeless. Something told me she was there to see me, and I to see her, and there was nothing and no one else that mattered, not even the other persons we had each become in the intervening years.

It made no sense that this feeling remained so fresh and immediate just under the surface of a forty-eight-year-old shell. I had no illusions that she shared this disorienting experience. And yet, each time I dared to look into her eyes I thought I saw it: a kind of tragic joy, mirroring the strange drunkenness that seemed to overtake me.

We made small talk about our lives and careers, but quickly found ourselves drifting into fond reminiscences. I struggled not to seem too overcome, pretended to be interested in meeting others, tried not to seem too possessive when others came over to talk to her—after all, we were strangers—and yet I found myself scheming like a shy teen to find an excuse to touch her hand. As the evening approached its end I managed a kiss good-bye. I was feckless and clumsy. I offered her a copy of my book, which I had brought along to show others, and which now served a different purpose, to communicate a special message. I wrote a few lame lines of dedication in it—a remembered pun I hadn't thought of since we had parted in college ("simply be you too full"), a pet name I hadn't forgotten (Raisin)—and tried to convince myself that this wouldn't betray my temporary insanity.

Returning that night to my parents' home, I couldn't sleep. Lying there in the dark, impossibly contradictory feelings swirled around me. At some point, I turned on the light and penned a brief poetic note. Many weeks later I would find the courage—or recklessness—to send it back across the country, back across the years. It read, *Three thousand miles for a stolen kiss, bittersweet taste of a lifetime missed.*

I realized that some part of me must have missed her deeply for all these years, because I now felt a painfully familiar loneliness swelling like a tender bruise on my heart. And yet what could I be thinking? How could I have these feelings after only an hour's meeting in thirty years? Months more would pass before the ripples from these emotions would reach shore.

I was a high school senior, full of certainty, hope, hormones, bluster, and shyness. Though I'd had girlfriends before, even my raging libido could not overcome my reticence to push these infatuations to the more intimate, blissful heights I had heard others boasting of in excited whispers. So I came to know my first real love, my high school sweetheart, through a mutual friend who provided each of us with the knowledge that the other was interested. All I clearly remember about our first day was that while we sat at a high school play together, she let me put my arm around her and that at her front door that night we kissed. And it was not just a quick and embarrassed first-date kiss but an unrushed pressure of our lips, a telling hesitation to part, despite the harsh glare of a porch light and the feeling of being watched while making this mutual discovery.

After that kiss, we were together every day. We explored each other thoroughly, mind and body, and yet in such cautious, careful increments we approached sexual intimacy only late that summer. Besides the still-burning images of her perfect young body and my initiation into adulthood in her arms, I remember mostly the mundane magic of just being together: snuggling on her living room couch, our fallen homework in a pile on the floor, with her sister's dated records playing in the background; the idle conversations on the phone in the dark, punctuated with long pauses and forbidden, whispered wishes. Most of all I remember our adventures together—tutoring, baby-sitting, hiking along driftwood-strewn beaches, visiting curious religious cults, engaging in philosophical discussion with groups of friends, sharing intimate train trips and family vacations, and working across from each other on the line in a fish cannery, our unshakable unity marked by the shared fragrance of smoked salmon.

But when you are young and just escaping the tethers of adolescence, the unexplored possibilities that the world offers seem too irresistible not to sample. Logically, the first taste could not possibly be the best. But how could we have known that in our first, simple explorations we had discovered a rare and uncommon synthesis of souls?

We fell apart as effortlessly as we fell together. I can't even remember how it happened. There were no fights, no ultimatums, no tearful good-byes. College life had managed to separate us in a casual and matter-of-fact sort of way. Different cities, different directions, new demands on our time. Though I still recall the sorrow of learning that she was dating someone else, and how I spent weeks composing poems to her that would win her back but that she would never see, I don't remember our last conversation or the moment when we at last embarked on separate lives.

She sits across a small table. We are surprisingly comfortable in our stiff-backed booth, in this bacon-and-eggs cafe on Whidbey

Island. We study each other's smiles, windblown hair, our eyes hesitating as they meet, embarrassed, but unable to turn away. We are like voyeurs peering into each other's open windows, and being seen in return. And what we see is too amazing to believe, too delicate and dangerous to comment on.

We had corresponded only a couple of times since the reunion, in ambiguous, poetic notes, but when I visited the area a few months later to spend the holidays with my family, I arranged to drive over to her house to chat. We delved more deeply into our biographies and what life had now provided. The afternoon turned to night and our casual stories turned to reflections on what might have been. As I stepped out the front door to leave that evening we held hands, and a message neither of us could yet put into words was communicated. We later wrote to each other of these unexpected feelings, and we both tacitly agreed to maintain a safer distance. Still, when I returned two months later for a conference nearby, I couldn't resist the chance to see her again, and arranged to take a ferry to a place where we could share a meal and a quiet walk.

We strolled along the deserted beach that day after breakfast, dodging the ceaselessly undulating blanket of waves and exchanging little stories from our separate lives, like precious gifts. We rested on a great silver driftwood log, and watched seagulls effortlessly soaring over the water. We looked out over the water to distant mountains, and our hands sometimes strayed to rest in contact, but only for a moment. She commented on her surprise at seeing an older man where she half expected to see a teenager. I had forgotten what she once looked like, and only recalled her as she now appeared. I didn't so much see her as her unchanging, pilgrim soul. I took dozens of photos that day with my new digital camera, but somehow the memory chip fell out and at home I found it blank. Our "last" good-byes that day were also impermanent.

I was troubled by a strange new silence and loneliness, and afraid of getting caught up in a sort of dime-store-novel fantasy. I knew that we both had become very different people from the high school sweethearts we once knew. It seemed inconceivable that we could be as compatible now as we were then. Could I trust the judgment of my heart to know fantasy from reality? And anyway, whether I admitted it or not, our separate worlds were bound up in complicated knots—marriages, children, homes, careers. As if these deterrents were not enough to make any unasked questions irrelevant, weren't the thousands of miles and three decades that separated us too vast to be breached in any practical way?

At sunset, looking out over the painted harbor beyond the restaurant that evening, we began to anticipate how quickly this dream together would fade in the harsh light of our other lives. We saw in each other treasures too delicate to reach out for because they were both too fragile and too precariously balanced among countless, even more fragile treasures. Yet something had profoundly changed for both of us. With arms linked tightly together to shield us from the evening breeze we began to share more than life stories. We spoke about the silent desperation of outwardly contented and responsible lives and acknowledged the invisible boundaries that neither of us had dared to cross, but yearned to. We shared the emptinesses, the unfulfilled hopes, the hollows around which our lives had been shaped, and noticed that something had begun to fill these spaces for the first time. To even hint at the existence of these feelings was enough to render them beyond denial.

Thirty years, three thousand miles, and three marriages separated us. How could adolescent love, forgotten and buried so long ago, find itself so easily rekindled in two middle-aged adults? Was it an illusion made real by the magic of nostalgia? Or just an illusion? Our dinner seemed like the last paragraph of a tragic fairy tale that even the waitress could not interrupt without apology. Along with the tears that dared not flow that evening, and with the torrent of hopes and wishes that had to be left unspoken, I felt my old life wash away as effortlessly as a sand castle is swept smooth by the incoming tide.

The illusory solidity of my life had been exposed to me, and I would never again be able to disguise the symptoms of this intense passion, no matter what happened. As I hurtled across the continent overnight, sleeplessly convulsed like a delirious addict in the depths of withdrawal, I realized that I had finally and firmly rejected the anesthetic provided by decades of detachment. I had opened myself up to a love I had forgotten could exist and with it there would come pain and joy, remorse and passion. Nothing would be the same again.

Traveling on the night train, somewhere between Vienna and Frankfurt. In the dark jerky rhythm of a tiny sleeping compartment we cuddle together in half sleep. I try to commit every image of sound and sight and touch to memory in these last hours together before we must fly off separately to opposite coasts of another continent. We have rediscovered life in German hotels and restaurants, on walks through Bavarian streets, aboard a tour boat cruising down the Danube, in Baroque parlors listening to chamber music, in an attic flat in Vienna enjoying breakfasts in the sun on the balcony above the trees of a playground. We have spent barely minutes apart in weeks, turning back every few seconds to touch each other, to grasp hands, to be sure this is real.

But we have also rediscovered life in hours spent together in rush-hour traffic jams or standing idly in long grocery lines, or accidentally bumping into each other while cooking supper, or brushing fingers while passing syrup across the breakfast table in the dim dawn light. Each episode is brief and more full than a lifetime. So it has continued. A romance told in many small, beautifully incomplete fairy tales. So it must continue for a while longer, until a hundred loose ends are severed and retied differently, until meetings and partings in airports become too commonplace to call up tears, until we find ways to endure the persisting remnants of our past lives that intercede between those few intense days and nights each month we are able to share.

Too soon each fairy tale ends with an unbearable last wave as one of us is swallowed by yet another silver airport throat, to survive raggedly alone until the next tale begins. Until, like a child drifting in and out of the telling of a bedtime story, I awaken to the dream of my first love . . . again.

AUTHENTIC SUCCESS

Shabbos dinner at Rabbi Shmuley Boteach's house is a chaotic affair. There are usually several adult guests, all of whom have brought children, along with Shmuley's own family—his wife, Debbie, and six kids. Chaotic, I should say, but joyous. There is wine, seemingly endless courses of food, many declarations of l'Chaim *("To life!"). But none of this begins before Shmuley conducts what he considers his most important ritual: blessing his children.*

One by one his kids stand before their father, a short, bearded man with piercing blue eyes. He summons his son, places his hands on the little boy's head, and pulls it near. The boy, eyes tightly shut, buries his face in his father's stomach. Across the table, my wife gives me a knowing look and nods: What could possibly be more comforting than resting your head on your daddy's belly and having him bless you? I can think of nothing. It should be a mandatory requirement of all fathers, like teaching your son how to catch. Particularly if, like Shmuley, like me, and like just about every other man I know, your father never blessed you.

Hero to His Children

Rabbi Shmuley Boteach

For what does it profit a man if he shall gain the whole world and lose his own soul?

Gospel According to SAINT MARK

It's Friday night and the serenity and rest of the Sabbath have just been ushered into my busy life. Around our family table, my wife and I have many guests. After the traditional hymns are sung, our guests are eager to partake of the meal, as am I. But there is one ritual left for which everyone must wait. Just before the blessing of the wine, I summon my six children to stand next to me as I place my hands over their heads and give them their weekly Sabbath blessing. My five daughters all receive a blessing to grow to be like the Jewish matriarchs: *May G-d make you like Sarah, Rebecca, Rachel, and Leah.* For my six-year-old son: *May the Lord make you like Ephraim and Menashe. May the Lord lift his countenance to you and be gracious to you, my son.*

Although I grew up in a traditional Jewish home, I did not receive a blessing from my father when I was a boy. I first witnessed it somewhere else, in my wife's home in Australia right after we married. My father-in-law called my wife to his side and she dutifully bowed her head as she received his blessing. An awkward moment followed when my father-in-law asked me if I wanted a blessing as well. At first I felt like I was betraying my own parents by accepting a blessing from a man who, after all, was not my father. I wasn't used to that kind of intimacy between a son and a father figure. But moved by my wife's example and a desire to please her, I bowed my head as well. Stifling a desire at this early stage of the marriage to show my in-laws that I was my own man, I delighted in submitting myself to the paternal blessing.

As a child I was not close to my father. He grew up impoverished in Iran and worked hard in the States to build up a fabric and dress business to support his family. The scars of his hard life always showed. He was rarely home. He had learned to survive by being tough and there was no hint that he wished to be otherwise, even around his own children. After my parents divorced when I was eight, we moved away with my mother from Los Angeles to Miami and I saw my father only three or four times a year. I grew up largely in his absence.

Feeling lonely and vulnerable as a result of my parents' divorce,

I married at the age of twenty-one; ten years later I was the father of
six children. I promised myself that I would not be like my father.
Though I appreciated his working hard to support his family, I vowed
never to put my work before my children. I wanted my kids to feel
that they were of infinite importance to me. My every desire would
bow to their needs. But one of the things you don't learn as a child
of divorce is that when you aren't given sufficient love in your early
years, your insecurities are deepened. Having grown up deprived of
attention, you embark on a career hell-bent on professional success
and the adulation—and love—that comes with it. Your need to be
noticed makes you a slave to the acquisition of status.

In life, every man is confronted with a simple dilemma. The greatest human need is to become a need. We all want to be wanted. We
desire to be desired. We love to be loved. We wish for status and
recognition—as Hegel said, we wish for our equals to corroborate our
uniqueness and humanity. But how to achieve that objective? There
are two paths. You can be either a hero to your kids or a hero to the
world. You can be a celebrity to thirty thousand adoring fans, or you
can be a celebrity to your wife and children. You can focus on becoming a success in your private life, often to the detriment of your professional life, or you can focus on advancing your career whatever the
repercussions to your spouse and offspring. To be sure, the two need
not conflict. Still, one must always choose which comes first: the public or the family. Whom do you wish to impress the most?

As a culture, we've already made a choice. The Western world does
not suffer much from poverty. But it does suffer from a lack of happy
marriages and secure children. A man is labeled a success in our society if he is the chairman of a multinational corporation and has his
own Gulfstream jet, even if he is on his fourth marriage and his children don't talk to him. The insecurities of one generation pass to the
next. Loveless children are like deflated stock issues that never
attracted the intention of investors. We grow up with an almost
incurable feeling of insignificance, which leads to a manic devotion

to professional success at any price. We feel that if people recognize us as we walk down the street, or if we host our own television show, or if the maître d' reserves us a special table, the demons inside us will finally be silenced. We're hell-bent on showing the world that we're special. And deserve to be taken seriously.

Something else nobody told me as a child: worldly achievement only excites those demons more. Once they see you working eighteen-hour days to make money or gain celebrity, they smell blood. We have him in our grip, they exclaim, we will never let go. The demon feeling of worthlessness is never assuaged, no matter how much money is poured down its cavernous maw. Little voices whisper in your ear that what you achieved yesterday is now gone and can never be reclaimed. You are already on the road to being forgotten. You therefore better get back on your horse if you are to achieve anything significant today and still retain the world's attention. Suddenly you are a young man grown old prematurely as your desire to distinguish yourself becomes an obsession that never affords you a moment of peace.

You will ask me how I know this. To be sure, as a rabbi I have counseled hundreds of men who are seized by the disease. But on this score I am myself the expert and speak from personal experience. A few years ago, I arrived in Oxford to serve as rabbi to the students. It was a prestigious appointment and I worked as hard as I possibly could to maximize its potential. During the day I taught classes, dispensed advice, and raised the money necessary to bring in world-famous speakers to lecture for our organization. I came home late, usually well after my children were asleep, and after eating dinner with my wife, would go straight to a computer to write my essays and books. I was a machine. And it paid off. I became one of England's better-known rabbis, eventually winning the prestigious *Times* Preacher of the Year competition. Some of my books sold in large numbers (you see, even here I seek to impress). I hobnobbed with world leaders and celebrities who were my guests at Oxford, everyone from Mikhail Gorbachev and Shimon Peres to Boy George and Jerry Springer.

Although the weekends were reserved for our children, my wife and I hosted about one hundred students weekly at the Friday-night and Saturday-afternoon Sabbath meals. I was sitting with my kids but shmoozing with the students.

I was well on my way to feeling distinguished, climbing the ladder of success and gaining the respect of my peers. But then an alarm clock went off. Our eldest child began exhibiting concentration problems at school. My wife was advised to take her to an education specialist. In the course of her session my little girl said, "I don't always like my friends. They tease me. I don't like school. Sometimes my sisters and brother bother me." The therapist then asked her, "What is it that you do like? What makes you happy?" And she answered, "When my daddy comes home and plays with me, I'm so happy. Nothing bothers me." My daughter was becoming like me. Feeling neglected and valueless, she awaited a father to come and make her feel precious. But he was too busy screeching to anyone who would notice that he was himself valuable.

When my wife recounted this to me I listened in stony silence. It was virtually the same thing I had told my teachers after I exhibited problems in school. I felt an abyss open beneath me. Was I going to transmit my insecurities to my children? Would that be their only birthright and genetic inheritance?

About a year later, I was on a book tour promoting *Kosher Sex*. I had been away from home longer than ever before, but convinced myself that my absence was justified because I was developing a reputation that would benefit my family. More than two weeks had passed since I'd seen my wife and children. I called Debbie in London and asked her to put on the kids. All my girls came running. "How are you, Tatty? Are you having a good time?" Then I asked for my six-year-old son. He couldn't be bothered to come to the phone. He was playing on his computer. My wife told me to call back later.

"No," I protested, "he's my son and he has to talk to me." So she pried him away from the monitor and persuaded him to talk to his father. Our talk was perfunctory and empty. Memories of the cold indifference I showed my father so many years earlier flashed before me. My son was learning how to busy himself in lieu of a father who was otherwise occupied. He was learning to live without me. I was being replaced by Super Mario Brothers and Pokémon. Just moments before I was soaring atop the world as a successful author. Now I had tripped on the cragged edges of parental failure and my heart was bleeding profusely.

Here I was, all grown up, looking into a mirror and seeing my father staring right back at me. The realization that I was a meager father who loved his children deeply but not enough to make them a priority in his life was accompanied by other insights. First, I was finally able to forgive my father for his neglect. I decided that my own failure deprived me of the right to judge him. In fact, I saw that we had much in common. All he wanted was a bit of recognition, a bit of attention, a feeling that he was important. As an immigrant, he wanted to prove himself. But like so many modern men, he had gone about it the wrong way. He empowered the external world to confer upon him a sense of specialness. He had never internalized a sense of self-worth. The world was his master and he its slave. As long as the world noticed, he was important. But the world has a very short memory and is easily distracted by someone else's spectacular feats.

The second insight: I was not the success I had imagined myself to be. In fact, I was a disappointment. I had failed my children. What good is winning the love of the world, only to lose the love of those whom you love most? Simple logic dictates that you can't really call yourself a success when those who matter most to you think the least of you. A father's first obligation is to make his children feel like the most special people in the world. Yet my children felt ordinary. I was a hero to the rest of the world and a stranger to my own kids.

Debbie and I once hosted the CEO of a large entertainment

corporation and his wife at our home for dinner. I asked him if he had to travel often, and he acknowledged that he did.

"So do you get a lot of time with the kids?" I asked him.

"Well, not enough," he conceded. "But whenever I'm in town I spend all my time with them."

To our astonishment, his wife cut in, "Oh, get off it. Who are you kidding? You're never with the kids. Even when you're with them you're not with them. They're being raised in a single-parent household. When you get home you're never off the phone. You love them, but you don't love spending time with them." Clearly embarrassed, he rushed to change the subject.

Having spent many years as a fundraiser, I've been able to observe the ebb and flow of success and wealth among modern men. One generation makes the money, the next generation squanders it. One of the ways I was able to raise money for our organization was to help successful parents with their problem children. Why is it that so many highly successful fathers raise so many troubled sons? The reason is simple: these men put all their time into making their marks on the world and almost no time in making a mark on their own children. One wealthy businessman told me that he would give our organization a donation if I would talk to his son, who was in the middle of a difficult divorce. After speaking to his son it became clear that what was really needed was for the father to show some hint of interest in his son's life. I went back to the father and told him so. But he responded, "Look, it's been so many years since he and I have really spoken. I wouldn't know where to begin."

"Well why don't you begin by listening?" I asked. "Make him feel that he's worth hearing."

"No, no," he told me. "That's for you to do in my stead."

And yet this was a man who gave away a fortune to charity. He had all the time in the world for everybody except his own children. And the reason: Who feels special when you win over those who already love you? No candidate for public office tries to get his own family to vote for him. The same is true of parenting your children. We so often take for granted their love and allegiance that we make no effort to bring them to our side. And they end up either as bitter adversaries or as lonely mediocrities whom no one has ever made to feel important.

It seems incredible that throughout history so many men have made the same mistake. They thought they would find glory by conquering the world, only to discover that in the course of expanding the frontiers of their own empire, barbarians had come and sacked their capital cities. Their wives, long numbed by their husband's neglect, sit alone at night fantasizing about other men making love to them. Their sons, pacified by TV and Nintendo, look longingly at every male schoolteacher as a possible father figure. Their daughters end up in tragic relationships with men who abuse their need for affection.

Who is the warrior trying to impress? Strangers who will abandon him the moment he suffers his first major defeat? Is it logical to assume that strangers and "fans" will continue to love us even when our family members have long since ceased to do so? Are we blind to the undeniable fact that when our "audience" applauds our money and power, it is not us they admire but our possessions? Your family and your closest friends are the only ones in the whole world who actually want you and not what you own. Our children want the greatest gift of all, the gift of our presence. But so many men today give their children objects in lieu of real affection, and then wonder why their children go off to college and only call when they need some cash.

Having glimpsed the oblivion that awaited me if I continued on my neglectful path, I vowed to try and change. I came home every night and helped my kids with their homework. The first few nights were great. Despite the humiliation of remembering virtually nothing about multiplication, division, and geography (am I really expected to know where the Zambezi River is?), I loved it. I felt needed. And I felt like a hero, one of those rare and great men who had his priorities right. But after a few nights, the jitters set in. I would walk into a Barnes & Noble and see all the new books coming out. I was being overtaken by my competitors. Here were all these authors churning out books, and I was doing homework with the kids that I could pay some high school student a few bucks to do for me? I started to rationalize my desire to pass the responsibility to someone else. Surely life is about the pursuit of excellence and maximizing my own potential. Wasn't I really wasting valuable writing time by adding 3 + 5 with my six-year-old? I had two outstanding book contracts that had to be fulfilled. They beckoned me. I felt a pit of nothingness opening beneath me and feared that I would fall into it and disappear into eternal insignificance.

What I have since learned is that attaining a measure of majesty and dignity in life does not exclusively involve worldly achievement. Nor is it dependent solely upon being a fantastic family man. It involves a careful balance of both. A wife who sees her husband spend the best part of the day at home playing with the kids will not be impressed. She also wishes to have a man with some modest worldly achievements to his credit.

To be sure, the need to distinguish oneself outside the home and live a life of professional excellence is expressly mandated by the biblical injunction to "fill the earth, subdue it, and have dominion over it." But the Bible also demands that we "cultivate the Garden of Eden and nurture it." Subduing the earth while tilling the home turf is what authentic success is all about. We must balance our predilection to seek distinction through dominance by creating enduring relationships.

Now, every week, when I offer my children the weekly Sabbath blessing, I place my hands on their warm little heads and wonder whether in the previous week I earned the right to call myself a father. Have I the right to ask the Lord to lift his countenance to them by virtue of being their biological origin or because I am the gardener who nourishes his saplings with great care and love, ensuring their healthy development? Now when I bless my son, I pray inwardly that he work hard, that later in life he advance in his chosen profession. But more important, I bless him so that even when he loses a promotion he will believe that he is still infinitely significant. After all, how could it be otherwise? His daddy proved it to him by giving him endless love, blessing, and attention. And his daddy was no ordinary guy.

He was a hero.

✧

There is a wonderful Jewish legend about King Solomon, who because he prayed for Divine wisdom rather than riches was given both by God. This secret knowledge included mastery over demons that stalked the earth. Now Solomon was entrusted by God to build the first temple, but he had a big problem. Jewish law strictly forbid the use of iron tools to cut altar stones. Now, one of the demons that Solomon subdued was a worm that possessed the power to split rocks. "Thus, the First Temple, the holiest site in Jewish history, had a team of demonic builders—suggesting that demons are not necessarily evil," Rabbi David A. Cooper writes in his fascinating book on Jewish mysticism, God Is a Verb. "The point of this story is that when we have power over demonic forces, they can be put to good use. On the other hand, when demonic forces have power over us, our lives can be miserable."

I thought of this legend while reading Rabbi Shmuley Boteach's moving yet unsettling essay because the demons that he so courageously wrestles with in his personal and professional lives are ones that I fight every day as well. We all do, to a certain extent, for the need to be admired, appreciated, applauded, and acknowledged is an equal-opportunity desire that does not distinguish between the sexes.

We think of achievement as a blessing, but we call ambition a curse. But what if ambition is a gift of Spirit? If sex can be both sacred and profane, if power blesses as well as destroys, why should the nature of ambition be any different? To be a true hero or heroine in the eyes of those we love, as well as in our own, we must not only master our demons but make them work for us.

—SBB

REDEMPTION

When asked what the smartest or wisest or luckiest thing they've ever done in their life was, many men—those who hope to be invited back onto the marital couch, at least—will say: "Marrying my wife." Their response is motivated by more than just tactfulness (or the possibility of sex), though. Long before personal experience convinced me it was true, I believed there to be an equivalency between the depth and satisfaction of a man's love life and the success he achieves in his chosen profession. And the success was entirely proportionate to the depth. Of course, this is not an entirely original idea. To Freud, success was defined by the ability to work and love. Leo Tolstoy once said men who can appreciate the satisfactions of both intimacy and industriousness can live "magnificently" in this world. Still, those of us fortunate to win the affections of a good woman, the right woman, are stunned to discover the almost immediate "magnificent" effects she has upon the rest of our life, and are happy and eager to spread the news.

One such acolyte is John Tierney, a columnist for The New York Times *who in his many explorations of city life has written often about homeless men. Over the years, he has become friendly with one man in particular and recently was surprised, and pleased, to learn that the man had turned his life around. How had he gone from social outcast to productive citizen? He had fallen in love. Tierney, who recently became a first-time father in his late forties, found interesting parallels between the homeless man's experience and his own.*

The Love of a Good Woman

John Tierney

Whoso loves believes the impossible.
ELIZABETH BARRETT BROWNING

What makes a man grow up? John Kovacs showed me the answer to that question, but it took a while. When I first met him, in 1990, neither of us was a model of responsible manhood. I was divorced and living alone, a thirty-seven-year-old with no savings, no assets except for the furniture in my apartment, and no desire to take care of anyone except myself. I was that species of commitment-phobic male referred to by women in New York as a toxic bachelor. John Kovacs was what social workers in New York referred to as a member of the homeless community, although he used a different label. "I'm a bum," he said.

John was forty-eight years old and lived in a railroad tunnel under Manhattan. On days when he did not have vodka for breakfast, he did odd jobs to get food for himself and the dog and fifteen cats that lived with him. He had been on the streets for most of his life. He told me of a father who had died when he was five, a mother who drank and attacked him with a butcher knife, a youth spent mainly in foster-care institutions until he ran away at age sixteen. He started smoking at age nine and had a drinking problem by his teens. In his twenties, he said, he spent six years in jail for auto theft and other crimes that he didn't feel like discussing. At times he had his own apartment and job, but he kept ending up back on the streets.

"I just made a few mistakes," he said. "I became a bum. You lose your job, you lose your friends, nobody really wants to be bothered with you. I was sleeping on park benches, subways, movie houses."

Then he found a quiet sanctuary inside an abandoned railroad tunnel that runs for two and a half miles beneath Riverside Park on the Upper West Side of Manhattan. He moved into a thirty-foot-long concrete bunker, once used by train crews, and scoured trash bins to furnish it with rugs, a bed, sofa, chairs, coffee table, kitchen cabinets, bookcases, and stuffed animals. He strung Christmas decorations across the ceiling and covered one wall with pictures from *Cat Fancy* magazine. Using kerosene lamps and a camp stove, he turned the bunker into an almost cozy home, if you didn't mind the dankness and the rats scurrying outside. By the time I met him, while reporting about homelessness for *The New York Times,* he had been living there for fifteen years. He occasionally talked about wanting to move out, but I didn't take him very seriously.

Then, a year after we'd met, he announced he was moving to a farm in upstate New York. "The air will be better up there," he explained with characteristic understatement. He'd been accepted into a program to turn the "homeless into homesteaders," run on a farm near Syracuse by a nonprofit group called the Earthwise Education Center. He said he was going to stop drinking. "I can do without the bottle when I want to. The only reason I drank down here was that I was lonely and bored. I don't drink when I'm working, and I'm ready to work. I'm ready to get my hands dirty."

One day he packed a few belongings—clothes, flashlights, kerosene lanterns, a radio, a hatchet, a first-aid kit, a Bible, and a Boy Scout handbook—into a shopping cart and wheeled it out of the tunnel into the daylight. He and his dog, Mama, climbed into the social workers' van. I'd never seen him looking so happy. "I feel good," he said. "I ain't coming back."

It made for a heartwarming story in the next day's paper, and John promptly became a media star. He and his dog appeared on local and national television. Sally Jesse Raphael asked him questions like "Animals are very important to people who live under the earth, right?" The film company of Barry Levinson, the director of

Diner and *Rain Man,* offered to buy rights to his story for $5,000
up front and $50,000 when filming began. John, who had left the
tunnel with $151 in his pocket, soon had an agent on both coasts.

Six months later he moved back into the tunnel with $22 to his
name. Nothing had worked out. The social workers at the organic
farm, determined to protect him from Hollywood's exploitation,
had advised him to hold out for more money from Barry Levinson,
so he ended up with zero. He stayed off the bottle and worked
hard, but he didn't get along with the social workers or the other
men in the program. When his roommates complained about the
smell of his dog, rather than bathe her he angrily moved out of the
farmhouse with her and began sleeping in a shed.

"John was always being John," the director of the program told
me. "We tried to stress four principles among the men, the four
C's—communication, consideration, cooperation, contribution—
but John didn't want to participate. He had an inability to communicate and follow instructions." The manager of the ranch that
employed John praised his energy on the job but said he seemed to
have a hard time trusting people. That diagnosis was seconded by
John.

"I really wasn't liked," John said. "I didn't get along with nobody
up there except when they wanted me to give them my money or
buy them food." As much as I sympathized with John's plight—I
wouldn't have enjoyed lectures about the four *C*'s either—I began
wondering if he'd ever turn his life around. I found out that he'd
blown previous chances. A woman living near the park told me that
she'd found a job and an apartment for John, but then he'd backed
out of the arrangement. Other neighbors and social workers tried to
help, too, but things never worked out. John would get angry just
talking about the jobs he'd quit.

He explained disagreements with his mantra: "I do things my
way." I tried telling him that he was not Frank Sinatra, that he was
going to have to compromise or stay in the tunnel forever. It some-

times occurred to me, after delivering these sermons, that I was not one to be giving advice. I was still alone in my apartment doing things my way.

But a couple of years later, in 1994, I fell into a serious relationship, and so did John. He met a middle-aged woman, a widow living near the park, when they were walking their dogs. He started spending nights at her place and moved some of his stuff out of the tunnel. I didn't expect it to last. Even if she didn't tire of supporting him, he would probably get angry at something and flee. For a man who had spent a third of his life living in a tunnel, coupledom would be a strain.

But I was wrong, as I discovered when I ran into John five years later. He was still together with his girlfriend. Now he had a job doing maintenance in several buildings, and he had his own apartment, which he took me to visit. "I've got a roof over my head," he said, relaxing on the couch. "I eat every day and buy food for the three cats. I've stopped drinking. I don't smoke much." The apartment was filled with furniture, a television and stereo, magazines, ceramic figurines of animals, and a poster with his exercise regimen.

John showed me pictures of his girlfriend and himself at her country house, and there was a flash of the old anger when he described a dispute they were having with their neighbors up there. But he got over it quickly. At fifty-six, he seemed healthier and happier than ever. He was not only supporting himself but also helping to take care of others. On the wall were photographs of four Central American children being sponsored by his donations to a charity program. We talked about them and the child that my wife and I were expecting. Then we took a walk down through the park and peered in through a gate at the tunnel. John scanned the darkness and pointed out the graffiti on the walls close to his old home. "I always told you I could get out of there, and I did," he said.

"When we used to sit down there in the bunker," I said, "I never thought I'd be listening to you talk about the problems at your country home." It was the first time I'd felt jealous of John. I, too, was now a responsible citizen, out of debt and working harder than ever to save money, but a country house was utterly beyond my means. "I went to work all those mornings you were drinking down here, and now you're the only one of us with a place in the country. How did this happen?"

John smiled and declined to make sense of life's vicissitudes. But he did offer a succinct explanation for what had turned him around, and it had nothing to do with any rehabilitation program or lecture about the four C's. It was the same thing that had made me grow up. "I met a woman," he said. "I was living like a bum, and I met this woman in the park, and I fell in love for the first time since I was a teenager. I knew I couldn't go out with her unless I got some money and changed my life. Let's face it. You can't bring a woman down to a tunnel."

DEATH

How did you imagine death as a child? Was it a state like dreaming? That image is as accurate as any we have during out later adult years, according to Adin Steinsaltz, the mystical rabbi who has spent much time thinking about and studying such things. For, limited by the perceptual abilities of the human brain, we cannot possibly fathom another form of existence that does not include the body we inhabit throughout life. Nor can we conjure the soul's liberation between death and what he calls Paradise.

Until that part of the journey begins, we can only dream.

Beyond the Chrysalis

Adin Steinsaltz

We are all resigned to death; it's life we aren't resigned to.
GRAHAM GREENE

Death, like so many other things, always has a double side. One is the general, rather abstract way of thinking about it. The other is the particular, the personal encounter, when death assumes a face and a name and suggests a very different reality. Then the general and abstract break down into specific details—the particular deaths of people around you, the deaths of relatives and friends, contemplation of, even the dread of, your own death. At times, one's notion of death often becomes incoherent, confusing, and, for some people, terrifying.

Having been born and raised in Israel in a stormy time, I had more encounters with death as a child than most other people face during a lifetime. Some of my first memories are of terrorist attacks, of other children disappearing mysteriously. "When will our neighbor again play the piano?" I would ask. The answer: "He will never again play the piano. He is dead." Coming home from a tranquil morning at the library one day, I remember having to take shelter in a doorway as shooting began. In the distance I could see people lying bleeding in the alley, some wounded, some dead. As the war went on, death seemed to weave itself into the fabric of life. It may have been frightening, but you cannot go on living in fear.

But even though I witnessed much death in childhood, there was no kind of horror connected to it for me. I remember once—I was quite small at the time, perhaps four—an old peddler came to our home trying to sell something and I took great pity on him. I blessed him, asking that he might be as speedily transported to Paradise as possible. I was wishing him well. I thought, What could be better than being in heaven? But he didn't take to it. He was shocked and angered, very offended. He demanded to talk to my parents. "What does the little boy want from me?" he asked. "Does he want to kill me?"

When I was older, for several years I lived under the shadow of death with a severe illness. I was to undergo surgery, and my doctors were worried. They said I had a little less chance than a Russian roulette player had of surviving—about one in four. What mattered to me was that I still had so much work to do, but the great fear, the horror of dying, I didn't notice. The night before the operation, I thought it would be worthwhile to write some kind of letter and give it to a friend to keep and if necessary to deliver. Then, as I do every night, I went to sleep. I am not a musical person, but a friend remarked to me that when I woke up I was humming some kind of song. Perhaps I was preparing myself. I didn't have any imagery connected to Paradise, but it seemed like a very nice place to be, a place that might be filled with song.

But I know that, to most people, death is frightening. It is irreversible, and there is something frightening about the idea of going somewhere and not being able to return. It is also totally unknown, and anything completely unknown is scary. But the most worrisome aspect of death is the notion of annihilation. One ceases to exist as a person. Everything stops. Everything disappears. We are unable to grasp that existence—the awareness that "I am here, I am alive, I know what is happening to me"—will not continue.

Of course, this notion of total cessation is connected with only one part of our existence—our bodily part. We all know of the processes of decay, of what happens to the body after it dies. Our existence, however, does not stop completely with death; another part, the nonbodily part, remains. In death, as in life, we are compound beings. One part is visible and has a particular way of being and communicating. The other, inner part is in many ways, though not entirely, what we call the "self." During one's lifetime that self is a combination of body and soul, and dwells neither entirely in the body nor entirely in the soul. The interface between the two creates our sense of self.

What we often don't realize is that life repeatedly mimics and prepares us for our own death. For instance, the cells of our body turn over completely every seven years. Materially, we are not the same person we used to be. This raises the kind of question Greek philosophers used to contemplate: *This is an ax I inherited from my grandfather. The handle was broken so I replaced it. The blade was rusted and dull so I replaced it, too. So is it my grandfather's ax?* How we think of the human body is not very different. When we look at pictures of ourselves, we are no longer the same person that we see, at least physically.

But whether we want to or not, we live, in so many ways, a spiritual life. Although most of our experiences in the body come through the bodily senses, we have a number of nonsensory experiences that belong more to the soul. These forms of perception include memory, imagination, thoughts, emotions, dreams. Our bodies may change continually in molecular form, but our spirit, our soul, endures. Take a particular man and ask: Who is this man? You will not define him as arms and legs and liver and spleen, but by his memories, his loves and hates, his tastes, his beliefs, the good he has done and the bad. He will continue to be described as that person after his body dies. The body is a part of what kind of person he is—strong, short, dark, bald—but it's the more changeable part.

Another reason death is terrifying is that the body, although it has undergone these many transformations, cannot fathom the dramatic change from life to another existence. Here it may be consoling to think of the changes a butterfly undergoes as it transforms from caterpillar to winged insect. For the caterpillar, changing into a butterfly is exactly the same as dying is for humans. In other words, the caterpillar cannot imagine life as a butterfly. When the caterpillar goes into the chrysalis, it dies; in a sense, it ceases to exist as a caterpillar. When it reemerges, it is the same caterpillar that reemerges—and yet it is not the same. It is entirely different. It has an entirely different life, an entirely different existence. Neither of the two stages is understood by the other. Not only is the caterpillar unable to imagine life as a butterfly, the butterfly cannot remember its life as a caterpillar, even though the caterpillar has begotten it.

The many transitions and deaths the body undergoes, along with its deterioration in old age, help us prepare for our departure from the body. As we get older, we have less and less contact with it; it becomes far less absorbing and enjoyable. We feel as though we're very slowly parting company. It's like a long relationship that fades away. We don't meet so often, we don't swap stories together, we become more remote, from time to time we have a little fight. So that when the time comes to say good-bye we're not really sorry. When we lose all our teeth, even if we were great eaters, eating becomes less enjoyable. So it is the way with the rest of the body.

As the body and its wishes and desires become weaker, the soul can shine undisturbed and old age can become a time of great tranquility and serenity. The desires and problems of the body, which have so often clashed with the intentions and desires of the soul, diminish and are no longer distracting. So the mind becomes clarified. But for those whose conscious minds were always, and wholly, defined by their bodies, it is a period full of anguish, since their desires remain with them and can't be satisfied.

I am fond of my body, I like the things I can do in it, and I have gotten attached to it. One reason the soul, the spirit, often lingers within the body after death is that the spirit has become sentimentally attached to it. It is like the man who has lost an old handkerchief and searches for it diligently, far more than is necessary. The handkerchief is not such a big loss, but it was *his*. I feel the same way about my body: it's just an old, used handkerchief, but it's mine. It's familiar, I'm attached to it the way I am to old furniture; it's comfy, it smells good. This is how the soul feels.

That's why, after seventy or eighty years of being bound up with life in a body, the soul, after death, often behaves as if it were still within a body. It carries on a sham existence—scheduling meetings and briefings, dealing with troubles with a spouse or children or a broken-down car—all in a nonphysical existence built entirely of bodily images, none of which is real anymore. One way to imagine this experience of a reality that is subjective, imaginary, and false is to think of the phenomenon of "phantom pain." When a part of the body is amputated, the amputee can often feel an itch or pain in the limb that no longer exists. This happens because the body retains the image of the limb, sometimes for a while, sometimes forever. After death, the soul carries with it a phantom image of its own existence.

A soul that is not prepared for moving on to another existence may carry this phantom imagery for a long time before it can be released. There are many stories about people who are caught in such a world. Although the soul knows that it is dead, it has difficulty extricating itself from the grip of the internal universe it has brought with it from life.

Once it does, it embarks on the next stage of its journey, in which it sees the reality of its life unimpeded by the boundaries of the physical brain. The soul has complete recall of the events of its life, but now with an understanding possible only from the vantage point of a different form of existence. In life, we can remember only what happened in the past. Now the soul can see its life as it was, with the additional perspective of knowing what will happen later. It can see both ways and now measures itself by different criteria. Things that preoccupied us in childhood become either funny little anecdotes, ridiculous and immaterial, or embarrassing and shameful incidents. We see our every mistake, blunder, stupidity. We realize how much time, effort, enthusiasm, and life were put into things that ultimately have no real value. The more we see, the more penetrating the understanding and the deeper the regret. Reviewing one's whole life in this way is terrifying, but it is part of the process of release, of dissociating the two partners, and of coming into a different existence.

Once we are out of the body we belonged to, we also begin to understand how enslaved we were to it. Imagine owning a car and having your whole life bound up with it, your entire daily schedule revolving around it: washing it, putting gasoline into it, driving it, parking it. It is as if the car is the whole of life, and you are just a driver. When this tremendous change in imagery occurs, the soul realizes that it is no longer subject to its vehicle, and it can then continue its life, moving on to an entirely different realm, disconnected from the body.

In Jewish thought, the stage after this release is called Hell. It is a continuation of this first, preparatory stage of understanding. Hell is not a punishment but rather—to use a modern idiom—like going into deep therapy. Once we gain a better understanding of our existence from the completely different perspective of the pure soul, once we realize how terrible some of our life experiences were, those memories that still stick to us from the past become too painful, and we want to get rid of them.

This second parting, dismissing one's former faults, is what we call the pains of Hell. Life's transgressions are not just a matter of having violated a law written in a book; the deeds make an imprint on the soul. Seeing one's mistakes in this way can be compared to waking up one day and seeing all kinds of terrible things growing out of one's body: thorns and horns and other horrible growths. One would desperately want to get rid of them, to cut them off, but this is not plastic surgery; the cutting off is accomplished only through the pain of understanding. That, in itself, is Hell. The deeper the transgression, the more deeply it is ingrained within the soul; the greater the attachment to the world, the stronger the impact on the soul; and, therefore, the greater the pain of cleansing, and the deeper the level of Hell.

This process goes on in a way we cannot really measure using earthly units of time. In Jewish thought there is no everlasting Hell. The time needed to purify each soul, and to turn into an entirely different being, depends largely on each person's life. For those who have relatively little to be ashamed of in their lives, it is short and easy; their souls did not have too many ugly blemishes and distortions. For others, who did not have the time and the ability to regret and to change in their lifetime, the process takes longer, like that of straightening somebody who is completely crooked. Only then, once a person has been cleansed, so to speak, can the soul move to the next stage, which we call Paradise.

Here, too, when imagining Paradise, metaphorical imagery does not make any sense when we are addressing matters that our conscious mind, tied to our physical senses and perception, cannot grasp. One who is born blind cannot understand what color is; one who is bound by matter cannot understand a spiritual existence! Whether the images that one has are images of wings and harps, or of being surrounded by beautiful orchards and gorgeous meadows, these are not just impossible for a soul, they are misleading to the literal-minded. Paradise can be known only as a different "world," in which the soul enjoys the light of the Divine Presence. Those who have experienced a moment of bliss, the supreme joy of encountering new knowledge, or the delight of a moment of deep spirituality, at least have a hint of it.

The body has a rather low threshold not only for pain but also for enjoyment; our bodily receptors make it impossible for us to tolerate too much of either. Without the body, when we are completely pure and free, not only is pain boundless, but so are enjoyment and pleasure. Just as the awareness of wrong becomes increasingly deep in Hell, the understanding and enjoyment of good grow constantly stronger in Paradise. Unlike Hell, which is a limited, finite stage because it has to correct and amend what happened in a finite span of life, the joys of Paradise are endless and everlasting. To use a physical metaphor, the absolute zero of temperature is defined and closed; but there is no upper limit to higher and higher temperatures. The freed, cleansed soul is now able to have a touch of Godhead, which is the absolute infinity that contains the wholeness of everything. While being connected and confined by the body and by the shadows of the world, the soul can hardly grasp it, but in another stage of existence, when these boundaries are no longer there, the soul can keep ascending for eternity.

JOY

A man I know describes the ultimate sensual (or is it sensuous?) experience: on a moonlit night, he mounts Ricky, his sleek Morgan quarterhorse, rides her out into the middle of a freshly mown meadow, and, while she grazes, stretches out across her back, his head resting on her hindquarters. The air sweetly perfumed by horse sweat and timothy hay, the visible universe pricked by the white light of a trillion distant suns, his head woggling on the horse's rear end as she shifts her weight, he falls into a swoon. Eros and the spirit mingle, and there is only joy.

And you thought horses were a woman's thing. Joy, we too often think, is an event we await, a mood that just comes upon us; if we're lucky, a reward for righteous living. But those who cultivate joy, who actively demand it, who look for that distinctive mingling of sex and the spirit at the heart of every positive human experience . . . well, they get what they're looking for. It is all around them; they only have to open themselves up to it. Joyfulness is a choice we make, says Thomas Moore. And an easy one at that.

Cultivating Life As an Act of Love

Thomas Moore

What is passion? It is surely the becoming of a person.
JOHN BOORMAN

I must have been an anaclitic baby—loving to touch and feel my mother's breast. Or was the breast denied me too soon? In any case, all my life I have loved to feel things sensually. I remember as a child rubbing my arms on my aunt's fur coat, and I remember the enchanting smell and scrape of hay on hot summer days on the family farm, and I remember the light in the evening on a field full of rabbits whose ears shone translucent as the projector sun sank behind the hill.

Until I was thirteen, when I left home to live in a monastic seminary, I didn't have much of an intellectual life. My father brought home books he thought I would love to read, but I left them on my desk unopened. In the seminary high school there was no breast in sight. The emotion of the place was cool, very cool, and the sensuality only serendipitous. Beeswax on the altar gave me something of a lift, but it was considered virtuous to deny yourself physical pleasures. At one point, we were not even allowed to shampoo our hair.

I was taught to enjoy deprivations, and at the same time I learned, perhaps a sublimation, to love the sensuality of words and the joy of ideas. Even today when I write I keep falling into a sea of abstractions. I have the habit of thinking too much and being awkward around all kinds of touches. I write books that some people think are self-help, and so I find myself often around people who hug and kiss freely. It isn't me. My sensuality is powerful beyond words but I can't get involved in casual hugging.

I really don't know if all this reserve came from the seminary or an Irish-Catholic family or from before I was born. I suspect the last, because the others in the seminary were very demonstrative and my family showed their affection easily. I remember my father being suddenly inspired many times to pick up my mother and carry her around the room on his shoulders as she screamed with feigned complaint, loving it. I loved it, too, but felt embarrassed.

I've noticed that people who are reserved often seem to be extremely sensual just beneath the surface, and I've imagined that behind closed doors these contained men and women might suddenly let go a ferocity of eros. That's true in my case, anyway. I've been therapist to people who are like that, too extremely contained in public but bursting with desire privately.

I'm attracted to the sensuality of the world: food, color, sounds, textures, and shapes. On my first trip to Italy I felt stunned. The sensuality everywhere put a perpetual smile on my face, and I wasn't used to the relaxation I felt in my body. I took in that world the way I take in a book at home. In Ireland I'm brought to life by the thick vitality of a pub and by the lonely air surrounding a rocky headland.

I've always been attracted to a spirituality that comes through the senses. Teilhard de Chardin's theology of the concrete world was overwhelmingly appealing to me. Immediately I recognized a similar spirituality in the Greek and Roman paganism I studied during my doctoral years at Syracuse. And, having been seduced into guilt and reserve by a misguided form of Catholicism for many years, I relaxed once again in the great tolerance of the body I found in pagan piety.

It's a mystery to me that during my monastic years, when I observed chastity to the very limit, I never felt deprived or abnormal. I explain it by referring to the obvious eros in community living, but I'm not sure about that. I do believe that chastity is an essential ingredient in sex, even for the married, and that it doesn't contradict sexuality at all. During those years I had moments when my desires took over and made me think and do silly things, but I never felt consciously twisted by the suppression of a sex life. Even now I look back on those celibate years with some longing for the sensual delights I knew then. I can't describe them, but they had to do with enjoying the security of a warm and familiar community. I think of this kind of sensuality when today our little dog comes running to the family when we arrive home after an excursion and he is excited and aroused. Community and family can be turn-ons.

My studies in paganism now lead me to believe that lovemaking is essentially the conjuring of a spirit. Sex is theurgy, an evocation of the spirit who then fills the persons present and the occasion with the gifts proper to that spirit. In sex we invoke the spirit of sex—I like to refer to the Greek goddess Aphrodite—who becomes present and permeates the couple with desire and pleasure and even physical response. If the spirit is not effectively summoned, the sex is only human and intentional and therefore inadequate, perhaps mechanical. Sex is inherently spiritual.

I also have come to appreciate the important work of Freudians who examined minute reactions of people with almost neurotic attention, teaching us how to see the most subtle signs of meaning. Today these same Freudians are frequently dismissed because their therapeutic techniques can't be shown to work. But their contribution is to show us how to reflect, how to notice the slightest twitches of meaning, and how to consider the poetry of our everyday lives.

I love living in a world that doesn't work, and I have no need for any proofs or demonstrations. I'd rather live by elegant ideas and people than by objective proofs and experts. The very idea of having to demonstrate the reliability of an idea seems grossly anxious and therefore highly neurotic. Modern scientific psychology is infinitely crazier than Freud and his followers ever were.

The Freudians also taught us that we can see everything through the filter of sex. Or I might say that everything is sexual from a certain point of view, and that if we want a good sex life we have to do everything from desire and pleasure, and that our lovemaking should not be separated at all from everything else we do. It's a caricature of Freud to say that a cigar is never a cigar. The point is, nothing ever is what it is. It is all poetry, and one genre of lived poetry is sexuality.

These are the qualities of sex: desire, pleasure, sensuality, fantasy, indulgence, physicality, love, and union. There are many others, but these suffice to show how any activity in a day's time could be sexual if these qualities were present. How can you live all day long in

413

a mechanical, functional society, perhaps work in a drab and inhumane environment, and then come home to make love? Can a person be so compartmentalized? I don't think we'd have as much public, guileful sexuality if the whole of life were more erotic.

I am led from a congenital overabundance of eros to a notion of the erotics of everyday life. But we don't live in a highly erotic culture, because for some reason—everyone blames it on the Puritans—we believe that we have to work hard to justify our lives and, focused on work and function and information, we reserve the erotic life for later, and often later never comes. I also suspect that because we chase eros out of the workplace and the church and public life, it comes back to haunt us as an emotional complex or an obsession. We live in a functional world and force sex into its compulsive forms. It's not present, deep, and affirming, and so we find it puerile and exaggerated in movies and novels and absurdly in the way on the World Wide Web.

If work, cities, education, politics, and banking were acts of love, we might be less depressed and less aggressive. It makes sense that the loss of eros would give rise to depression. It is less clear but no doubt true that, as used to be said five hundred years ago, aggression can be tamed by the spirit of sex. We need that taming badly, because superficial sex goes in the opposite direction—it engenders violence.

I have prayed to and meditated all my life on a sexless God. It may seem obvious to many people that God should be sexless, but in fact most presentations of God around the world are highly sexual. Desexing God in certain places has hurt both religion and sex. Religion becomes repressive and guilt-producing, while sex becomes secular and mechanical. Religion and sex need each other.

I agree with the mystics around the world who say that the ultimate lover we seek is divine. In my church I would read the Song of Songs at every ritual and bless the sexuality of everyone present—everyone, no matter what their lifestyles and so-called preferences.

I would not base my spirituality on the control and suppression of sexuality because that is a sure way to enslave the spirit and turn inadvertently from religion to ideology. I would not make a religion based on fear, because there is no life in that nervous approach. I say "in my church," but we all have our own church. Emerson said, "Every church is a church of one member."

My philosophy, gathered from congenital appetites and preferences and from a variety of experiences over sixty years, comes down to this: at the heart of life runs a counterpoint, like a Bach invention—a discovery, a crafting, a moment of beauty—a counterpoint of spirituality and sexuality. My living of this counterpoint is in every instance imperfect, but that is the blessed human condition.

I recommend a life that is thoroughly, but not obsessionally, sexual and spiritual. If one is missing, the other will become problematic. And my definition of each is infinitely broad. The point is to trust deep desire and always aim for genuine pleasure. Anything less is a worried way of life, and that doesn't help anyone.

I'd like to return to some old words—*joy* and *holiness*. Both are susceptible to sentimental interpretations, but I mean something more solid. Joy rather than entertainment, holiness rather than health. Our sexuality will bring us joy and spirituality holiness. We don't need anything else.

And now a footnote: I am writing this abbreviated little confession as a person. Honestly, I don't know what it means to be a man. Today, gender is in such confusion that it is loaded with neurotic implications, and to enter that realm is to risk raising an emotional complex better avoided. I write as a person who is not at all simple. My masculinity is a small aspect of the whole picture, and in the current cultural context I don't think it's worth bringing up. I think that for a period of time we need to give up talking as and about men and women. We have too many other things of importance to work out first.

Let us be human. Let us be individuals. Let us be together. Let us each be free of criticism and constraint in our honesty to sort out our values and our meanings. Let us be free to be outrageously spiritual and outrageously sexual, to the point where the two will seem inseparable and a deep division in the human heart will have been healed.

✦

Thomas Moore's exquisite essay on the soul of our sexuality reinforces my own deeply cherished belief that our deepest longings, unexpressed desires, and romantic impulses are sacred invitations to know Divine intimacy through a spirituality of the senses. Ancient spiritual traditions—from the Egyptians to the Celts—have always recognized the sacredness of sensuality and looked to the senses as the Sacred's private portals to reverence and redemption. To be spiritual is to be passionate. To be passionate is to honor God. Passion is holy—a profound Mystery that transcends and transforms through rapture. We need to accept that a sacred fire burns within us whether we are comfortable with this truth or not. If we don't give outward expression to our passions through reveling in our senses, the fires of hell present no problem— we'll experience self-immolation in the spontaneous combustion of our souls.

As Oscar Wilde reminds us, "Nothing can cure the soul but the senses, just as nothing can cure the senses but the soul."

—SBB

THOUGHTS FOR THE ROAD

Ten Things Every Man Should Keep in Mind at All Times

Jake Morrissey

1. Right-y, tight-y; left-y, loose-y.
2. A career is not a substitute for a life plan.
3. Shouting doesn't help.
4. Laughter does.
5. It is inevitable that the people you love will occasionally let you down.
6. It is inevitable that you will occasionally let down the people you love.
7. Health is the first wealth.
8. It takes too much energy to hold a grudge.
9. Amortize, ameliorate, or purge all regrets every five years.
10. Flowers always help. So does "I'm sorry" and "Thanks."

WITH THANKS AND APPRECIATION

As for me, I know of nothing else but miracles.
WALT WHITMAN

Every book seems a miracle after it is finished, but this one more so than others. Perhaps it is because *A Man's Journey to Simple Abundance* is the launch book of my publishing imprint with Scribner, The Simple Abundance Press, and I have fretted over it more than any of my other books.

I have always been reluctant to participate in literary collaborations. So many horrific battlefield stories abound (where death becomes more desirable than publication) that many writers won't even consider them. Obviously, the collaboration phobic never have had the good fortune to work with the fifty-two incredibly gifted and generous men who contributed to this book.

But there is only one real explanation for how and why this book came together as beautifully and seamlessly as it did: unmerited grace. So let me begin by thanking the Great Creator—in whom I move, write, live, love, find my being and my meaning. I continue to be humbled and moved by the daily miracles in my life. Franz Kafka was once asked if he prayed. "I write," he said. As for me, I write and publish: everyday prayer incarnate.

But individual thanks need to be extended for the blessings of this book. First and foremost to Michael Segell, who edited this book with such passion and perseverance, and persuaded some of the most important contemporary male writers of our day to take a leap of faith with us. I could not have done it without you, Mike.

And to his wife, Winifred Gallagher, who was part of the mystical chain of chance that led me to him.

Thanks to Kathy Schenker for helping me persuade Sting to take a risk on the page and to Trudie Styler for making it a reality at a lovely luncheon on a summer's afternoon in Italy.

A special word of acknowledgment and appreciation to my wonderful new colleagues at Scribner. My publisher Susan Moldow, personal editor Nan Graham, and associate publisher Roz Lippel collectively circumvented the laws of heaven and earth so that this book could be brought into the world far earlier than seemed humanly possible six months ago.

If the full extent of Scribner's vice president of publicity Pat Eisemann's kindness and consideration toward me was public knowledge, it would bring out the green in the eyes of other writers, so I'll never tell. Your determination to recast what books should be considered "classics" is a source of inspiration. Art director John Fontana's intuitive understanding of how much subtle nuances mean to me made our cover meetings and photo session among the highlights of this book's evolution. Thanks to design director Erich Hobbing for always responding to my suggestions for the interior with such grace. The imprint's editorial assistant Ethan Friedman has my undying gratitude for taking on the thankless task of sorting out all the thorny bits so that only this book's bloom is visible.

Writers know, in good conscience, that each book that bears their name out in the world would not have been the same without the enormous gifts of time, creative energy, emotion, and goodwill, of an invisible benefactor. For *A Man's Journey to Simple Abundance*, my unseen abettor and creative co-conspirator was Jake Morrissey, the editorial director of Simple Abundance Press. Thank you for running interference for me daily (Knute would be proud) and for perpetuating the illusion that I have command not only of the English language but of my senses. Your thoughtfulness, intelligence, and wit is evident on every page, and I hope that this is just the first of many happy publishing projects together.

"Late in life, with indomitable courage, we continue to say that we are going to do what we have not yet done," the French philosopher and poet Gaston Bachelard wrote. "We are going to build a house." To everyone at Scribner, please know that your warmth, enthusiasm, creative risk taking, and genuine respect for my work makes my threshold crossings on the twelfth floor seem as if I'm entering not just a dwelling place but a House of Belonging. And to Carolyn Reidy, president and publisher of Simon & Schuster, thank you for turning over the soil of publishing convention so that the roots of our co-venture will be sturdy and long-lasting.

Finally, there is always one person in a successful career whose contribution to your well-being is so vast you don't know how to begin expressing gratitude. Edith Wharton said it best: "I suppose there is one friend in the life of each of us who seems not a separate person, however dear and beloved, but an expansion, an interpretation, of one's self, the very meaning of one's soul." For over a decade, this extraordinary person has been my literary agent, business manager, and dear friend, Chris Tomasino. Thanks, toots. Where we're going, we don't need roads.

Blessed am I among women, writers, and publishers and I know it. I only pray that all who helped me love this special book into full being can read my affection, appreciation, and gratitude between every line.

—SARAH BAN BREATHNACH

SELECTED BIBLIOGRAPHY

The following is a selected bibliography of the works in print written by contributors to *A Man's Journey to Simple Abundance,* as well as other works that I mentioned by name. I intend this bibliography to be used as a starting resource for readers interested in further exploring the work of the contributors to this volume. The editions listed here represent, in many cases, a currently available reprint of the work, and not the original publication, although every effort has been made to be complete and accurate.

My sources for the quotes that appear throughout the book have been rich and varied. My favorite collections of quotations are: *The Beacon Book of Quotations by Women,* compiled by Rosalie Maggio (Boston: Beacon Press, 1996); *Bartlett's Familiar Quotations,* 16th ed., edited by Justin Kaplan (Boston: Little, Brown and Company, 1992); *The Columbia Dictionary of Quotations,* compiled by Robert Andrews (New York: Columbia University Press, 1993); *The Oxford Dictionary of Quotations,* 5th ed., edited by Elizabeth Knowles (Oxford, England: Oxford University Press, 1999); *The Oxford Dictionary of Phrase, Saying, and Quotation,* edited by Elizabeth Knowles (Oxford, England: Oxford University Press, 1997); and *The Oxford Dictionary of Literary Quotations,* edited by Peter Kemp (Oxford, England: Oxford University Press, 1997).

—Sarah Ban Breathnach

Aldrich, Nelson, W. *Old Money: The Mythology of Wealth in America.* Allworth Press, 1996.

Ban Breathnach, Sarah. *Simple Abundance: A Daybook of Comfort and Joy.* Warner Books, 1995.

———. *The Simple Abundance Journal of Gratitude.* Warner Books, 1996.

————. *Something More: Excavating Your Authentic Self.* Warner Books, 1998.

————. *The Illustrated Discovery Journal: Creating a Visual Autobiography of Your Authentic Self.* Warner Books, 1999.

————. *The Simple Abundance Companion.* Warner Books, 2000.

Barras, Jonetta Rose. *Whatever Happened to Daddy's Little Girl?* One World, 2000.

Bass, Rick. *The Book of Yaak.* Houghton Mifflin, 1996.

————. *The Deer Pasture.* W. W. Norton. 1996.

————. *In the Loyal Mountains.* Houghton Mifflin, 1997.

————. *The Wilderness of Colorado.* Houghton Mifflin, 1997.

————. *Winter: Notes from Montana.* Houghton Mifflin, 1997.

————. *The Lost Grizzlies: A Search for Survivors in the Wilderness of Colorado.* Houghton Mifflin, 1997.

————. *The Sky, the Stars, the Wilderness.* Houghton Mifflin, 1998.

————. *The New Wolves.* The Lyons Press, 1998.

————. *Where the Sea Used to Be.* Houghton Mifflin, 1998.

————. *The Watch.* W. W. Norton, 1999.

————. *Colter: The True Story of the Best Dog I Ever Had.* Houghton Mifflin, 2000.

Bausch, Richard. *The Fireman's Wife and Other Stories.* W. W. Norton, 1991.

————. *Rebel Powers.* Vintage, 1994.

————. *The Last Good Time.* Vintage, 1995.

————. *The Selected Stories of Richard Bausch.* Modern Library, 1996.

————. *Good Evening Mr. & Mrs. America and All the Ships at Sea.* Thorndike, 1997.

————. *Take Me Back: A Novel (Voices of the South).* Louisiana State University Press, 1998.

————. *In the Night Season.* HarperCollins, 1999.

————. *Real Presence (Voices of the South).* Louisiana State University Press, 1999.

————. *Someone to Watch Over Me.* Harperperennial Library, 2000.

de Beauvoir, Simone. *The Second Sex.* Vintage, 1989.

Bell, Robert H. *Jocoserious Joyce: The Fate of Folly in Ulysses (Florida James Joyce Series).* University Press of Florida, 1996.

————, ed. *Critical Essays on Kingsley Amis,* MacMillan, 1998.

Blount, Roy, Jr. *Roy Blount's Book of Southern Humor.* W. W. Norton, 1994.

————. *Crackers.* University of Georgia Press, 1998.

————. *Be Sweet: A Conditional Love Story.* Harcourt Brace, 1999.

Boteach, Rabbi Shmuley. *The Wolf Shall Lie with the Lamb: The Messiah in Hasidic Thought.* Jason Aronson, 1994.

————. *Wrestling with the Divine: A Jewish Response to Suffering.* Jason Aronson, 1995.

————. *Wisdom, Understanding and Knowledge: Basic Concepts of Hasidic Thought.* Jason Aronson, 1995.

————. *Dating Secrets of the Ten Commandments.* Doubleday, 2000.

————. *Kosher Sex: A Recipe for Passion and Intimacy.* Main Street Books, 2000.

Brown, Larry. *Dirty Work.* Algonquin, 1989.

————. *Big Bad Love: Stories.* Algonquin, 1990.

————. *Joe.* Warner, 1992.

————. *On Fire.* Warner, 1995.

————. *Facing the Music: Stories.* Algonquin, 1996.

————. *Father and Son.* Algonquin, 1996.

————. *Fay.* Algonquin, 2000.

Cahill, Tim. *Road Fever: A High Speed Travelogue.* Vintage, 1992.

————. *Pecked to Death by Ducks.* Vintage, 1994.

————. *Jaguars Ripped My Flesh.* Vintage, 1996.

————. *Pass the Butterworms: Remote Journeys Oddly Rendered.* Vintage, 1998.

————. *Dolphins.* National Geographic Society, 2000.

Cheever, Benjamin. *The Plagiarist.* Collier Books, 1994.

————. *Famous After Death.* Crown, 1999.

Chödrön, Pema. *When Things Fall Apart: Heart Advice for Difficult Times.* Shambhala Publications, 1997.

Deacon, Terrence. *The Symbolic Species: The Co-Evolution of Language and the Brain.* W. W. Norton, 1997.

Dickey, Christopher. *Expats: Travels in Arabia, from Tripoli to Teheran.* Atlantic Monthly Press, 1991.

————. *Innocent Blood.* Simon & Schuster, 1997.

————. *Summer of Deliverance.* Simon & Schuster, 1998.

Dyer, Anthony. *The Big Five.* Trophy Room Books, 1996.

————. *Men for All Seasons: The Hunters and Pioneers.* Trophy Room Books, 1996.

Evans, Harold. *The American Century.* Knopf 1998.

————. *War of Words: Memoirs of a South African Journalist,* with Benjamin Pogrund. Seven Stories Press, 2000.

Harrison, Jim. *Legends of the Fall.* Delta, 1980.

————. *Country Stores.* Longstreet Press, 1993.

————. *American Christmas.* Longstreet Press, 1994.

————. *The Shape of the Journey: New and Collected Poems.* Copper Canyon Press, 1998.

————. *Just Before Dark: Collected Nonfiction.* Houghton Mifflin, 1999.

————. *The Road Home.* Washington Square Press, 1999.

————. *Dalva.* Washington Square Press, 1999.

————. *Sundog: The Story of an American Foreman, Robert Corvus Strang.* Pocket Books, 1999.

————. *The Beast God Forgot to Invent: Novellas.* Atlantic Monthly Press, 2000.

Johnson, Robert A. *She: Understanding Feminine Psychology.* HarperCollins, 1989.

————. *He: Understanding Masculine Psychology.* HarperCollins, 1989.

————. *We: Understanding the Psychology of Romantic Love.* Harper San Francisco, 1989.

————. *Inner Work: Using Dreams and Active Imagination for Personal Growth.* Harper San Francisco, 1989.

————. *Balancing Heaven and Earth: A Memoir.* Harper San Francisco, 1998.

Klaber, William. *Shadow Play: The Untold Story of the Robert F. Kennedy Assassination,* with Philip Melanson. St. Martin's Press, 1998.

Kramer, Peter D. *Moments of Engagement: Intimate Psychotherapy in a Technological Age.* Viking Penguin, 1994.

————. *Listening to Prozac.* Viking Penguin, 1997.

————. *Should You Leave?* Simon & Schuster, 1999.

Levoy, Gregg. *Callings: Finding and Following an Authentic Life.* Harmony Books, 1997.

Liebmann-Smith, Richard. *The Question of AIDS.* New York Academy of Science, 1985.

Main, Bruce. *Revolution and Renewal: How Churches Are Saving Our Cities.* John Knox Press, 2000.

Marinovich, Greg. *The Bang-Bang Club: Snapshots from a Hidden War,* with Joao Silva. Basic Books, 2000.

Marshall, Garry. *Wake Me When It's Funny: How to Break into Show Business and Stay There,* with Lori and Penny Marshall. Newmarket Press, 1997.

Menaker, Daniel. *The Treatment.* Washington Square Press, 1999.

Moore, Thomas. *Care of the Soul: A Guide for Cultivating Depth and Sacredness in Everyday Life.* Harperperennial, 1994.

————. *Soul Mates: Honoring the Mysteries of Love and Relationships.* Harperperennial, 1994.

————. *Original Self: Living with Paradox and Authenticity.* HarperCollins 2000.

Norman, Geoffrey. *Two for the Summit: My Daughter, the Mountains, and Me.* Dutton, 2000.

Norris, Gunilla. *Being Home: A Book of Meditations,* Harmony Books, 1991.

Price, Reynolds. *A Generous Man.* Atheneum, 1966.

————. *Permanent Errors.* Atheneum, 1970.

————. *Things Themselves.* Atheneum, 1972.

————. *Names and Faces.* Atheneum, 1973.

————. *Love and Work.* Atheneum, 1975.

————. *The Surface of Earth.* Atheneum, 1975.

————. *Early Dark.* Atheneum, 1977.

————. *A Palpable God.* Atheneum, 1978.

————. *The Source of Light.* Atheneum, 1981.

————. *Vital Provisions.* Atheneum, 1982.

————. *Mustian.* Atheneum, 1983.

————. *Private Contentment.* Atheneum, 1984.

————. *Kate Vaiden.* Atheneum, 1986.

————. *The Laws of Ice.* Macmillan, 1986.

————. *A Common Room.* Atheneum, 1987.

————. *Good Hearts.* Atheneum, 1988.

————. *Clear Pictures.* Atheneum, 1989.

————. *The Tongues of Angels.* Atheneum, 1990.

————. *The Use of Fire.* Central Bureau voor Schimmelcultures, 1990.

————. *New Music.* Theatre Communications Group, 1990.

————. *The Foreseeable Future.* Ballantine, 1992.

————. *Blue Calhoun.* Atheneum, 1992.

————. *Full Moon.* Theatre Communications Group, 1993.

————. *The Collected Stories.* Atheneum, 1993.

————. *A Whole New Life.* Atheneum, 1994.

————. *The Promise of Rest.* Scribner, 1995.

————. *The Three Gospels.* Scribner, 1996.

————. *The Collected Poems.* Scribner, 1997.

————. *Roxanna Slade.* Scribner, 1998.

————. *Learning a Trade.* Duke University Press, 1998.

————. *Letters to a Man in the Fire: Does God Exist and Does He Care?* Scribner, 2000.

Reid, Elwood. *If I Don't Six.* Doubleday, 1998.

————. *What Salmon Know: Stories.* Doubleday, 1999.

————. *Midnight Sun.* Anchor/Doubleday, 2000.

Segell, Michael. *Standup Guy: Masculinity That Works.* Villard, 1999.

Shepard, Jim, ed. *You've Got to Read This: Contemporary American Writers Introduce Stories That Held Them in Awe.* Harperperennial, 1994.

————. *Kiss of the Wolf.* Harcourt Brace, 1994.

————. *Batting Against Castro: Stories.* Knopf, 1996.

————. *Nosferatu.* Knopf, 1998.

————. *Writers at the Movies: 29 Contemporary Authors Celebrate 26 Memorable Movies.* HarperCollins 2000.

Siebert, Charles. *Wickerby: An Urban Pastoral.* Three Rivers Press, 1999.

————. *Angus: A Memoir,* Crown, 2000.

Smith, Huston. *Beyond the Post-Modern Mind.* Theosophical Publishing House, 1989.

————. *The World's Religions.* Harper San Francisco, 1992.

————. *Forgotten Truth: The Common Vision of the World's Religions.* Harper San Francisco, 1993.

————. *The Illustrated World's Religions: A Guide to Our Wisdom Traditions.* Harper San Francisco, 1995.

————. *Huston Smith: Essays on World Religion,* edited by M. Darrol Bryant. Paragon House 1995.

Steinsaltz, Adin. *The Talmud: The Steinsaltz Edition; A Reference Guide.* Random House, 1989.

———. *Essential Talmud.* Jason Aronson, 1992.

———. *The Thirteen Petalled Rose.* Jason Aronson, 1992.

———. *The Strife of the Spirit.* Jason Aronson, 1996.

———. *Talmudic Images.* Jason Aronson, 1997.

———. *On Being Free.* Jason Aronson, 1997.

———. *Talmud, the Steinsaltz Edition: Tractate Sanhedrin (Talmud, Steinsaltz Edition, Vol. 19, Part 5).* Random House, 2000.

Tierney, John. *God Is My Broker: A Monk-Tycoon Reveals the 7½ Laws of Spiritual and Financial Growth,* with Christopher Buckley and Brother Ty. Random House, 1998.

Visotzky, Rabbi Burton. *Reading the Books: Making the Bible a Timeless Text.* Schocken Books, 1996.

———. *The Genesis of Ethics.* Random House, 1997.

———. *The Road to Redemption: Lessons from Exodus on Leadership and Community.* Crown, 1998.

———, ed. *From Mesopotamia to Modernity: Ten Introductions to Jewish History and Literature.* Westview Press, 1999.

White, Mel. *Stranger at the Gate: To Be Gay and Christian in America.* Plume Books, 1995.

———. *Hotel Honolulu: The Diaries.* Outwrite Publishing, 1996.

CONTRIBUTOR BIOGRAPHIES

NELSON W. ALDRICH, JR., is the editor of *The American Benefactor* and the author, most recently, of *Old Money: The Mythology of Wealth in America*. He lives in New York City with his wife and youngest daughter.

Environmentalist and writer RICK BASS is the author of *Colter: The True Story of the Best Dog I Ever Had; The Sky, The Stars, The Wilderness;* and *The Book of Yaak*. He has won the PEN/Nelson Algren Award and the James Joyce Fellowship Award.

RICHARD BAUSCH is the Heritage Professor of Writing at George Mason University in Fairfax, Virginia. He has written eight novels, including *Violence, Rebel Powers, Good Evening Mr. & Mrs. America and All the Ships at Sea,* and *In the Night Season;* and five story collections, including *Rare and Endangered Species, The Fireman's Wife,* and *Someone to Watch Over Me*.

ROBERT H. BELL, William R. Kenan Professor of English at Williams College, recently received the Robert Foster Cherry Award for Great Teachers. He is also the author of books on James Joyce and Kingsley Amis.

GREG BESTICK has been, at various times, a land surveyor, a community activist, a technology entrepreneur, and an executive for computer software companies. He is currently consulting to Internet businesses and working on a collection of short stories.

ROY BLOUNT's latest book is *Be Sweet: A Conditional Love Story.* He has been described as having "done more different things than any other humorist-novelist-journalist-dramatist-lyricist-lecturer-reviewer-performer-versifier-cruciverbalist-sportswriter-anthologist-columnist-screenwriter-philologist of sorts he can think of."

RABBI SHMULEY BOTEACH is the author of the best-sellers *Kosher Sex* and *Dating Secrets of the Ten Commandments,* as well as other books. He served as rabbi at Oxford University for eleven years, won the London *Times* Preacher of the Year 2000 contest, and is the founder and director of the L'Chaim Society, a Jewish education organization that hosts leading world figures and statesmen. In addition to his other achievements he has taken Michael Jackson to synagogue, helped Mikhail Gorbachev light a menorah, and debated pornography with Larry Flynt.

Former Marine and firefighter LARRY BROWN is the author of seven books, the latest of which is *Fay.* He is the recipient of the Mississippi Institute of Arts and Letters Award for Literature, the Lila Wallace–Reader's Digest Award and two Southern Critics Circle Fiction Awards.

Travel-adventure writer TIM CAHILL's books include *Jaguars Ripped My Flesh, Pecked to Death by Ducks, Pass the Butterworms,* and *Dolphins,* a companion book to the IMAX film of the same name, which he also co-wrote. He has slept with a grizzly bear, swam with dolphins, and braved oil-well fires in Kuwait, among other feats.

CORKY CARROLL is a five-time U.S. surfing champion, three-time international surfing champion, surfwear designer for Corky Carroll Surfwear, and columnist for the *Orange County Register.* He is also a singer/songwriter who has recorded sixteen albums, and has worked as an advertising director, tennis pro, ski instructor, car dealer, and actor.

BENJAMIN CHEEVER is an essayist, reviewer, and the author of three novels, *Famous After Death, The Plagiarist,* and *The Partisan.* He is currently working on a nonfiction book.

TERRENCE DEACON is a world-renowned neuroscientist and the author of *The Symbolic Species: The Co-Evolution of Language and the Brain.* He conducts research at Boston University and Harvard Medical School.

CHRISTOPHER DICKEY is a longtime journalist noted for his wartime coverage in Central America and the Middle East; he is currently the Paris bureau chief for *Newsweek* magazine. He has written a number of books, including the novel *Innocent Blood* and several works of nonfiction: the critically acclaimed *Summer of Deliverance, Expats: Travels in Arabia from Tripoli to Tehran,* and *With the Contras.*

ANTHONY DYER is a professional hunter and rancher in Kenya and author of *Classic African Animals: The Big Five* and *Men for All Seasons.* An eager conservationist, he is currently participating in wildlife monitoring projects in Kenya.

HAROLD EVANS, former editor of the *Times* (London) and the *Sunday Times* and former president and publisher of Random House, one of the world's largest publishing houses, is author of the best-seller *The American Century.* He is working on a prequel, *We the People.*

ROGER EVANS considers his foremost professional accomplishment to be hacking out a living in commercial real estate while residing in a small mountain town in Idaho, where, with growth the perennial pariah and the doors to paradise slammed shut, it is an annual exercise in resourcefulness to survive.

MILLARD FULLER is the founder of Habitat for Humanity, an organization dedicated to providing housing to those in need around the world. He is the recipient of the Presidential Medal of Freedom, the nation's highest civilian honor, and the Martin Luther King, Jr., Humanitarian Award.

JIM HARRISON is the author of *The Road Home, Dalva, Legends of the Fall,* and *A Good Day to Die,* among other books. His work has been translated into eleven languages.

JAKE JACOBSEN is a hermit.

KEITH JOHNSON is a former editor at Time, Inc.

ROBERT A. JOHNSON, a renowned Jungian analyst and author of *He, She,* and *We,* is "proceeding with the transfer of *doing* to *being,* which I see as the main task of entering old age. It feels like pioneering to me. I love what I am learning in this ancient art."

GENERAL JAMES JONES is a four-star general and the 32nd Commandant of the U.S. Marine Corps. He has served abroad in Vietnam, Iraq, Germany, and Bosnia and is the recipient of numerous honors, including the Defense Distinguished Service Medal and the Silver Star.

WILLIAM KLABER is the author of *Shadow Play: The Untold Story of the Robert F. Kennedy Assassination.*

PETER D. KRAMER is the author of the upcoming novel *Spectacular Happiness* (Scribner, 2001). His previous work includes *Should You*

Leave?, Moments of Engagement, and the international best-seller, *Listening to Prozac.* He maintains an outpatient psychiatric practice in Providence, Rhode Island, where he is clinical professor of psychiatry and human behavior at Brown University.

ROSHI JAKUSHO KWONG is the founder and abbott of Sonoma Mountain Zen Center in Santa Rosa, California, and was a student of Suzuki Roshi, who founded the first Zen monastery in the West.

RICHARD LIEBMANN-SMITH, a former magazine editor and television writer, is the quintessential "writer living in New York," which is to say he presently resides in Los Angeles and barely writes at all.

BRUCE MAIN is executive director and founder of UrbanPromise Ministries, Inc., an inner-city, Christian-based youth outreach program in Camden, New Jersey; Wilmington, Delaware; Toronto, and Vancouver. He has recently published *Revolution and Renewal: How Churches Are Saving Our Cities* with Dr. Tony Campolo, and will publish *If Jesus Were a Sophomore* in 2001.

GREG MARINOVICH won the Pulitzer Prize for spot news photography in 1991 and is author of *The Bang-Bang Club.* He has worked around the world, photographing Bosnia, Somalia, South Africa, Chechnya, and other troubled regions.

GARRY MARSHALL has written and directed some of television's most popular shows, including *The Mary Tyler Moore Show.* He is the director of *Pretty Woman* and *Runaway Bride.*

DANIEL MENAKER, a former *New Yorker* senior editor, is now senior literary editor at Random House and the author of two collections of stories, *Friends and Relations* and *The Old Left,* and a novel, *The Treatment.* He has won two O. Henry awards.

STEPHENS MILLARD is a Silicon Valley entrepreneur and co-founder of five NASDAQ-traded companies. He is a consultant to various venture capital firms and was previously a vice president of the Mead Corp.

THOMAS MOORE made "care of the soul" part of the cultural vernacular in 1994. His latest book is *Original Self: Living with Paradox and Authenticity.* Currently working as a writer and lecturer, Moore served as a monk for twelve years and holds degrees in theology, musicology, and philosophy.

BILL MORRIS is the author of *Motor City* and *All Souls' Day* and has worked as a newspaper reporter, columnist, a New York City bicycle messenger, and a Nashville disk jockey. He has recently completed two new novels: *Deuce and a Quarter* and *Mr. Mediocre,* the third and fourth installments in the Buick Quartet. He lives in Brooklyn, New York, and still drives a lipstick-red and black '54 Buick.

Sports and adventure writer GEOFFREY NORMAN's latest book is *Two for the Summit: My Daughter, the Mountains, and Me.* He has written for many national magazines and is editor-at-large for *Forbes FYI.*

GALLAGHER POLYN is a writer living in New York with his girlfriend.

REYNOLDS PRICE, a former Rhodes scholar and currently James B. Duke Professor of English at Duke University where he has taught for over forty years, has recently published his thirty-fourth book, *Feasting the Heart.* He won the National Book Critics Circle Award for his novel *Kate Vaiden* and his first novel, *A Long and Happy Life,* winner of the William Faulkner Award, has never been out of print since its first publication in 1962. He is a member of the American Academy of Arts and Letters.

ELWOOD REID is the author of *Midnight Sun, What Salmon Know,* and *If I Don't Six.* He is a former Big Ten lineman for the University of Michigan Wolverines, and has worked as a carpenter, bouncer, cook, bartender, and writing instructor.

Former air force fighter pilot BRUCE "BUCK" RODGER now flies the world's largest airplane, the 747-400, for United Airlines. His latest recreational trek took him to the Amazon jungle, where he spent time in the canopy observing wildlife, saving a three-toed sloth, and working on blowgun techniques with the Yaguar Indians.

JIM SHEPARD's most recent novel is *Nosferatu.* He is editor of the anthology *Writers at the Movies: 29 Contemporary Authors Celebrate 26 Memorable Movies.* He is professor of English at Williams College.

CHARLES SIEBERT is the author of *Angus: A Memoir* and *Wickerby: An Urban Pastoral.* He lives in Brooklyn, New York.

DR. CHARLES SIMONYI, a renowned programmer, is heading the Intentional Programming team at Microsoft, exploring a new way to write software. Active in promoting basic as well as applied science, he has endowed two professorships, one in the understanding of science at Oxford University and one in theoretical physics at the Institute for Advanced Study in Princeton.

HUSTON SMITH, visiting professor of religion at the University of California at Berkeley, is author of *The World's Religions* and *Cleansing the Doors of Perception: The Religious Significance of Entheogenic Plants and Chemicals.* A leading scholar of the history of religion, he has taught at Washington University, Syracuse University, and the Massachusetts Institute of Technology.

EDDIE STATON is the founder of MADDADS, a nationwide organization with more than fifty thousand members dedicated to preserving and resurrecting our communities. Members organize community activities and conduct street patrols, which report crimes to the police, paint over graffiti, and post a challenge to the behavior of drug dealers and gangs.

ADIN STEINSALTZ is the author of more than sixty books, including *The Thirteen Petalled Rose* and *The Essential Talmud*; he is now doing the first modern translation of the Talmud.

Legendary rock-and-roll musician and former member of the Police, STING needs no introduction. His latest album is *Brand New Day* and he and his wife, Trudie Styler, are active in a number of international charities, including the Rainforest Foundation.

JOHN TIERNEY is a columnist for the *New York Times*. He is the coauthor, with Christopher Buckley, of the comic novel *God Is My Broker: A Monk-Tycoon Reveals the 7½ Laws of Spiritual and Financial Growth*.

RABBI BURTON L. VISOTZKY is professor of biblical studies at Union Theological Seminary in New York City. His most recent books are *The Road to Redemption* and *From Mesopotamia to Modernity*. He is also a member of the executive committee of CancerCare, Inc.

MARK WINEGARDNER is the author of several books, including the recent *The Veracruz Blues*. His upcoming novel, *Crooked River Burning*, will be published in January. A regular contributor to

GQ, Winegardner has also published in the *New York Times Magazine, Playboy, Ploughshares, TriQuarterly, DoubleTake,* and many other magazines. He is professor of English and director of the creative writing program at Florida State University.

DR. MEL WHITE is founder of Soulforce, a former speechwriter for Jerry Falwell, Pat Robertson, and others, and author of *Stranger at the Gate: To Be Gay and Christian in America.* He has won the ACLU's National Civil Liberties Award.

INDEX

ABOUT THE AUTHORS

SARAH BAN BREATHNACH's (pronounced "Bon Brannock") work celebrates quiet joys, simple pleasures, and everyday epiphanies.

What began as a personal safari to unearth her authentic self, transformed into her number-one *New York Times* best-sellers *Simple Abundance: A Daybook of Comfort and Joy,* and *Something More: Excavating Your Authentic Self.* These were followed by her best-selling *Simple Abundance Journal of Gratitude, The Illustrated Discovery Journal,* and *The Simple Abundance Companion. Simple Abundance* has been translated into twenty-eight languages around the world.

Sarah is also the founder of the Simple Abundance Charitable Fund, a nonprofit bridge group between charitable causes and the public, dedicated to increasing awareness that "doing good" and "living the good life" are soul mates. Since 1995, the Simple Abundance Charitable Fund has supported the vision of more than 100 nonprofit organizations by awarding more than $1 million in financial support. The Simple Abundance Charitable Fund is underwritten with proceeds from Sarah's speaking engagements, royalties, and products.

Sarah Ban Breathnach is the publisher of the Simple Abundance Press, a groundbreaking joint venture with Scribner, as well as president and CEO of Simple Abundance, Inc., a consulting firm specializing in publishing and multimedia projects.

She divides her time beween Maryland and New York.

MICHAEL SEGELL, a former contributing editor and "Male Mind" columnist at *Esquire,* has written for *Rolling Stone, Time, Sports Illustrated,* and *The New York Times.* The author of *Standup Guy: Masculinity That Works,* Segell is a columnist for MSNBC, contenville.com, and the lifestyle editor at the New York *Daily News.* He lives in New York City.